Gaming in Academic Libraries:
Collections, Marketing, and Information Literacy

Edited by Amy Harris and Scott E. Rice

Association of College and Research Libraries
A division of the American Library Association
Chicago, 2008

The paper used in this publication meets the minimum requirements of American National Standard for Information Sciences-Permanence of Paper for Printed Library Materials, ANSI Z39.48-1992. ∞

Library of Congress Cataloging-in-Publication Data

Gaming in academic libraries : collections, marketing, and information literacy / edited by Amy Harris and Scott E. Rice.
    p. cm.
  ISBN 978-0-8389-8481-9 (pbk. : alk. paper) 1. Libraries--Special collections--Electronic games. 2. Academic libraries--Collection development. 3. Academic libraries--Marketing--Case studies. 4. Academic libraries-- Public relations--Case studies. 5. Information literacy--Study and teaching (Higher)--Audio-visual aids. 6. Library orientation for college students-- Audio-visual aids. I. Harris, Amy. II. Rice, Scott E.

    Z692.E4215G36 2008
    025.2'1877--dc22
                              2008041626

Printed in the United States of America.

12 11 10 09 08   5 4 3 2 1

TABLE OF CONTENTS

v   Introduction
Amy Harris, University of North Carolina at Greensboro

Game Collections and Curricular Support

1   Chapter 1: Making Book: Gaming in the Library: A Case Study
Natalie Gick, Simon Fraser University Surrey Campus

26   Chapter 2: Lessons Learned From Starting a Circulating Videogame Collection at an Academic Library
David Baker, Duncan Barth, Lara Nesselroad, Rosemary Nigro, Lori Robare, Ann Zeidman-Karpinski, University of Oregon

39   Chapter 3: Positioning the Library as a Source for Industry and Career Information for the Videogame Business
Tracey Amey, Pennsylvania College of Technology

52   Chapter 4: Gaming in the Classroom: A Model for Support in an Academic Library
David Ward, Mary Laskowski, and Christian Sandvig, University of Illinois at Urbana-Champaign

66   Chapter 5: Gaming in D.H. Hill Library, NC State University
Joe M. Williams and Mary C. Chimato, North Carolina State University

Gaming as Marketing

76   Chapter 6: Get Game@zsr—How We Did It and What We Learned Along the Way
H. David "Giz" Womack and Lynn Sutton, Wake Forest University

88   Chapter 7: Hosting Game Events in a Small, Liberal Arts Academic Library
Sheree Fu, The Libraries of the Claremont Colleges

108   Chapter 8: Shaking Up The Library: How Quake Introduced Students to the Library
        Vanessa Earp, Kent State University and Paul Earp, University of Akron

116   Chapter 9: Games in the Library: Creating an Awareness of Library Resources for Lifelong
        Library Users
        Sharon Mazure, Fairmont State University and Amy Hughes, Northern Arizona University

127   Chapter 10: Geocaching
        Linda Musser, Pennsylvania State University

Gaming as an Information Literacy Tool

135   Chapter 11: Your Library Instruction is in Another Castle: Developing Information Literacy
        Based Videogames at Carnegie Mellon University
        Donna Beck, Rachel Callison, John Fudrow, and Dan Hood, Carnegie Mellon University

149   Chapter 12: The Fletcher Library Game Project
        Bee Gallegos and Tammy Allgood, Arizona State University

164   Chapter 13: Bioterrorism at UF: Exploring and Developing a Library Instruction Game for
        New Students
        *Sara Russell Gonzalez, Valrie Davis, Chelsea Dinsmore, Cynthia Frey, Carrie Newsom, and
        Laurie Taylor, University of Florida*

175   Chapter 14: Education on a Shoestring: Creating an Online Information Literacy Game
        Scott Rice, Appalachian State University

189   Chapter 15: The 'Blood on the Stacks' ARG: Immersive Marketing Meets Library New
        Student Orientation
        Jeremy Donald, Trinity University

212   Chapter 16: Leveling Up: Increasing Information Literacy Through Videogame Strategies
        Paul Waelchli, St. Norbert College

229   Authors

INTRODUCTION

Gaming has become popular in many different types of libraries, but how does it fit in with the mission of academic libraries? The majority of the focus on gaming in libraries has been concentrated on public library programs. Books have been written on public library gaming programs, and the library blogs seem to contain almost daily news about more public libraries experimenting with gaming.

This book aims to show how librarians in colleges and universities of varying sizes, populations, and locations have successfully incorporated gaming into their libraries. It is our hope that academic librarians will find at least one idea that can be incorporated into their library.

In an attempt to encompass the variety of ways games are being incorporated into libraries, this book has been divided into three sections: Game Collections and Curricular Support, Gaming as Marketing and Gaming as an Information Literacy Tool. Though there are surely other ways games and gaming are being used in libraries, these three categories represent the most common and popular.

Collections

Game collections are springing up in academic libraries around the country. They typically serve one of two purposes, serving populations of students who are gamers or supporting degree programs in game development. In Chapter 1, Baker, Barth, Nesselroad, Nigro, Robare and Zeidman-Karpinski write about establishing a gaming collection at the Science Library at the University of Oregon. Natalie Gick (Chapter 2) writes about building a game collection and a dedicated gaming room at Simon Fraser University, a relatively new university near Vancouver, Canada. She discusses the acquisition, cataloging, marketing and maintenance of a collection that supports both students in the School of Interactive Arts and Technology and student gamers. The collection at Simon Fraser consists not only of videogames but computer games, consoles, and an arcade game. Tracey Amey, in Chapter 3, discusses supporting students who are interested in a career in the videogame industry at Pennsylvania College of Technology by collecting books, journals and magazines that could help students find jobs after graduation.

They have also hosted workshops about finding a job in the videogame industry and used game nights as a marketing tool to reach out to gamers and let them know about the library's other services.

Librarians at the University of Illinois at Urbana-Champaign created a collection of videogames and consoles in response to student requests for such a collection and were also able to support an undergraduate course entitled "Communication Technology and Society" by providing both copies of a game to be played by class members and computer lab space for students to play in groups. Ward, Laskowski, and Sandvig write about this process in chapter 4. Williams and Chimato (Chapter 5) discuss building a gaming collection at North Carolina State University, where the creation of a new learning commons led to the purchase of large monitors and consoles that students can use while in the library. NCSU has also run several successful gaming events, including a LAN party and a *Madden NFL '08* tournament.

Marketing

Games and gaming events are also being used to market the library and its services. Since students are playing games, librarians can use them to bring students into the library. One such example is Get Game@ZSR, a gaming event held at Wake Forest University. In chapter 6, Womack and Sutton write about starting Game Night at Wake Forest in the fall of 2005 as a way to bring first-year students, particularly men, into the library. This event has grown and changed since then and continues to be a successful outreach program. The Libraries of the Claremont Colleges hold weekly Game Nights as a way to market the library as a social space. The Game Nights are well-attended by students, as well as faculty and their families. Fu discusses this successful program in chapter 7.

Earp and Earp, in chapter 8, write about an exam week gaming program at Texas A&M University- Kingsville. For this program, the library set up a networked game for students to play during exam week. Approximately ninety students participated in this event the first time it was held. At Fairmont State University in West Virginia, Mazure and Hughes have employed a three-pronged approach to using gaming to market the library to students. They purchased a Nintendo Wii to mount permanently in the library's student lounge for students to enjoy during breaks. They also hosted two events designed to bring students into the library: a library carnival and a murder mystery. For the carnival, librarians set up carnival-style games and gave small prizes to students who won the games or played all the games. In the murder mystery, students used library resources to solve a mystery. They write about these successful attempts at outreach in chapter 9.

Musser and the librarians at the Earth and Mineral Sciences Library at the Pennsylvania State University (chapter 10) have found a unique way to reach out to students and the public using a geocache hidden inside the library. A geocache is a hidden box that people search for using global positioning system technology. The librarians have seen a great deal of interest in their geocache and have even created an open house activity for new students around it.

Information Literacy

Information literacy is another area in which the impact of gaming has been felt. Online and alternate reality games (ARG) are being used to orient students to libraries' physical and virtual spaces and to teach and reinforce information literacy concepts.

At Carnegie Mellon University (chapter 11), Beck, Callison, Fudrow and Hood write about the Library Arcade, two mini-games they created with students from their Entertainment Technology graduate program. One game was designed to teach students about the Library of Congress Classification System, and the other gives students the opportunity to choose the best resource for a given information need. This game has been popular with students and librarians alike. Another game that has received attention from librarians and students is *Quarantined: Axl Wise and the Information Outbreak*, a game created by librarians at Arizona State University West. In chapter 12, Gallegos and Allgood write about testing the gaming waters by creating a board game for students to play, then creating *Quarantined*, an online game where a student must use various types of information to find the cause of an on-campus epidemic while avoiding getting sick or being placed in quarantine. At the University of Florida, Gonzales, Davis, Dinsmore, Frey, Newsom and Taylor (chapter 13) created another game with a biohazard theme. Their game, entitled *Bioactive*, is a primarily text-based, interactive fiction game where students must find the antidote to a poison that has been stolen from a science lab. This game will be used in conjunction with first-year classes.

In chapter 14, Rice writes about *The Information Literacy Game* that was created at the University of North Carolina at Greensboro. This board game-style electronic game, designed to be played by one to four players, teaches students about meeting information needs, formulating database searches, citing sources, and general library information. This game can also be adapted and modified by other libraries.

Librarians from two libraries have incorporated gaming into their information literacy programs without creating electronic games. Donald at Trinity University (chapter 15) created an Alternate Reality Game called Blood on the Stacks, where students use library resources to solve the mystery of a missing canopic jar. This game was used as part of New Student Orientation at Trinity. In chapter 16, Waelchli writes about incorporating gaming strategies into instruction sessions at the University of Dubuque. The librarians there incorporated these strategies in a variety of ways, including using personal response systems to allow students to vote on the path of the class.

Gaming in academic libraries is a trend that will likely continue as more librarians become aware of its usefulness both as a tool for marketing and outreach as well as for teaching information literacy skills. It is our hope that this book will provide ideas for librarians interested in gaming and continue the conversation in the academic community about gaming in the library.

Editors' Note: The game system names and other gaming-related terminology throughout the book are written according to the *Videogame Style Guide and Reference Manual*, available at http://vgstyleguide.com/

 CHAPTER 1

Making Book: Gaming in the Library: A Case Study
Natalie Gick

Introduction
The Games Room and Collection at the Fraser Valley Real Estate Board Academic Library, Simon Fraser University Surrey Campus, was initially established in 2001, making it one of the older gaming collections in an academic library, and perhaps the oldest. The room and collection support teaching, learning and research at the university. The collection is intended to be representative rather than comprehensive, and to include both current and legacy games and equipment. Holdings and circulation are indicated in the chart.

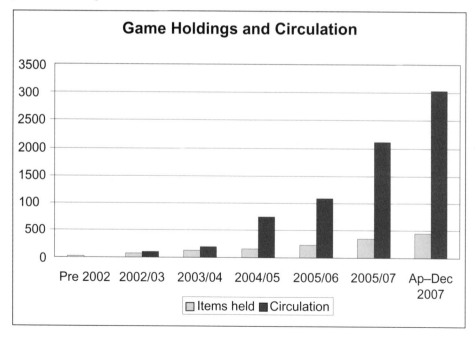

Circulation has steadily increased since the collection was created.

This chapter will cover the development and configuration of the games room over time, partnerships on campus, selection and processing of games, managing gaming equipment, programming, and challenges encountered along the way.

Academic Environment

Simon Fraser University (SFU) is a comprehensive, mid-sized university with approximately 20,000 FTE located in the Vancouver area of British Columbia, Canada. Surrey is the newest campus, established in 2002 but inheriting some programs, faculty and students from Tech BC, a university established in the late 1990s. SFU Surrey began in 2002 with 200 full-time equivalent students, has 1500 now and plans to expand to 5000 by 2015.

While the Campus offers programs across the disciplines, including education, business, applied science, science, arts and social sciences, the oldest and largest department is the School of Interactive Arts and Technology (SIAT) with 800 students. Historically affiliated with Tech BC, this department is the reason the gaming equipment and collection exist and they partner with the Library to support the initiative.

Within SIAT, students and faculty in the Media Arts stream are the primary users of the gaming collection as they are interested in the computational and cultural aspects of new media. Graduates are expected to be skilled in both the critical analysis and the creation of new media such as electronic games and other interactive multimedia.

Gaming courses, offered in both the undergraduate and graduate programs, include several game design courses plus courses on narrative, animation and immersive environments. Faculty are also researching games and game design, interactivity, narrative and the use of computer graphics, animation and simulation.[1] In addition to courses and research, many SIAT students are planning to work in the games industry when they graduate.

Games Room v1: Tech BC

The games room and collection at SFU Surrey is an inherited idea. The campus was originally its own institution (Tech BC) and the games room was originally proposed by a Tech BC student in 2001 to support study not only in game design but also in storytelling, computer modeling and team management, and to support potential employment in the gaming industry. The Tech

BC games room was set up in an office in their library with a couple of computers and software and legacy consoles bought second-hand by the students themselves.

Due to concerns about the legality of circulating games, Tech BC attempted to identify and contact the owners of the rights to games to ask for permission to circulate the games. However, determining who had the rights—creator, producer, licensee—proved extremely difficult, as was finding current contact information for any of these people and then convincing them to allow loans. Tech BC successfully negotiated permission from Electronic Arts (EA) to circulate their games for one week loan periods, probably because of close ties between the university and the local EA office. This was their only success. Tech BC did not allow games from other publishers to leave the campus but students could use them in the Library or borrow them for short periods.

Games Room v2: SFU Surrey

After the transition from Tech BC to SFU in 2002, the Library moved, and the gaming hardware and software spent the next year in boxes. Once the two PCs, Super Nintendo console and a small collection of games for both platforms were unpacked and identified, investigation into what exactly to do with them began, starting with the games.

SFU Library Collections Management had concerns about the legality of circulating games, especially PC games which have 'click-through' licenses. An attempt was made to read the licenses to see if loans might be allowed, but they were difficult to decipher and varied too much from game to game to make this a practical use of time. Literature and web searches were conducted but turned up no other Canadian libraries circulating games, and therefore no legal precedents nor examples of procedures. The fallback position was to follow Tech BC's example. Two games item types with corresponding loan rules were created in the catalog. Borrowing was limited to students and faculty at the Surrey Campus only, to take advantage of Tech BC's agreement with EA. The loan period on EA games was one week and non-EA games had a four hour, same-day loan period. Once the loan policies were set the boxes of games began to be processed, labeled and catalogued. Large stickers on the games indicated which could only be borrowed for four hours.

A former server room located in the new Library became the second games room, proving that all you need is about seventy square feet, power and a network connection. Furniture was found in storage, and Academic Computing Services installed the PCs and connected them to the campus network. Initially, users were given administrative rights so they could install games themselves. A television was found for the Super Nintendo console. The PCs, console and controllers were locked to the tables with cable locks for security. The games room opened and immediately became well used.

Once the games room had been reopened, students began asking for new games and consoles. The Games Research Cluster on campus, composed primarily of faculty and graduate students, were consulted as to what games and platforms were required. A wiki was set up to allow everyone in the cluster to contribute and it was soon populated with suggestions, some from the book *Chris Crawford on Game Design.*[2] In addition to PC and Super Nintendo, PlayStation 2 games were requested, and a console was found in campus storage and installed in the games room. Amazon and EB Games online were searched, and all of the requested games available for the existing platforms were ordered via Library Acquisitions.

To address the need for new consoles and computers, a joint proposal for funding from the Games Research Cluster and the Library was made to the School of Interactive Arts and Technology, the home department for the research cluster and most of the students on campus:

> The Game Space supports research and learning at SFU Surrey. Access to a variety of games and platforms is important to our School. Games are an important example of interactive multimedia with aesthetics and design principles that need to be explored and understood. Several of our graduate and undergraduate courses include the study of games. The Games research cluster examines interface and performance variables in game experience. A broad collection of innovative games, both historical and current, will be a valuable teaching and learning tool…

> The current Game Space has a few old computers, one or two legacy game platforms, and a PS2. The library is willing to continue to provide a small room for now, incorporate a larger Game Space room into the next round of space planning, circulate gaming software within the library, and allocate a portion of the ongoing acquisitions budget to the games collection (if there is hardware to support the games).

The Games research cluster has reviewed this concept, and supports this development…

We would like your support for the purchase of a mixture of current game platforms, legacy game platforms and game-compatible PC's. We are forwarding the enclosed list for your consideration…

1.	Gamecube	350
2.	X-Box	350
3.	Gameboy Advance	200
4.	1 contemporary game-compatible PC's w/ monitors *	2,000
5.	Legacy Game Platforms **	1,100
6.	Pentium II 266 w/ Win 98 / 17" Computer monitor	350
7.	1 additional contemporary game-compatible PC's w/ monitors *	2,000
8.	Neo-Geo Cabinet system	800
9.	CPS2 Cabinet system	800
10.	2 additional contemporary game-compatible PC's w/ monitors *	4,000
11.	Chairs and furniture as needed	?
TOTAL		$11,950

* Note: The PC's on this list are scalable in quantity. One will enable solo play, two will enable head-to-head play, four will enable multi-player gaming.

** Seven legacy platforms, as available: Choose from NES [Nintendo Entertainment System], SNES [Super Nintendo Entertainment System], Sega Genesis, Atari or Coleco Vision, Arcade cabinet, [Sega] DreamCast, N64 [Nintendo 64]. [3]

The proposal was successful and the Nintendo GameCube, Xbox, Game Boy Advance and two PCs were purchased immediately and two more PCs were added later. The Neo-Geo and CPS2 cabinet systems were not purchased due to concerns about copyright on the games.

The games room was incredibly popular, used from Library opening to closing, at far over the room's planned capacity. The cooling system initially installed for servers was very useful in preventing the room full of gamers from overheating. No expansion space was available in the current location, but in 2004 planning began for a new campus and library, which was to include a new expanded games room.

Games Room v3: New Campus

In 2006 the new campus was completed and the library was moved. The new games room is approximately 700 square feet, or ten times the size of the old one. Two walls hold shelving for the game boxes and sixteen desks and thirty-two chairs are arranged in two rows. The double walls successfully soundproof the room, allowing gamers to play without headphones and not disturb other library users. For safety reasons, the door is windowed and a window was installed between the Loans area and the games room, allowing staff to easily check on activity inside.

Currently, the library has about 500 games, six PCs, seven consoles, two handhelds and one arcade machine. Gaming equipment is kept secure by using a lock or loan system: either attached to a desk with a cable lock or kept in a staff area and circulated from the Loans desk if too small or awkward to be locked down. Game boxes are shelved by platform and call number but the actual games are kept at the Loans desk for retrieval by staff, in order to keep them secure.

Loan rules on games were changed at the time of the move, to better reflect the academically diverse new campus and more integration with the other campuses. Attempting to comply with the old agreement Tech BC negotiated with EA was abandoned, along with loan rules that distinguished between EA and non-EA games and restricting game loans to faculty and students from the Surrey campus only. Games may now be borrowed by any current SFU faculty or students. Console games are treated similarly to DVDs or videos and loaned for three days to undergraduates and one week to faculty and graduate students. Because PC games are more like software, they are loaned for 4 hours (not overnight), to limit them to use on campus only.

Games room and gamers. (Photo courtesy of Dominic Wong, Simon Fraser University.)

Interestingly, students will often bring in their own laptops, consoles, controllers and games and play in the games room. This allows them to increase the number of people who can play a game at once and also provides access to games or consoles not owned by the library. Gaming is a very social activity, and the games room gives it a home on campus.

Partnerships and Collaboration

As mentioned before, the library collaborates with other partners on campus in support of the games room, specifically the School of Interactive Arts and Technology, Academic Computing Services and the SFU Surrey Gaming Club. These partners provide direction, funding and technical support.

The library provides the administration, planning, space, furniture and televisions, and purchases, processes and circulates the games. Most of the gaming courses and research are part of the School of Interactive Arts and Technology, so they make recommendations on some of the games needed, provide direction on which platforms are required, and have funded the purchase of almost all of the consoles. Even when the school does the funding, Academic Computing Services often sources and purchases the equipment. Computing services also provides the PCs and installs and supports all the equipment.

A committee of three representatives from the SFU Surrey Gaming Club liaises with the library on behalf of the students. They suggest purchases of games and equipment and volunteer to help with programming. In addition they provide a mechanism not only to discover any problems and issues occurring in the use of the games room but also to discuss and provide input on possible solutions and then communicate the solution back to the other students. For example, students and staff complained about food consumption in the games room. A discussion was held with the representatives on why a no-food policy was going to be implemented, they communicated it to their fellow students and for the most part the new policy was accepted without complaints. A student-library consensus is generally better accepted by students than a straight library directive.

Games

Game holdings include 130 PC games, most published after 2000, plus a gift of 350 late 1990s PC games received as a donation and waiting to be processed and catalogued. Console game holdings currently sit at approximately 350. The largest collections are for the PlayStation 2 (PS2) and the Xbox; other collections include PlayStation 3 (PS3), Xbox 360, GameCube, Super Nintendo and Wii games. Generally only one copy of each game for a particular platform is acquired, but updated versions and editions for different platforms are also purchased. The collection is being actively developed and should grow to 700 games this year, in addition to the donated games.

The collection is intended to include both new and legacy games. Libraries have always been archives of materials: generally items are purchased when new and readily available, but they are also stored for future use by students and researchers when long out-of-print and unavailable for purchase. Because the collection was started well after computer games first appeared, it does not include a representative sample of older games; currently the oldest games in the collection are from the mid-1990s, plus some emulated 1980s games in the reproduction arcade. This is an area of the collection requiring development.

Selecting Games

The initial Tech BC games collection was selected by students, mostly by browsing local second-hand games stores. To expand the collection in 2004, the campus Games Research Cluster, mostly composed of faculty with some students, were asked to suggest notable games for the collection and provided a long list. Faculty continue to request game titles, usually for use in specific courses. Graduate students doing extended research into a genre or aspect of gaming will also request games, generally ten to twenty at a time. Undergraduates also request games, usually the newest, most popular releases. All these requests are accommodated, budget allowing.

Faculty and student requests are welcomed, but as with our print collection they are not relied on exclusively. Librarians also select materials, including games, to develop a collection reflecting and supporting the teaching, learning and research interests of the campus community.

Jamie Anderson, a librarian who worked on the games collection for a number of years, suggests that in addition to asking your users what they want, you also monitor the following selection sources:

- Metacritic[4] provides links to hundreds of games and reviews, with rankings on a scale of 1-100
- Game Developers Choice Awards[5]: annual best of as selected by game developers
- British Academy of Film and Television Arts Video Game Awards[6]
- School Library Journal reviews of games.

Purchasing Games

Games are selected and purchased on a title-by-title basis. The initial Tech BC game collection was primarily second-hand copies purchased locally, but as with print, SFU Library always attempts to purchase new copies of games. Until 2006, most games were purchased online by the Library Acquisitions department from either Amazon or EB Games[7] and paid for with a library credit card; others were acquired from Baker and Taylor. Recently a number of game orders have been blocked because shipping certain games from another country to Canada is prohibited, so until this is resolved games are only being ordered from Amazon's Canadian site.

While experts at ordering materials, Acquisitions staff are often unfamiliar with games and initially some confusion ensued around which versions and platforms were to be ordered. To alleviate this confusion, game orders now clearly state the version and platform required and provide a link directly to the exact game required on the vendor's web site.

Different acquisition methods are used as required. Games not available from online sites have been purchased by telephone from Electronics Boutique retail locations and either picked up or shipped. If new copies of games are not available, used copies are purchased, and once an out-of-print game required for a course was purchased on eBay by Acquisitions staff. Games required immediately can often be purchased by credit card at retail stores within walking distance of the library.

Cataloguing Games

Cataloguing staff download records for games from OCLC. Records are available quickly (when checked the day after the game was released, a *Halo 3* record was available). In addition to downloading, Cataloguing staff augment records in a number of ways to assist patrons and loans staff to easily find games and game keys and to track the physical parts of the games.

Initially, games were difficult to find in the Library catalogue unless the search was for a specific title, as they were identified neither by unique subject headings nor general material designations. Searches often found books about gaming or even just about computers. PC games were particularly problematic as the word computer appears so frequently in the catalogue; PlayStation games and others with unusual key words retrieved fewer false hits and were easier to find. As patrons often asked what games the library owned in general or for a particular platform, e.g. Xbox, public service librarians asked Cataloguing if the records could include this information. In response, Cataloguing had the public service librarians provide an authority list of platforms, from which they selected the appropriate one for each game and included it in a searchable local MARC 690 field. This allows not only the keyword search for games by platform but also the ability to generate current lists of all our games for a particular platform on the fly, using a query string such as "X?SEARCH=pc+game" for example. These lists are linked from our games page[8] to enable users and staff to find games quickly, and they are always up to date.

The second local addition to the records are game keys. Keys are unique numeric or alpha-numeric sequences sold with some PC games in order to prevent copying by unauthorized users.

The key is required to install the game and while they are sometimes recorded on the game discs, often they might be on a small slip of paper or other ephemeral material in the packaging and can be easily lost. Without the key the games cannot be legally installed, keys are difficult or impossible to replace, and usually the game must be purchased again. To avoid this problem, Cataloguing records game keys in a local MARC field so staff can find them and suppresses the field so keys are not being published to the web in the catalogue record.

Game keys are not the only part of a game that can be easily lost; games include booklets with valuable information on installing, configuring interfaces or playing. For current games, all this information would be easily found on the web, but not necessarily in the case of older games.

Games Processed and Shelved. (Photo courtesy of Simon Fraser University.)

Because the library's intent is to have an archival, not just current, game collection, booklets need to be retained. Cataloguing supports this by creating separate item records for all the significant physical parts of the game. Item records are created for game discs and booklets but not for posters or promotional materials. Each item record has its own barcode, so both discs and booklets are checked out to patrons and checked back in when they are returned. The circulation system tracks any unreturned parts and notifies the patron to return them. Appendix A contains a MARC sample record along with the notes created by Cataloguing for creating game records.

Gaming Equipment

The move into a larger space allowed for additional gaming equipment. More PCs were planned for the games room as part of campus computing expansion, and funding for additional consoles and legacy systems was requested from the School of Interactive Arts and Technology. A total of six new PCs were installed at opening, and a laptop hub was installed later to meet demand from students wanting to use their own machines. Funding was approved for new consoles, which were purchased over time. Currently seven are installed in the games room, each with a television: Super Nintendo, GameCube, PS2, PS3, Xbox, Xbox 360 and a Wii. A new reproduction arcade machine preloaded with 50 vintage games was ordered before the move and installed soon after opening.

Not all the library's gaming equipment is kept in the games room. Two handheld consoles, Game Boy Advance and Nintendo DS, are part of the collection but because they are too small to lock down, they are kept at the Loans desk and circulated from there. At the request of faculty, additional games consoles have been purchased, processed as part of the library collection and are loaned to students in particular courses to allow them to complete assignments. These include a PS2 with the Eyetoy accessory and three Wiis.

In addition to the regular game controllers, the library owns and circulates some special interface equipment, like the Eyetoy mentioned above. For the very popular game *Guitar Hero*, there is a guitar for the PS2 and one for the Xbox 360, plus plans for a second Xbox 360 guitar to allow dueling. A Logitech racing wheel, pedals, and gear shift were purchased for graduate student research in the summer and are now available to any student. Remotes and nunchuks were acquired for the Wii. Funding for two *Dance Dance Revolution* (*DDR*) dance pads has been approved; like the guitar, two will allow competition. This equipment is meant for in-library, or at least on-campus, use, and is loaned for four hours and not overnight.

When the new library and games room were being planned, some space was allowed for new and large interfaces, but not enough. At the time only *DDR* was considered. Space was allocated based on existing PC or console games played sitting down, with keyboards or controllers, in groups of one to four. That two people might be moving around and swinging their arms mimicking a game of tennis using the Wii was not envisaged. To accommodate the Wii, two desks were removed and another reoriented, but unfortunately, players still have to be careful not to hit walls, shelves or other people while playing.

Acquiring and Maintaining Equipment

Consoles have generally been sourced and purchased from retail outlets by Academic Computing Services. Acquiring new consoles is not usually urgent, and they wait for prices to decrease and/or stocks to increase. For high demand equipment required immediately for a course, like the Wii, sourcing is often time consuming as stocks quickly sell out and the only available units might not be close by. Additional controllers and interface equipment are generally the responsibility of the library, and are purchased from local retail or online sources. The reproduction Arcade Legends[9] machine was found on the web in response to faculty requests for legacy (or emulated-legacy) platforms.

Maintaining equipment has been relatively simple so far, but will become more of a problem as the systems age. No repairs have been attempted because replacements have been readily available and inexpensive. The consoles have been very dependable, especially given the amount of use they experience, with one exception. The new PS3 stopped working mid-game less than a week after purchase. The store replaced it with a new one and also replaced the game that was stuck inside the old one, without issue. Controllers have worn out regularly and have been replaced every couple of years, and recently the old PS2 stopped working. With its demise, two new PS2s were purchased inexpensively, one to replace it and one as backup, plus additional controllers. A new GameCube and extra controller was also purchased at a bargain price, again as a backup system, and once the Xbox comes down in price a backup will also be purchased. Trying to maintain equipment to access old formats is not a new experience for libraries, however the gaming consoles have been less of a concern because they are consumer goods and much more common than institutional equipment, so a supply of used equipment is expected to be more easily available.

Up to now, no issues have arisen around playing older games on PCs with newer operating systems. Maintaining one PC with Windows 2000 was contemplated when the others were upgraded, but a few games were tested on Windows XP Professional and worked. So far, no one has complained of any difficulty playing an older game from the collection, although this could be because they are only playing the newer games. Running older operating systems can have major security implications, so if the need arises, a workaround will have to be found.

PC Hardware & Software

As mentioned above, Academic Computing Services provides, configures and installs the PCs in the games room. The six PCs are Dells and were leased in 2007. According to Shelley Sluggett, the campus IT Coordinator, "Bigger, faster and stronger works best," and their current hardware configuration is:

- 2.8GHz
- 160 GB hard disks
- 2 GB RAM
- NVidia Quadro FX540 graphic cards
- 19" flat-panel displays

To manage the software, a master image has been created for gaming PCs. The image is stored on an Academic Computing Services server and is updated as necessary with patches and new software versions. At least every one to two weeks, the PCs in the games room are formatted and re-imaged from the master. Software currently installed is:

- Windows XP Professional operating system
- selection of media players: QuickTime, DivX, Real Player, Windows Media Player, Audacity
- Adobe Acrobat
- 4-5 popular games and demonstration versions of others

In addition to using the PCs, a laptop hub (NetGear network switch) with additional ports is available in the games room, so students can connect to the campus network using their own machines.

Signs are posted in the games room outlining acceptable use of campus computers and the campus network. Students using the gaming PCs must log in and be authenticated. As with all the computers on campus, computing services monitors the bandwidth being used, and anyone who appears to be downloading overly large files or otherwise misbehaving is disconnected, has their account suspended, and must see computing services to have it reinstated.

Once logged in to the gaming PCs, students have administrative rights so that they can install games. Because students have been known to download software they have not legally purchased, even though signs have been posted forbidding this, the PCs are regularly re-imaged to remove all illegally-acquired software.

PC Games Management

Three different models for managing the games software on the PCs have been tried: students installing, staff installing and a combination of the two. Initially, in version 2 of the games room, students had administrative rights to the PCs so that they could install games themselves. Unfortunately, this resulted in illegal software being downloaded. Administrative rights were revoked, and all of the PC games in the collection were preloaded by computing services onto all of the computers in the games room. However, this solution only lasted a year; as the collection grew all of the games could no longer fit on a single computer. Games were on average four to six gigabytes, and the hard drives were not large enough. Even when the games all fit, loading a hard drive to its maximum had caused performance issues. Dividing up the collection over the PCs and loading different games on different computers was contemplated, but this would have required multiple images to be created and stored and would have multiplied the time required for installation and maintenance.

Next, a hybrid model was devised and implemented and is still being used now. In addition to the software listed above, we preload some of the most popular games, about six currently, onto the games room PCs. Sometimes these are installed by computing services as part of the image, and sometimes they are installed by library staff after the re-imaging. When students want to play other games, they check them out from the Loans desk and install them themselves. If the game requires a key and it is not recorded on the packaging, the students ask the library staff to enter the key for them.

Multiplayer Gaming

Multiplayer gaming occurs in the games room, but the number of players is limited by both the number of copies of games and the number of number of PCs and laptop ports. As mentioned before, the library usually only purchases one copy of a game, so students need to provide their own additional copies for multiplayer gaming.

For additional space, once or twice a semester the SFU Surrey Gaming Club asks Academic Computing Services to set up one of the campus computer labs for gaming. The students are told to supply as many copies of the games as they can gather together and show them to computing services staff, who then give them administrative rights on the same number of computers in the lab to allow them to install the games. The following morning administrative rights are revoked, and the computers are re-imaged to remove the games.

Online Gaming

Because excessive use of bandwidth compromises network access and quality for the rest of the university community, bandwidth-intensive non-academic activities like online gaming are not allowed on campus. Students once attempted hosting an online game in the games room, but computing services detected it and the port was immediately shut down.

Programming

Games and equipment are used both inside and outside of the library for university events and for student recruitment. Open gaming, often using projectors for more visual impact, is a regular feature at Campus open houses, clubs and services days and even staff functions. Consoles are set up, games which are attractive to many and without a steep learning curve are chosen, and student volunteers are recruited to help teach people to play. Other than that, the event is completely unstructured and people play for a while and then move on, except for the occasional young person who stays for the whole event. Lately the Wii has been the most popular console for these events, followed by the Xbox 360.

In an attempt to recruit local high school students to the university, last spring and summer the library and the School of Interactive Arts and Technology co-hosted monthly High School Gaming Nights, actually held in the afternoons. One of the SFU Surrey Gaming Club members was hired to coordinate and supervise these events. He created posters that were sent to two local schools, and in summer two advertisements were placed in local newspapers. The program suffered from a lack of publicity and an inconsistent schedule but by August a few regulars had become established, along with some surprising but welcome visits from elementary school

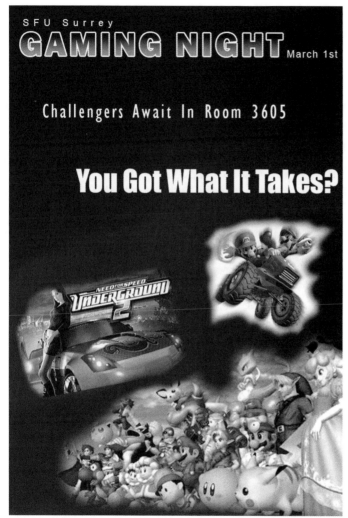

SFU Surrey
GAMING NIGHT March 1st

Challengers Await In Room 3605

You Got What It Takes?

Gaming Night Poster. (Courtesy of Michael Chang, SFU Surrey Gaming Club.)

students. The program was not resumed in fall but may be scheduled again in the future.

Challenges

Managing the games room has had its challenges, including noise, heat, monopolization by a single group and abuse of privileges. Gaming is loud, and as it seemed neither appropriate nor realistic to quiet it to an acceptable level for a library, the games room was very well sound-proofed and located on the outer edge of the library. Gaming is also hot and unfortunately this was not planned for, so the ventilation is the same as elsewhere on campus. Air fresheners are proving effective, and air purifiers are being considered.

The games room is consistently occupied by the same group of primarily male users. They can unintentionally appear intimidating to new people and be uncommunicative with staff. Attempts have been made to try and make it a

Students Gaming. (Photo courtesy of Dominic Wong, Simon Fraser University.)

more inclusive space, for instance targeting women by purchasing games of interest to them and offering programming open to all at campus open houses and other events. Other planned strategies include purchasing *Dance Dance Revolution* and hosting women's nights periodically, if a woman can be found to coordinate them. Another issue is that the primary users are a tight-knit group and sometimes they attempt to manage the space internally without consulting staff. Not communicating issues appropriately can lead to problems escalating unnecessarily. For the most part, however, they behave well.

Some students have abused their privileges by showing disrespect for staff and instructions. A common example of this was reluctance to leave in time for the library to close. A more serious incident in 2007 involved students opening up the wiring troughs and disconnecting the PCs in order to connect their laptops to the network. The first time it happened, a sign was posted by computing services warning that this was an unacceptable use of university property and was not to happen again. Unfortunately, the same offense occurred again. When it was discovered by staff, students were asked to leave and the games room was closed down, which proved a very effective means of communicating the gravity of the situation to the students. Staff from the library and Academic Computing Services met with the SFU Surrey Gaming Club representatives. The underlying issue for the students, lack of enough computers, was discovered and addressed by the installation of a student-accessible laptop hub. In addition, a code of conduct was drafted by the library in consultation with the student representatives. Once the code was agreed on, it was posted on the web and in the games room and communicated to other students by the Gaming Club representatives. The text of this code is available in Appendix B.

The code has had a positive effect: problems with eating and reluctance to leave on time have decreased considerably, unauthorized access to wiring or networks has not occurred again and Gaming Club representatives regularly communicate with library staff.

Future Development

Future development of the games collection and room and their management will depend on the requirements of gaming research and teaching and student development on campus. A statement from the 2004 proposal is still the guiding principle: "A broad collection of innovative games, both historical and current, will be a valuable teaching and learning tool."[10] Staying current with the plethora of new consoles and games is a challenge to both budgets and staff time, but this is being pursued more successfully than the development of a legacy collection, so one future goal is the acquisition of more second-hand equipment and significant classic games. If the actual legacy systems are not available or are problematic, the second option is collecting emulations of classic games on new platforms.

In addition to developing the collection, procedures will need to be adapted to meet new needs. Already, teaching has required the purchase and circulation of gaming consoles to students for use outside the library in addition to the permanent units in the games room. No doubt other changes will be required in the future. In addition, for the games room and collection to be most effective, access needs to be maximized. Attempts should be made to acquire games meeting diverse interests; an inclusive and welcoming environment in the games room should continue to be maintained and improved; and programming should be used to entice new users.

Conclusion

The history of SFU Surrey's games room and collection has been one of experimentation and trial and error, made worthwhile by the appreciation of faculty and students. Throughout this time, all available games and equipment have been heavily used. Gamers are often lined up at the library door at opening and do not leave until closing. All day long controllers and games are being checked in and out at the Loans desk. At times students are using the games recreationally, to "blow off steam"[11] to use their own words, but the games and equipment are also used for course assignments and for research. In addition, for students planning a career in the gaming industry, a broad knowledge of games is an asset. For these reasons, the games are expected to persist on campus, and for the library and other partners, no doubt new challenges will arise, old solutions will be discarded, and new solutions will be implemented.

Notes

1. School of Interactive Arts and Technology, "School of Interactive Arts + Technology," Simon Fraser University, http://www.siat.sfu.ca (accessed January 4, 2008).
2. Chris Crawford, *Chris Crawford on Game Design* (Indianapolis: New Riders, 2003).
3. Jim Bizzocchi, e-mail message, February 11, 2004.
4. CNET Networks Entertainment, "Metacritic Games Homepage", CNET, http://www.metacritic.com/games/ (accessed January 5, 2008).
5. Game Developers Conference and Gamasutra.com, "Game Developers Choice Awards", Game Developers Conference, http://www.gamechoiceawards.com/ (accessed January 4, 2008).
6. British Academy of Film and Television Arts, "British Academy Video Games Awards 2007", http://www.bafta.org/awards/video-games/ (accessed January 5, 2008).
7. GameStop, "EB Games", http://www.ebgames.com/ (accessed February 4, 2008).
8. Natalie Gick, "Fraser Valley Real Estate Board Academic Library Games Room and Games Collection", Simon Fraser University, http://www.lib.sfu.ca/about/surrey/gamesroom.htm.
9. BMI Gaming, "Arcade Legends," http://www.bmigaming.com/arcadelegends.htm (accessed February 5, 2008).
10. Jim Bizzocchi, e-mail message, February 11, 2004.
11. Video interview with students by Warren Bandzmer, Simon Fraser University, April 3, 2007.

Appendix A

A sample MARC record with the notes created by Cataloguing for creating game records. Local additions are in bold text.

Electronic games	
-	the descriptive cataloguing will be the similar to other electronic resources
III Grid:	Mat Type = m
Leader	Rec TYPE = m
007	co cga—for optical discs that are 4 ¾ in., in colour and with sound Co caa—for 3 1/2 in disc, g = a, in colour and with sound see MARC manual for other formats
007	cb cza—for chip cartridge, in colour and with sound
008	File TYPE = g
245	|h[electronic resource]—whether on CD or on came card/chip
246	Add other titles: 246 13 |iTitle on manual: |aCompu-math decimals 246 13 |iAlso known as:|aMAXLIK
250	Put edition (including version information) in edition statement Version 2.0 [Version] 1.1 Interactive version Gamecube version Only indicate this if it is definite from the item that the game was issued in different versions for different platforms

300	1 computer chip cartridge 1 CD-ROM |b sd., col. – if easily determinable |c size —diameter for CDs and DVDs (usually 4 ¾ in. or 3 ½ in.) +|e1 user guide

500	Always note source of title (priority order).
	    Title from disk label
	    Title from container
	    Title from guide
	Give the source of the edition statement if it is different from the source of the title proper.
	Edition statement from container…

516	Always include a 516 Game.
520	Include a brief summary if easily determined. If summary is quoted from container or web site indicate source: 520 "[summary]" – container. 520 "[summary]" – Web site.

538	Always include Systems details note.
	e.g.: 538 IBM PC, Windows 95, 10XCDROM
	    (always note only the lowest designation, ie if item says Win 95 to XT use Windows 95)
	    Only include if information is readily available on the item (often in the fine print!)

593	**CD key (not for public display) – III tag = y**
650	Subject headings Accept headings in record If game is computer simulation of a real thing, add heading for thing.

	e.g. Baseball|xComputer simulation. Automobile racing|xComputer simulation If these headings are in record already with |vSoftware, leave as it. If no subject heading add one.
690	Platform: PC game Playstation 2 Playstation 3 Game boy Advance Nintendo DS Nintendo Gamecube Xbox Xbox 360 Super Nintendo Wii.
710	Heading for Game manufacturer.
Call no.	Check LC schedules. Games are organized by platform (see below) and some individual games already have cutters assigned. Use those if possible. If the item you are cataloguing in not listed, fit the first cutter into the schedule. Always use two cutters First cutter for the Main title of the game Second cutter for the version of the game… E.g. GV1469.323 PlayStation GV1469.3233 PlayStation 3 GV1469.338 Wii GV1469.339 Xbox GV1469.3391 Xbox 360

Item records: so far the games are for Surrey, so consult the Surrey list	
	N.B. Surrey has 2 Itype codes/locations for games: one for PC games (41), one for all others (40)—see details on Surrey list … **There should be an item record for the game and one for the manual (user guide/instructions, etc.). Put 'manual' in the v field. Do not make records for the safety instructions, advertising, or other ephemeral material.**[1]

1. Penny Swanson, "Electronic Games."

Appendix B
Games Room Code of Conduct

Code of Conduct:
In order to ensure a pleasant environment and to respect the rights of all members of the campus community, the Library and SFU Surrey Gaming Club ask that all users of the Games Room respect the following Code of Conduct and other relevant policies established by SFU Library and by Simon Fraser University.

Appropriate behaviour in the Games Room means:
- Treating all users and staff with respect
- Being inclusive of others wanting to use the games room and sharing the equipment fairly with all users
- Refraining from behaviour that may be interpreted as intimidating, disruptive or offensive to other users, for example yelling or swearing
- Communicating issues and suggestions and immediately reporting abuses, problems and problem users to Library staff
- Preventing damage to computing resources and unnecessary use of staff time by:
  - not interfering with the staff installations of the computers, wiring or networks
  - not seeking unauthorized access to computers, wiring or networks
  - not violating copyright or patent protection and authorizations or license agreements and other contracts
- Complying with Simon Fraser University Policy GP-24 Policy and Procedure on the Fair Use of Information Resources
- Using SFU materials, equipment and facilities with care and respect and refraining from damaging or seeking unauthorized access to any resources
- Refraining from consuming food
- Disposing of personal garbage or recycling in the appropriate containers
- Exiting the Library promptly at closing time and during emergency situations or drills[1]

1. Natalie Gick, "Fraser Valley Real Estate Board Academic Library Games Room Code of Conduct," Simon Fraser University, http://www.lib.sfu.ca/about/surrey/gamescodeofconduct.html (accessed January 5, 2008).

 CHAPTER 2

Lessons Learned from Starting A Circulating Videogame Collection at an Academic Library

David Baker, Duncan Barth, Lara Nesselroad, Rosemary Nigro, Lori Robare, Ann Zeidman-Karpinski

Introduction: Why Are We Doing This?

A number of things came together in order for us to create a circulating videogame collection: we became aware that we had very little to offer in this subject area in which there is pervasive social interest and which has many potentials for academic study; we noted that use of the library collection was consistently falling; and we learned that a handful of other libraries were also coming to similar realizations and buying video collections or hosting videogame events. Our hope was that by demonstrating our willingness to delve into an area that might be perceived as fun and not academic, we would generate good will in our student users, causing them to see the library as a positive, helpful space. We knew not every student using the games collection would return as a user of other library services, but we also were certain that a student who never came here in the first place would never make use of our collections or services, so we hoped the presence of a games collection would improve library usage. What follows is an account of how we set up a collection at the University of Oregon's Science Library. This collection is in its infancy and continues to evolve; changes in how it is managed occurred even while editing this chapter. We share here what we have learned in creating this incredibly popular and well-received collection.

How We Did It: Circulation

Choosing What to Purchase

We purchased four popular gaming systems: Wii, PlayStation 3, and XBox 360 units, and the hand-held Nintendo DS, and games that could be used on these consoles. Since the gaming market is shared relatively evenly among the producers of these platforms (Nintendo, Sony, and Microsoft, respectively), we elected buy one of each rather than choose a particular manufacturer on which to focus.

We selected games initially based on currency and perceived popularity, with an eye to having a varied selection of game types, such as action/adventure, sports, and role-playing, for each game system. Initially we purchased forty games, of which some are available for multiple platforms, and some of which are unique to one gaming system.

Circulation Policies

We decided early on that if we were going to circulate gaming consoles, we needed to make these things possible:

1. The inclusion, in any checkout of a console, of all the pieces that would either always or usually be needed, for the most likely video monitor options.
2. A means of verifying that each of those pieces was present at check-out and check-in, without creating a ponderous filing system.
3. A fines structure that would effectively encourage prompt return.
4. Limitations on any one user's borrowing power, so that one enthusiastic person couldn't check out every gaming console at once.
5. A loan period that would suit both our need to make the materials widely available and the borrower's likely desire to be able to keep their game for several days, or over a weekend.

We ultimately decided on several policies and procedures. For each console, we purchased a commercially available kit to hold the console itself, assorted wires and controllers, and user manuals. For the DS, this box came with some useful accessories, such as charging adaptors for home and car, earbuds, and game cases. For the other systems, the case was not as comprehensively useful, possibly because while the DS is a hand-held (and therefore deliberately portable) game, the manufacturers do not expect the larger consoles to be treated as portable. Still, we assembled a kit containing AV hookups (standard and High Definition), two controllers, a power supply, and a means to recharge batteries during use. At the check-out point, we maintain a list of contents for each case, and check off the presence of each piece, then require the borrower to sign an agreement that stipulates that all the pieces are present as marked off, that they will notify us at once if a part gets damaged or lost, and that they will return all the parts. This signed page also includes information about overdue penalties.

In addition to the consoles, we also purchased extra controllers, in order to foster the opportunity to use the games for social or group interaction.

The circulation policy we adopted was a three-day loan for both games and game kits and accessories, with steep daily overdue fines.

Storage and Security

Another issue we had to come to a decision about was how to display the materials while keeping them secure, and how to effectively check out the game disks (in nearly all cases, these are ordinary CD/DVD-size disks), which are not good candidates for barcodes.

Our initial approach, which is working well for the size of the collection, is as follows: we purchased sturdy plastic sleeves designed for display of VHS or DVD paper-board covers, and cloth DVD-size sleeves. For each game, we separated the game disk, which we placed in the cloth sleeve, from the various instruction booklets, which we barcoded for circulation and placed in the plastic sleeve. Neither of these remained attached to the hard plastic box in which the game was originally purchased. The game disk sleeve is kept behind the circulation desk, in a drawer designed for DVD/CD storage; this drawer is in a locked cabinet in which we also store the game consoles and peripherals. The plastic sleeve with the instruction booklet is kept on a publicly-accessible shelving unit (also designed for video display), along with the hard plastic case, onto which we affixed labels that indicate they are display boxes. This allows our patrons to tell (by presence or absence of the plastic sleeve with the barcoded booklet) whether something is checked out, but also allows them to see, visually, what games we have even when they *are* checked out; patrons bring the plastic sleeve to the counter and we retrieve the matching game in the cloth sleeve, which fits neatly into the plastic sheet. At this time, we merely divide up the shelving unit by platform, because there are not more than twenty games for any one platform; as the collection grows, we will probably need to be more concerned with organization by either call number, genre, or title—or something else we haven't yet thought of.

Lessons

We did anticipate that the small size of the collection might represent a problem if many students were interested in borrowing. Many games—and all four consoles—have been checked out fairly constantly, frustrating patrons who wanted them and found the system for reserving the games and consoles (the booking system) difficult to use. Further, staff also found the interaction between the circulation and booking modules to be confusing. This has required flexibility in thinking about how we want to manage our loan rules; the change made during the editing of this chapter (therefore, no conclusions regarding effectiveness have been drawn) has been to alter the loan period to one of many hours (currently sixty), rather than three days, in the hope this will maximize use and make patrons less frustrated. Success of this new loan policy remains to be seen.

In addition, while we anticipated that some users would object to the decision to include videogames in an academic collection, we didn't realize there might be staff resistance to circulating these materials. How we addressed patron concerns is addressed later on in this chapter. The average age of the permanent staff of this library is forty-five, and some staff in this demographic were unfamiliar with the content and the format of games and gaming equipment. We resolved this problem by carefully labeling all the parts in the game kits, and by reassuring staff that if they followed the checklists for circulation by comparing label to list, they would be getting everything they were supposed to, and that some difficulties with this new process were expected.

How We Did It: Acquisitions
Hardware
Because the purchase of gaming materials is outside the usual purview of acquisitions in an academic library, creating a work flow for the University of Oregon's Science Gaming initiative proved challenging initially. The most obvious issue to overcome involved the purchase of game consoles and associated peripherals. Our Acquisitions Unit is accustomed to purchasing all kinds of materials formats: books, DVDs, CD ROMs, maps, photographs, electronic resources, and journals. What distinguished these purchases from the usual library acquisitions was the fact that in addition to individual game titles, which are comparable to any other software, and which were categorized as "computer disks" in the form field on Millennium™ Innovative Interfaces Inc), our catalog system, our project also involved ordering actual hardware that would normally be purchased through Facilities/Purchasing or Library Systems.

The Acquisitions Department was the logical choice to take on the responsibility of purchasing these items for several reasons. Due to the nature of our work flow, we had an established relationship with Metadata Services and Digital Projects (MSDP) and were therefore in a very good position to work closely with them—and close collaboration was absolutely essential in expediting this project given the timeframe we had for getting the systems up and running. It also made sense that the people responsible for ordering these items would need to develop a solid knowledge of the various game systems and accessories involved in supporting this initiative. We all had high hopes for this project, and it seemed like ordering gaming materials was in our future! We wanted to make sure this new "expertise" remained within our department so that future purchasing would be that much easier. Finally, regardless of who actually purchased the equipment, Acquisitions would still be responsible for creating order records, allocating funds, and paying bills—so keeping the ordering within our unit was the most logical option.

The first step in establishing an Acquisitions work flow for the gaming materials was to decide how to create order records for things like videogame consoles and controllers which were not going to be cataloged by MSDP, but which needed to be accounted for in Millennium so that we could encumber the appropriate fund indices and process payments in Banner, the university's accounting system. We decided to create a generic bibliographic record under the title "Science Gaming Materials" and attach individual order records for any purchases that were not actual videogames, including game consoles, specialized controllers (such as dance pads and guitars), protective cases, cables, and miscellaneous accessories. In creating these order records, a generic fund code was used in the fixed-length field of the record, and the specific index was placed in an internal note field. In addition, we used the identity field to indicate exactly what was being purchased—for example, three Wii Nunchuk controllers.

Software

Once a process was established for acquiring the hardware, we turned our attention to creating a routine to deal with the ordering and processing of individual game titles. Initially, a few games were purchased through the university bookstore, in conjunction with the game consoles and peripherals. The person responsible for content used Amazon.com to create a wish list that contained the bulk of the titles she was interested in purchasing and our ordering specialist was able to purchase items directly off this list. The Amazon wish list feature was very useful because it listed exactly which titles needed to be ordered and how many copies were required. It can also be used to rank each item (highest to low). Since our ordering specialist was not familiar with videogames prior to this project, the clarification provided by the wish list was helpful in avoiding confusion and possible duplication when we were asked to order the same title across several platforms.

In consultation with MSDP, it was decided that Acquisitions would not spend time searching and importing individual records from OCLC for each game title, which is our usual procedure when ordering new materials. Instead, our ordering specialist keyed brief order records for each game that could then be overlaid by catalogers when items were received and sent for cataloging. This allowed us to focus our efforts on acquiring the gaming materials as quickly as possible, while providing catalogers with information that could help them determine how the games would be cataloged in our system. Because we were able to use the information from Amazon to create order records in Millennium at the time of purchase, once the games were received they could be immediately routed to MSDP after a very quick update of the receive date field in the record. This helped us minimize the amount of time the materials spent in our unit and allowed us to streamline our work flow.

Lessons Learned—Acquisitions

The most unexpected problem we had was the absence of secured storage space in Acquisitions. Although we deal with a wide variety of media and formats, expensive videogame systems provided a unique challenge to our limited departmental space. These items were simply too expensive and tempting to be left alone on the shelves the way most of our other unprocessed materials are. When they were not being worked on by staff, the consoles and games were kept in the only lockable space available to us—the department head's office. This was inconvenient for both the Acquisitions staff and the department head since he was not in the habit of regularly locking his office, and we were required to find a key whenever he was away. For future projects involving the acquisition of tempting items such as videogame systems, set aside a space where items can be locked away securely and conveniently. Because of the limited time frame for implementing the gaming project, we paid extra to have the games shipped quickly from Amazon.com. As a result, we incurred significantly higher shipping costs than we would have had we had time to use the free shipping option.

Another very important lesson learned from this project was the need to work closely with our colleagues in other departments, such as Library Systems and MSDP. Collecting videogames is uncharted territory for those of us in academic libraries, and the challenges involved transcend any one department. Working with the cataloging staff as we began to develop our work flow allowed Acquisitions to take full advantage of the knowledge and resources MSDP could offer, while at the same time encouraging their staff to start thinking about the unique issues involved in cataloging videogames. By working collaboratively, we were able to acquire everything that was essential to building a solid foundation upon which the videogame project could grow, and we were able to do it in a remarkable short period of time.

How We Did It: Cataloging

In many ways, cataloging and processing the new collection of videogames was fairly routine. We had experience cataloging computer files and so were not dealing with an entirely unfamiliar format. However a number of issues arose which required special attention and the limited time frame for cataloging and processing presented challenges as well. Equipment for viewing the games was a fundamental concern for catalogers. According to AACR2, most information in the catalog record is taken from the item itself (the title frames in particular) rather than the container, so catalogers need to be able to run the game, especially when doing original cataloging. Catalogers have dedicated equipment for playing videos and DVDs, for example, and we needed to develop a plan for providing this access to the games.

In the initial phase, we were able to address this need by keeping the newly purchased game consoles in Acquisitions while the first batch of games was cataloged. (As noted above, the consoles and games were locked up when we were not working on them.) As the collection grows, we will need to find a different solution. The consoles are now located in the Science Library, which is across campus from the cataloging operation. Assuming that consoles will wear out with frequent use and need to be replaced, we are considering the idea of ordering replacement consoles in advance of need and storing them in cataloging. When needed as a replacement, a console could be rotated in as the circulating "copy" and another replacement console ordered.

Given that there was catalog copy available in WorldCat for most of the titles purchased, it was also important to consider when it was necessary for catalogers to view the games. It is essential for original cataloging, and important when working with catalog copy that requires significant editing (minimal level cataloging, or records that clearly contain errors). We are comfortable with trusting other libraries' work when working with full level copy in most cases, and so discovered that we did not need to view many of the titles cataloged.

For most titles, copy was available in WorldCat at least for one platform (Nintendo, Xbox, etc.). Fullness and quality of the cataloging varied, as is often the case with nonbook formats.

Our cataloging normally follows AACR2 and the Library of Congress Rule Interpretations, but the Library of Congress has not begun cataloging videogames. In the absence of the model provided by LC for many other formats, there is great variation in cataloging practices among libraries. We found it necessary to develop field-by-field guidelines to supplement the usual standards to help catalogers make decisions about editing copy and creating original records. Guidelines address such topics as the wording of system requirements notes and summary notes, ESRB ratings, and subject and genre access. Guidelines also documented the choices we made about classification and coding in our local system.

We wanted patrons to be able to access videogames using either subject or genre in the catalog. However, using controlled vocabularies to accomplish this presented a number of challenges. Library of Congress Subject Headings (LCSH) are established for some individual games, but such headings are to be used for works about the games (such as strategy guides) rather than for the actual games. LCSH also includes headings that represent form or genre (what an item is, rather than what it is about), including Video games, Nintendo video games, and Sony video games. Again, these should be used for works about videogames when coded as subject headings (MARC tag 650) in the bibliographic record. One of the most frequent errors we found in catalog copy for individual games was the inclusion of headings such as Nintendo video games coded as subjects. It is possible to bring out the form or genre of an item using LCSH by coding the headings as form/genre headings (MARC tag 655). However, the vocabulary for genres of videogames has not been developed in LCSH, since to date LC has not collected or cataloged games. The gaming community makes extensive use of genre terms to categorize games, such as "Racing," "First-person shooter," "Tactical role-playing," etc., but there is not consensus on the terms or consistency among sources. This is an area that is ripe for development within LCSH and would be of great value to academic libraries and the gaming studies community. In the short term, we chose to use one genre term, Videogames, consistently on all records for individual games. This serves a practical need as it allows users to retrieve all of the records for games with one search on the heading in our genre index. While the collection is small, this approach is adequate. As the collection expands, the need for more specific genre terms will increase. We plan to revisit this decision and consider the feasibility of proposing new genre terms for inclusion in LCSH.

Classification is often a question when dealing with non-book formats. We use Library of Congress Classification for most of our collections, but accession numbers for most non-book formats. We discussed the advantages and disadvantages of each approach. LC classification clearly provides better collocation with other resources and would help in collection assessment, which often uses call number ranges. However, all of the titles would go in one number, GV1469.35.A-Z, given the current scope of our collection. Few have Cutters already established (Mortal Kombat is one exception, GV1469.35.M67), so catalogers would spend more time formulating Cutters and shelflisting. In terms of shelving, it could be more difficult to quickly locate a particular call number in the collection for retrieval and re-filing, given the similarity of call numbers. Accession numbers were determined to be more practical for our needs. The format for call numbers is the term "GAME" followed by a five-digit accession number, with the name of the platform (Xbox, PS3) at the end. Call numbers are indexed in the non-LC call number index in our OPAC, so all games can be found by searching the term "game" in this index.

In order to maximize access to the collection, we used two additional approaches that are not typical in our cataloging. Recognizing that users searching the catalog might be most interested in retrieving all games that can be played on a specific system, we developed a standard way of referring to each platform and used this form in both the system requirements note and a 753 field, System Details Access to Computer Files. A keyword search on a term such as "Nintendo Wii" limited to the material type "Software/Data" retrieves all games for the Wii platform. This could also facilitate the use of canned searches on the terms from a web page. Also, anticipating that users might have questions about borrowing the games and equipment, we included a link to a Game and Equipment Policies page in all records to help answer questions about circulation.

How We Did It: Systems And Set-up
Setting Up the Consoles for Check Out
Each of the four consoles we planned to loan presented different problems from a setup perspective. Our two main goals in this phase were:
1. To create an easy and straightforward experience for our patrons, from their initial setup experience to their in-game experience
2. To secure the system software of each console against accidental or intentional abuse by borrowers.

These goals sometimes came into conflict; for instance, in order to maintain security for the Xbox 360, it was necessary to disable access to the "Live" experience, in which users could play in real time against others on their own systems elsewhere. This was not transparent to users, nor, in fact, to staff, at the outset, making for a frustrating user experience when an expected and significant aspect of the gaming experience was not available.

Hardware

How do we set up each system so our patrons can understand it, so our staff can support it, and so we make options as widely available as we can without presenting unacceptable security risks? The choices we encountered included such technical details as whether to optimize for a television screen with a 4:3 or a 16:9 aspect ratio, and whether to include connection cables to support more than merely the most likely video/audio setups our patrons might possess. Beyond that, we needed to consider to what extent we needed to provide training and troubleshooting, to both patrons and to our own staff. .

We decided it was important to support various potential setups, and that patrons who were already technically savvy would know probably more than we did about how to best set up for their less standard arrangements. We also noted early on that for all four consoles, the manufacturers have fairly exhaustive documentation available online. Therefore, we purchased materials that allowed a broad range of options, but set defaults, where possible, for the most likely options (a 4:3 aspect ratio; a non-high-definition/surround-sound AV connection). We also considered including laminated instructions for set-up, and ultimately decided instead to wait and see, allowing patrons to ask us questions and attempting to troubleshoot ourselves (using the on-line manuals if necessary). To date, we've found that our assumption that high-end users would have high-end knowledge has been accurate.

Software

As each system has out-of-game software, much like a computer's operating system, how should each system be set up to ensure the best experience for our patrons while keeping them secure from abuse? To a degree, each console had certain similar options (parental controls, network setup for internet access); but each also presented fairly unique access and security problems. The most important part of setting up each system's software was to enable password-protected parental controls. If this were not enabled prior to checkout, it would be possible for a patron to enable them, set a password, and lock the library out of our own console.

Another major concern was our need to ensure that any patron data left behind on a console was kept as private as possible. To do this, we set each console up to retain as little patron data as possible while still allowing the hardware and software to function as intended. In the end, we found there was actually very little we could do to specifically prevent the retention of patron data, if the patron was determined to load and leave their data on the consoles. The best solution seemed to be to simply advise that the consoles should be treated as one might treat a publicly accessible computer workstation, with the understanding that many people would have access to the information on each console.

Things They All Had in Common

With each system, we tried to take into account how patrons would be connecting the hardware to output devices. As each console ships with different output capabilities (composite, component, HDMI), and each also ships with different cabling to support those capabilities, we simply tried to note which cables we didn't yet have and so recommend their purchase.

How to Answer the Question, "Why Are You Spending Money on Games?"

It is actually an inexpensive way to lure people who might otherwise not be library users into the library. And if they come in for videogames, regularly or erratically, eventually they will stop and ask a question or check out a book or look for an article. We have books and other resources that we've paid $5,000 for that have gone unused, so the per item cost per use of videogames has been relatively inexpensive.

Our interactive multimedia department has used a videogame to get ideas for a learning object they are animating for a large anatomy class on campus. We hope to be able to highlight the academic connections to videogames, as well as the connection to a local videogame company. Through internships with that local company, students can learn how to make games as well as play them.

This is also a way of fostering the Learning Commons ideals in the Science Library for relatively little money. If we have something here that students want to use, will they use the library as a space to do other things in? We hope so. The University of Illinois at Urbana-Champaign Undergraduate Library had that experience. Those students who are regular users of the collection take a proprietary interest in maintaining it and the space. We think the same thing is happening at the University of Oregon.

We also think that more and more disciplines will use videogames to teach other things, e.g., the use of simulations and games in the fields of anthropology, sociology, and environmental studies to understand social behavior and causal relationships in complex systems. Business students could use simulation games like *Tycoon* for the same purpose. Anatomy/human physiology could use games like *Trauma Center* to practice decision making skills. The possibilities are seemingly endless and we look forward to seeing how they develop.

Why this is Important, and Why We are Doing it

Within minutes of setting up the display case, a student asked me why we had them. He then confessed that he was studying videogames on his own time. Then he asked about checking out a console.

Generally the skepticism we've encountered comes from a near-moral high ground that very much elevates the noble academic mission that everyone in the university's employ must aspire to. The truth is that this kind of academic morality is very selective, and most often comes from a natural position of self interest; i.e., How is this going to benefit me, my department, my research, et cetera. This can be tough to argue against because the library can't tell anyone what to research, or how to research it. So if a history professor doesn't see the point of the game collection because it doesn't further her research, she is correct in her assumption that it is useless to her.

The comparison that we've used most is between this collection and our film collection. The nature, subject, and quality of each individual production can vary wildly. Each piece might only be useful to a handful of disciplines. It is relatively new media whose relevance is largely pushed by consumer demand, and is subject to format changes and price wars. And yet we have invested considerable funds in expanding our video collection. Much like movies, videogames have become socially and culturally relevant as well as financially profitable.

Videogames will grow and change, but they are not going away. Hopefully they will change for the better. One way to do that is to make them, and the discourse surrounding them, smarter. A significant percentage of what is written about gaming is simple service journalism.

Consumers need to know when a game is coming out, will their controllers work with it, if it is any good, etc. But real game criticism is still in its infancy (see Chuck Klosterman's article and Clive Thompson's response. http://www.esquire.com/features/ESQ0706KLOSTER_66 and http://www.wired.com/gaming/gamingreviews/commentary/games/2006/07/71290)

Educated people are woefully ill-equipped to discuss and critique videogames, in part because the academic world still traditionally considers them unworthy of notice. What that doesn't take into account, of course, is that academia is not the arbiter of cultural relevance. It is necessary, as an academic institution, to acknowledge and react to the cultural growth that happens around us and outside us. Ultimately, questioning the importance of an academic understanding of videogames sounds just as silly as questioning the importance of an academic understanding of our culture. Is this kind of understanding strictly necessary to our existence? Of course not. But can we benefit from the ideas and hard work of others whose interest leads them to seek tools to further our collective understanding through critical discourse and scholarly debate? Simply: yes.

If we can help provide the tools, of course we should do so.

Appendix

For more information on the gaming program at the University of Oregon, please visit https://scholarsbank.uoregon.edu/dspace/handle/1794/5456

Positioning the Library as a Source for Industry and Career Information for the Videogame Business

Tracey Amey

Introduction

Libraries all over the country, including university libraries, have seen the benefit of adding gaming tournaments to their programming or including games in the circulating collection, but the field of gaming, as a developed, persistent industry, is largely ignored. Many academic librarians believe that adding some titles on game design and game research is enough. For an accurate reflection of today's videogame field, it is not enough. A business that has captured the imagination, attention and time of so much of the academic population, including students, faculty and staff, deserves a collection development policy that supports its considerable expansion and evolution.

In 2005, at the Pennsylvania College of Technology (Penn College) in Williamsport, PA, we decided to create a collection development policy that reflected the state of the videogame industry, from its origins to its current unrestricted growth. The motivation behind developing such a collection was to position the campus library as the number one resource place for this highly influential industry. We had questions coming from all representatives of our campus community, students, faculty and staff that pertained to any number of questions about the industry. How did one go about breaking in to the field? Where could one find research on the influence of games on learning? Did the library have any books on DirectX, the graphics software? In response, we developed a policy directing us to focus on a variety of types of materials:

- Professional journals
- Current design program books
- Retrospectives or titles chronicling the history of the videogame industry
- Non-print media to represent the visual aspects of videogames
- Key Web sites that provide current industry events and developments

- Published academic research on the educational and social influence of gaming
- Titles representing expansions into new fields for videogames, such as fiction or movies

The underlying intent of the policy was to not only support new classes on game design offered in the computer science curriculum, but also to provide the resources to help students and faculty become literate on the deep and wide range of information resources related to the industry.

The incitement for this new policy came first from the students at Penn College. As students neared graduation, they came to the library looking for resources on how to find a job in the videogame industry. While traditional resources such as *Occupational Outlook Handbook* and VGM's *Opportunities in* series provided basic information on the computer science field, these titles did not provide information on the unique culture of the game design field or how one went about finding a job in a field where following traditional job search paths may not be the best strategy. All one needs to do is watch the series of streaming media shorts on how to break into game design from Paul Barnett, Creative Director at Electronic Arts (EA) Mythic, to see how the tried and true methods for getting an entry level position would not necessarily be the best choice in this field.[1]

The series consists of words of advice on how to get a job in the videogame industry, available from a creative director at one of the most successful companies in the field. This would make a great resource for anyone starting their job search strategy. The catch is that this information is available only on the internet. In a nutshell, collection development policies for the videogame industry must include a view that encompasses all the fields that are intersecting and cross-pollinating with the industry in order to be truly relevant to the end user. This policy should include gaming's influence on fields such as education, advertising, fiction writing and movie making.

Along with the growing divergence of the field itself, a collection development policy for this industry must also commit to collecting diverse resources in a wide variety of formats. Traditional resources, such as books, are not always the best mode to reach the technology-savvy users the collection will appeal to, nor are books the first place the industry promotes itself. To that end, this chapter will provide examples from all formats and kinds of resources, from printed materials to Web sites and streaming media.

This chapter will not, however, attempt to identify a complete title list of resources for the game industry. Indeed, that would be impossible and against the nature of the ever-evolving videogame field. Instead, it will focus on resources that are the best starting places to find the most current, relevant information and resources. These resources will continually lead to specific titles on the most recent software that is being employed by coders and designers or to the current academic research on videogames. These sources have been selected as places you can turn to time and again to keep current with the industry. Keeping current and relevant with the field will aid in promoting the library as a continually valid resource center for all your users.

Along with these specific resources, this chapter will also have sections on outreach opportunities and ways to promote the library's collection and position the library as the campus source for your users' information needs regarding the videogame industry.

Building a Gaming Industry Collection
Journals

If you subscribe to one professional journal in the videogame industry, there is no question that it should be *Game Developer Magazine (ISSN 1073-922X)* published by CMP Media. *Game Developer* is the print journal source for developers, programmers, marketers and job seekers in the gaming field. Each issue has articles that range from the latest shadowing techniques to the pros and cons of the contractual career path. The interviews and roundtables as well as the "State of the Industry" articles series provide the industry leader names. Even the advertisements for upcoming conferences and for open positions are gems for anyone trying to start a career in the field. This title is one of the best for keeping current on the information and developments in the field. It is a resource you should not only have, but read regularly to keep abreast of any new resource collection needs.

The Easter eggs of *Game Developer* (in electronic media, an "Easter egg" is a hidden feature or novelty), are the journal's annual lists and salary surveys. The surveys cover award winners for best programs, tools, books and hardware. Top publishers are listed every year in the October issue. There is also a Fall Career Guide supplement published annually. All this information is vital for a library to be aware of if its goal is to be a viable resource center. Finally, what every would-be game designer wants to know is covered in every April in the Salary Survey issue. This issue alone is worth the modest subscription price of approximately $50 and holds important, difficult-to-find-elsewhere information for any type of library and user. The most recent salary information was published in the April 2008 issue and can be found in the journal published annually at approximately the same time every year.[2]

Research publications are often mentioned in game industry journals and the trade publications alone can help you keep abreast of the current trends in videogame research, but consider adding to your collection one or two peer-reviewed titles as well. *Games and Culture: A Journal of Interactive Media* is a peer-reviewed quarterly journal publishing research in the field of game studies and *Game Studies, the International Journal of Computer Game Research* (ISSN 1604-7982, http://gamestudies.org/) is an online research journal you can add to your RSS reader.

Finally, there is no better source for what is up and coming and who is hot than the popular gaming journals themselves. *Games for Windows (ISSN 0744-6667), PC Gamer (ISSN 1080-4471), Game Informer (ISSN 1067-6392), Electronic Gaming Monthly (ISSN 1058-918X),* and *Game Pro (ISSN 1042-8658)* are examples of popular videogame magazines and are inexpensive. These titles are excellent resources for keeping on top of anticipated releases, and they demonstrate your library's willingness to support the user experience of gaming.

Programming Titles

An important aspect in Penn College's collection development policy was to actively maintain titles, whether in print or electronic format, on the current software used in game design. This included not only resources exclusively on game design software, but also resources on software used by players after a game has been released into the market, such as modification creation software.

Many popular games now allow users to create what are known as "mods," or modifications, to game titles. These can be user interfaces or graphics modifications or new maps and environs that a player creates to change the look or experience of the original game. The modification creator then makes them freely available to other players. Users can utilize all types of software to create these modifications. The academic library can support these efforts by providing the titles that may be tutorials or how-to's for gaming software. The importance of the library supporting this kind of activity is not simply supporting students' hobbies. In fact, creating mods can lead to a career in the game design field.[3] Game design companies regularly ask for any mods a potential recruit has created to be included in their portfolio as a means of evaluating the individual's abilities. Mod creation is, in fact, a serious exercise.

For many years now, DirectX has been the Windows standard gaming program used for graphics and sounds. However, Microsoft periodically releases new versions of DirectX. As new video cards and games are released, they often take advantage of the most current release of

DirectX. It is important to keep resources on the most current DirectX available. Professional trade journals, such as *Game Developer* and game development Web sites (to be discussed later) are often the best sources for information on upcoming releases of DirectX.

Another popular graphics language currently being used is OpenGL. This 3D language has become a de facto standard supported in Unix, Windows and Macintosh computers. XNA and the Unreal Engine are other game design programs to be aware of in your collection development policy. Again, getting familiar with the trade publications will keep you abreast of new software developments.

History of Gaming

You wouldn't think an industry that began just over twenty-five years ago would necessarily have a lengthy narration, but as with many aspects of the videogame business, this one is unique. The industry has naturally developed as quickly as the computer industry that is its backbone and at this time, the tables have turned in many respects. The videogame industry is challenging the computer industry, requiring improvements in components such as processor speeds and graphic cards to meet the needs of the videogame community. However, videogames have a beginning unique from that of the computer industry and the titles that follow document some of that history. For the most part, they are considered to be classics by the very audience that watched and read them. Again, this is not necessarily a checklist, but these are titles to be aware of, as the games or developments they represent play a significant role in the history of the field.

Doom, the game that many say started the videogame revolution, and its creation at the hands of John Romero and John Carmack, is chronicled in the classic title *Masters of Doom: How Two Guys Created an Empire and Transformed Pop Culture*. *Doom* is considered by many gamers to be the grandfather of all personal computer games, and its importance should not be overlooked. Similarly, *The Ultimate History of Video games: From Pong to Pokemon—The Story Behind the Craze That Touched Our Lives and Changed the World* is a tribute to "all things videogame" from the very beginning. From personal anecdotes from the original game designers themselves to the founding of the big names in videogames, like Sega and Nintendo, this book covers the early history of the industry, and is, again, representative of the industry's history.

Undeniably, Japan has had a defining influence on videogames. This influence should be acknowledged in any good gaming collection. *Power-Up: How Japanese Video Games Gave the*

World an Extra Life by Chris Koehler incorporates rare insights into the design industry in Japan. Koehler lived in Japan and speaks Japanese. Consequently, his book is one of the few English-language books with a real insider's look into videogame design history in Japan.

Equally important to books in the gaming industry is visual media. Videogame design and production does not simply center on releasing a piece of software anymore. Games are often seen as potential movies. Of course, one movie that first portrayed the potential of computers and their interconnectivity is *Tron* (Disney Pictures, 1982). Many things make *Tron* worthy of including in a videogame industry collection. First, its very use of computers in production represents Hollywood's first toe in CGI waters. Secondly, the story itself is about computer games and the ability to connect to other game players. While the film missed winning an Oscar, it has long been considered important not only for its portrayal of videogames, but mostly for its groundbreaking use of computers in filmmaking.[4]

Tron, of course, spawned a successful videogame. The films-to-videogame phenomenon has long been a staple of the videogame industry. However, the games-to-film genre has had some commercial success with film series such as *Resident Evil*. You may also want to consider titles such as *Lara Croft: Tomb Raider*, *Mortal Kombat* and *Doom* as successful examples of videogames made into motion pictures.

And finally, there is *World of Warcraft*. What history of the videogame industry would be complete without at least an acknowledgement of the behemoth that is Blizzard's massively multiplayer online role-playing game (MMORPG)? At the time of this writing, several books that focus on the phenomenon that is *World of Warcraft* are in the publication process. At Penn College, we currently have several books on the game, including research publications and strategy guides. Given the historical significance of this videogame, I am certain much more research on it will be published in the future, and we intend to watch for titles attentively.

Other Recommended Titles

The following titles represent what I believe are essential books for anyone who is developing a gaming resources collection. They not only help the reader understand the videogame phenomenon (which is vital if you are attempting to become a viable resource center for the industry), but they are also significant to the field in and of themselves.

Published in 2004, *Got Game? How the Gamer Generation is Reshaping Business Forever* by John Beck is one of the first titles to take a research approach to explaining the impact of videogames on the behaviors and attitudes of those raised from infancy with videogame controls in their hands. Beck looks at gamers' behaviors from a positive stance and asks older generations to think about how best to get through to this very different group of potential employees and customers.

In 2003 at the first Austin Game Conference, Raph Koster presented "A Theory of Fun" as the keynote. The subsequent book (*A Theory of Fun*, Paraglyph Press, 2004) has become a must-read for any would-be game designer, or in fact, anyone interested in why it is people play games and what they get out of them. This title is not only a slice of videogame industry history as a manifestation of the first Austin conference, but it also makes academic research in the field accessible to all.

Web Sites

The gaming industry moves at a rapid pace and there is no better way to keep on top of industry developments than by using the Web. At Penn College, we made the decision to incorporate game-related Web sites into our online catalog. Part of our positioning strategy was to provide our users with a single place to go to find all kinds of resources about the videogame industry, whether they were physically in our collection or not. With that goal in mind, including Web sites important to the videogame field in our catalog was essential. The Web sites below are not only good resources to include in any game discipline collection, but they are also excellent sources for the news, events and information that any librarian interested in the industry should be aware of and have in their RSS reader.

Leading the teeming pack of gaming sites is *Gamasutra.com*. The CMP Game Group, publishers of *Game Developer Magazine*, has this to say about its site and I could not think of any better way to put it:

Gamasutra.com provides features, industry news, product news, job listings, comprehensive resume and contractor databases, and a directory of schools and training programs relevant to game developers. In essence, Gamasutra addresses everything game developers need to improve their skills, interact with other developers, learn about products, find work and locate services in their areas.[5]

Along with *Gamasutra*, we have included the Web site for the Entertainment Software Association in our catalog (http://*theesa.com*). The ESA is one of the top sites for statistical data about the game industry, from sales data to the demographics of game players and buyers. If you see data quoted on the industry, chances are the source is ESA.

Trade shows and conventions are also very important in the industry. The Electronic Entertainment Expo (E3) is covered internationally and is considered the place to unveil upcoming games and company plans. Although attendance is by invitation only, coverage is available from a variety of Web sites including official coverage at E3 Insider (http://*e3expo.com*). Another industry conference that must be followed is the Game Developer Conference (http://*gdconf. com*). For those hoping to break into the industry, there is always a career pavilion and several career events at the conference as well as an online list of companies at the career exhibit for those unable to attend in person.

Finally, the last component I feel would be valuable to include, but not strictly necessary, is a representation of how the gaming industry has branched out into other areas of publishing. Any gamer will get excited at the thought of getting their hands on a strategy guide for a newly released title. I include these in Penn College's collection for two reasons. The first is that they represent a career path for someone who is interested in game development, but may not be interested in being a designer and secondly, it stimulates interest in other titles related to gaming. The cost of strategy guides is relatively minor, but including these titles in an academic collection can lead to the campus community discovering other titles about gaming in the collection. Along those lines, we have also included fiction works and soundtracks that are related to some of the most popular games, such as *Halo* or *World of Warcraft*.

Collection development in the game industry must, I believe, be conceptualized outside traditional physical representations. The industry itself exists so wholly outside the printed word that to attempt to represent it in the same manner in an academic library collection goes against logic. The latest and most sought after information exists, at this time, on the Internet. The industry itself is represented in software and in non-print media. So to conceptualize your collection development policy, look and listen to the gaming world around you as your guide. The users themselves will tell you where you will want to take your collection.

Outreach Opportunities
Faculty Outreach

As student demand for classes about gaming increased, the faculty of Penn College looked to the library for resources not only related to the design aspects, but also information about the field as whole. The videogame industry was a new area for everyone, and the entire campus community required a place they could learn about all of its aspects, not just practical design applications and software. To introduce the faculty to the industry, a bibliography of library resources was created. This list was used by the computer science faculty in formulating a new curriculum for a proposed four-year degree on gaming and simulation. A current list of Penn College's videogame industry resources can be found on the web at http://home.pct.edu/~tamey/resources/video_game_resources.pdf.

In the spring of 2007, the library wanted to offer students a workshop on how to land a job in the videogame industry, one of the most frequent career requests we received from our computer science students. Our Computer Science faculty were consulted during the planning stages of the workshop. Soliciting their input provided not only valuable information for the workshop, but also opened the door for faculty/librarian collaboration outside the traditional classroom. The faculty had the chance to see how the resources of the library could complement the information literacy needs of our students outside the standard research paper. Our collection, with its depth of coverage of the industry, provided an educational experience for the faculty as well as the students. Indeed, the workshop was attended by the faculty in addition to students, because the faculty also felt they had a great deal to learn about the field.

These opportunities, such as the resources list and the workshop, threw open wide the door between the Computer Science faculty and me, their subject librarian. By providing a resource list, the faculty was able to see how deep and wide our collection ranged. Our collection represented sectors of the videogame field previously unknown by the faculty. The workshop provided the opportunity to show faculty information literacy at work: preparing students to use information resources in a real-world setting by incorporating them into a career workshop. Projects proposed by the library are now enthusiastically welcomed by the faculty and promoted to their students in the classroom. Also, the faculty continuously consults with the library first as their source for current, relevant, and reliable information on the videogame field.

Student Outreach

One of our challenges at Penn College at the start of our project to build a gaming collection was the lack of any curriculum related to gaming. Without our traditional access road of the formal information literacy classroom experience, reaching students interested in the field— and there were many of them—called for new methods. First, I became involved as an advisor for the campus gaming organization. This provided me with direct access to those students already aware and highly interested in the field. At informal discussions during club meetings, I asked them directly what the library could do to support them. First, they asked for a place to play their videogames as a group. Library gaming tournaments have been known to be wildly popular for some time now, but we looked for additional opportunities to have gaming experiences piggy-back off of previously untapped events in the library. We included a gaming component in the library's Casino Night as well as providing our TV-equipped study rooms during off hours for group console playing.

They also asked for books that supported not only videogames, but also pen-and-paper role playing games, such as *Dungeons and Dragons*. After attending one of their scheduled gaming sessions, their reasons for wanting the books became apparent. Gamers are good multi-taskers and more than one student would be playing a videogame on a laptop while seated at a table simultaneously playing a pen-and-paper game. We made a small investment of a few basic volumes of role-playing game books, which were instantly popular. Our openness to purchasing these books made the students see the library in a different light.

Finally, these discussions provided valuable information as to what the students were actually doing in these videogames. As stated previously, "mods," or modifications, are highly popular among videogame players. Players create, share and use them freely. I found students anxious to share all kinds of valuable information, such as what software they used to create mods or what games had the most mods available. This information fed directly into our collection development policy. If the game industry looked to hire the creators of the best mods, then we wanted to have the resources for our students to create these mods. Again, supporting our students with these non-traditional academic resources paid off with a collection of books that flew out our doors.

Many students also expressed interest in finding a job in the videogame industry, but felt they had no information on how they could go about getting one. These discussions led to the library's first information literacy workshop for gamers. The presentation, entitled "Got Game? What You Need to Know to Break in to the Gaming Industry," was designed to give students who were interested in working in the videogame field information that went beyond *Occupational Outlook Handbook* or a traditional career book. The session covered such topics as the wide variety of jobs in the videogame field, jobs beyond game design, such as those involved in writing or marketing. It covered resources for basic job information such as the salaries of specific jobs. We also covered how to find out who the biggest game producing companies were and what the highest selling types of games were currently. The underlying goal of the session, never once directly discussed with the students, was to teach them to be literate in the information resources of the field of their interest. We discussed resources for job outlooks, professional trade publications, and even how to determine the reliability of information all within a workshop not related to any specific class. Instead, the class related to a specific industry. Our plan is to run the workshop every spring for graduating students. A copy of the PowerPoint used in the workshop is available at http://home.pct.edu/~tamey/. Also, an accompanying list of tagged web resources distributed to the class is available at http://gamingcareers.blinklist.com/.

The Library as the Source for Game Industry Information

The final piece of the initial project was to build campus-wide awareness of the library as *the resource* on campus for information on the videogame industry. We wanted our students, faculty and our staff to explore this new collection we built. Some of our efforts have already been discussed: faculty outreach and non-traditional workshops for students and advising gaming-related clubs. However, we also wanted the collection to have a highly visible and visual position on campus. We wanted to draw the community's attention to the gaming resources and ultimately, to the library. We wanted the collection to take them by surprise. After our initial acquisition of books and materials, we devised our first display dedicated to gaming.

The goal of our first display was to showcase the gaming industry's expansion into different arenas. Following the industry's lead, we created a graphically colorful display that highlighted the new areas that videogames had ventured into by showcasing professional journals in the field, research publications, and game design books. We judged our success by how quickly the resources were checked out or taken from the display. They went quickly.

Since this first display, we have actively planned and scheduled regular displays related to the game industry. Some of our displays have coincided with major game releases or events in the industry. We felt this showcased the library not only as a place for gaming resources but also as a resource for up-to-the-minute coverage of events in the industry. For example, the library celebrated the release of *Halo 3*, the highest pre-ordered videogame in the history of the market, with a display on the game's ubiquitous influence in artwork, in computer graphics, in videogame design and even in the research of play. We have also had displays on game design software releases such as DirectX 10 and XNA and highly anticipated game expansion releases such as *World of Warcraft's Burning Crusades*. The students and faculty have been very responsive and even the administration has taken note of our efforts.

Conclusion

The goal of Penn College's gaming collection development policy was twofold. We wanted not only to build a physical collection representing the entirety of the burgeoning field of videogames, but also to position the library as a vital, contemporary and persistent resource for information on the industry. While offering gaming nights in the library computer lab is an excellent way to bring students into the library environment, this project's goal was to show our user community that we recognize videogames as a field growing in influence and importance in the modern world, a field that is rapidly moving beyond its computer science roots and into education and social research. Our policy plan, which included physical and virtual collection building, outreach to faculty and outreach to students has turned Penn College's Madigan Library into the place students, faculty and administration look to first for the most up-to-date and important information available on the videogame industry.

Notes

1. Paul Barnett, "How To Get Into the Industry," IGN, http://media.pc.ign.com/articles/792/792352/vids_1.html (Accessed November 5, 2007).
2. Jill Duffy, "Game Developer's 6th Annual Salary Survey," *Game Developer* 14, no. 4 (2007): 7-13.
3. Hector Postigo, "Of Mods and Modders: Chasing Down the Value of Fan-Based Digital Game Modifications," *Games and Culture* 2, no. 4 (2007): 300.
4. Ellen Wolff, "*Tron* Then and Now," *Millimeter* 35, no. 4 (2007): 30.

5. "CMP Game Group Asserts Editorial Authority in Game Industry by Winning a Webby Award for Gamasutra.com and a Maggie Award for Game Developer," United Business Media, http://ubm-technology.mediaroom.com/index.php?s=43&item=1698 (Accessed December 18, 2007).

 CHAPTER 4

Gaming in the Classroom: A Model for Support in an Academic Library

David Ward, Mary Laskowski, and Christian Sandvig

Introduction

The explosive worldwide impact of videogames in the past decade (with yearly sales reaching $12.5 billion in 2006[1]) has begun to reverberate in the collections and programming of libraries. But while a spring 2007 study found that over 70% of public libraries supported gaming in some way[2], evidence of academic library participation (such as a strong presence in the scholarly literature[3] or the LibSuccess Wiki section on gaming[4]) has so far been scant. Fortunately, interdisciplinary scholarly interest in gaming research and classroom integration, fueled by positive reports from scholars and entities such as the Federation of American Scientists[5], grant opportunities from notables such as the MacArthur Foundation grant for Digital Media, Learning and Education[6] and the Library of Congress National Digital Information Infrastructure and Preservation Program (NDIIPP) Digital Preservation Program grant[7], and events such as the ALA TechSource Gaming, Learning, and Libraries Symposium[8], have created many opportunities for libraries to position themselves as centers for scholarly research and classroom support of gaming. This chapter details an investigation into specific roles the academic library can play in support of scholarly teaching activities related to gaming, and investigates the opportunities, advantages, and overall viability of positioning academic libraries as a physical and virtual hub for pedagogical gaming support.

Library Environment

The Undergraduate Library at the University of Illinois at Urbana-Champaign began its involvement in campus gaming activities in the Spring of 2006, with an initial purchase of one hundred games (the top twenty-five best sellers for Xbox, Xbox 360, Nintendo GameCube, and the PlayStation 2 (PS2)) and related hardware to form its research and teaching collection. The collection has since grown to approximately 250 games in the Fall of 2007, and now includes portable games (PlayStation Portable (PSP) and Nintendo DS) as well as PC/Mac games. The impetus for the collection was the formation of a campus mailing list for gaming researchers, begun in the Fall of 2005, as well as patron demand and interest in gaming. Gaming nights, featuring competitions, prizes, and speakers from the campus gaming research group, were held in the Spring and Fall semesters of 2006 and Fall 2007, following the examples of public and academic libraries such as the Ann Arbor District Library (http://www.aadl.org/aadlgt/) and Wake Forest University.[9] Finally, the library established a gaming Web site[10] in Spring 2006 to chronicle library and campus collections, research, and teaching activities related to gaming.

Project Background

"Communication Technology and Society" is an undergraduate general education course (SPCM 280). It enrolls a maximum of one hundred students, is taught yearly, and employs one instructor, two to four graduate teaching assistants, and one to two undergraduate teaching interns. Students meet weekly in two plenary weekly large lectures and one smaller discussion section. The course is organized around an introductory survey of the implications of various historical and modern communication technologies from stone tablets to videogames. In topic and structure, it is similar to courses offered by most Departments of Communication and some Departments of Library and Information Science at many universities.[11] In the course, students are frequently required to learn about newer information technologies by using them. These include Web page design, blogs, wikis, and various search engines.

After teaching the course twice, the instructor wanted to add a unit that would include videogames as a topic of study but also potentially use videogames as a way to teach other course material. This opportunity came about because the 2005 bestselling PC/Mac multiplayer game *Civilization IV* (hereafter *CIV IV*) included a simulation of communication technology and society. In the game, players can make decisions about investing in the development of writing, libraries, mass media, or the Internet. They can construct cultural projects like stone monuments and networks of broadcasting stations. These features exist in the commercial version of the game available in stores. Pedagogically, this technology was intended by the instructor as a simulation that would support the goal of making students more responsible for their own learning (often called "active learning") and develop critical thinking about new media.[12] It should be noted that this is an unusual and difficult ambition. Most university courses that experiment with digital media are small seminars, not large lectures.

The collaboration between the instructor and the library came from a humble beginning: every other place the instructor had asked for support had turned him down. Specifically, the class unit on gaming required student participation in a collaborative gaming environment, necessitating a gaming lab to be established where the modified version of *CIV IV* could be loaded on multiple PCs and LAN gaming supported. The class objectives also required an environment where students could access the game during a wide variety of hours and have access to basic technical support for getting it up and running.

The class needs were a perfect match for pre-existing services and recent improvements in the technological infrastructure of the Undergraduate Library. Specifically, the library processes and houses a large centralized reserve collection, which included multimedia items such as videos. Additionally, a forty-computer library classroom was completed in early Fall 2006, and the video cards had been upgraded in late 2006 to run Second Life, and their specs allowed them to handle *CIV IV* as well. The library also had a small gift fund specifically for gaming activities that could be used to develop any needed infrastructure for the course. Finally, as home to the gaming collection for the university, the librarians and staff were familiar with many of the technical and functional needs required to circulate and provide access to videogames.

In a 2006 meeting, the authors outlined a plan to provide access to *CIV IV* in a variety of formats, including placing the game on course reserve and utilizing the library classroom as part of the lab sections of the course. Library Information Technology (IT) was brought in to discuss support and troubleshooting needs, and part of a student worker's time in the IT department was allocated to support the project. Meetings continued throughout the Spring 2007 semester to make sure the access mechanisms devised kept up with the evolving needs of the course, as more details about how *CIV IV* was to be used pedagogically and technologically in the course were fleshed out.

Methodology
Initial Setup
Implementation began with an assessment of which existing library services and facilities would work for the class, and which new services and facilities would have to be created. The initial plan was for the library to purchase multiple copies of the game for reserve (a total of four were

purchased), and to equip a stand-alone library PC (the beginnings of a library "gaming cluster") to dual boot with both standard and gaming capabilities. In early Spring 2007 a conference call was arranged with representatives of Firaxis (the game's creator) and 2K Games (the distributor). The representatives were enthusiastic about the game being used in a university-level environment (the previous version of the franchise, *Civilization III,* was used in high school classes[13]), and agreed to send an additional thirty copies of the game for use in the class to be used as needed.

These thirty copies were used to provide access to the game in multiple ways, and added to the reserve collection for in-library use. Additionally, the library's instructional classroom was modified so that the profile for each of the forty computers in it was set up to include an installation of *CIV IV* which, along with the "gaming cluster" PC, required an individual disc to be loaded in order for the game to run.

The classroom space was used in two different ways. First, it served as a teaching lab for each of the course sections, where the instructor and his teaching assistants introduced the game to students, and walked them through playing it in group (LAN) based scenarios. Second, during the Spring 2007 semester the library established lab hours specifically for the course in the evenings after regular teaching activities in the room were done. The lab hours were staffed by library graduate assistants, who effectively served as room monitors and did little to no instruction on actual gameplay, outside of helping students load it initially. These evening hours were offered Sunday, Monday, and Tuesday nights for the duration of the assignment. The game was also available as an online download via Steam (http://www.steampowered.com/v/index.php), which allowed for students to install it to their desktops directly from the Internet.

The final option students had for playing the game was to purchase a copy for themselves to load on their home computer. In sum, the options the students had for accessing the game were: checking out a one-day overnight reserve copy (three PC and one Mac available); using the gaming cluster PC in the library; coming to a class lab session in the library instruction lab and using one of the donated copies processed for reserves; buying the game outright; or downloading a copy via Steam. This resulted in two options for in-library use (gaming cluster, lab hours), and three options for personal use (purchase a copy, use Steam, or check out a library overnight reserve copy and use at home).

Library Technical Services

Processing games for the library collection or for use as reserve materials involved implementing a number of new procedures and enhanced training for processing staff. In most cases, the games in the new gaming collection were ordered title by title through a local game store due to problems identifying and ordering specific versions online or through traditional book vendors. Additional issues resulted from the fact that games, even more than other media formats, quickly go out of print, and there is a wider variety of playback equipment to maintain to provide in-library support for the various gaming platforms.

The media catalogers had to develop procedures for cataloging games, many of which required original rather than copy cataloging due to the lack of game title holdings in library collections. Specific issues included standardization of new subject terminology for ease in searching the library online catalog, assignment of new prefixes for call numbers, and creation of appropriate public notes to designate which platform(s) a title is held for.

For this collaborative project, the library-owned copies of the game were rush ordered and cataloged, repackaged for security, and given appropriate item types, statuses and locations in the library online catalog as placed on reserve under the instructor's name and course number. The copies received from the distributor for the course were treated as though they were instructor personal copies and were given brief "quickbib" bibliographic records in the online catalog. In order to facilitate the use of these thirty copies both individually and for group lab use, the games were cataloged both as a set with one barcode for speedy checkout to the instructor or teaching assistant for the course, and as individual records with unique barcodes and copy numbers for individual use by the students. They were given a checkout period of four hours, which is twice the standard reserve loan of two hours, in order to facilitate class use without needing to renew the items. As the project (and growth of the gaming collection in general) progressed, a number of additional staff were trained in how to correctly identify, order, receive, catalog, mark, and shelve games for the various platforms.

The primary pedagogical goal for the instructor in this project was to develop student fluency in thinking critically about non-linear digital media, a large and increasing part of most students' lives. To that end, students spent three weeks with the game, writing one short paper each week (each 250 words). The assignments were designed to promote independent discovery of the way the simulation worked, and then to encourage students to critique or commend the simulation by making reference to course lectures and readings. Students played a modified version of the game designed to make gameplay faster and hence to fit in a fifty-minute class period.[14]

Staff Training

All public services staff and several technical services staff required some degree of training prior to the class coming in to use *CIV IV*. The public services staff training consisted of a description and walkthrough of the various options for using the game, as well as encouragement to play the game on the gaming cluster to become familiar with questions students might ask. One point that was stressed during training was that library staff were expected to know all of the options for getting the game into students' hands, but that they were not responsible for providing assistance/advice on actually playing the game once students successfully got it launched. Library graduate assistants received additional training on using the game in the lab environment and were pointed to the online class page with instructions for setting up games for the class to use with students. As much as possible, the copies of the game on reserve were set up to mirror other media reserves the library held, in terms of checkout periods, marking, and charging/discharging procedures.

Evaluation Plan

The project employed a mix of qualitative and quantitative methods for both formative and summative assessments. In line with the project's research goal of determining best practices for collaborations with academic classroom use of gaming, measurements were developed jointly during the implementation phase of the project to analyze student use of the library options for gaming, track staff time allocated towards the class, monitor facilities and technology required, and determine whether the library proved a suitable partner from the instructor's perspective.

Students in the class were given two web-based surveys of forty items each about gaming and the assignment. The confidential surveys were administered during class time using a pre-test/post-test design (given before and after the three weeks on gaming). There was no incentive for participation. It included a demographics panel, questions about the game, questions about library use, and a panel on computing skill.[15] The teaching staff were also debriefed extensively after the project. Finally, one lecture period at the end of the semester was used to host a university-wide forum on the effectiveness of the project in which students and teaching staff participated with invited experts on digital media and learning.[16]

Findings

The collaboration between the instructor and the library worked well, and the results indicate an important role for academic libraries in supporting this kind of coursework. The pedagogical results of this project were mixed, but were promising enough to continue to develop the use of CIV IV in subsequent offerings of the course.

There were ninety-two students enrolled in the course, and fifty-seven of these participated in the *CIV IV* project.[17] A total of forty students completed the in-class survey (a response rate of 70%). The class was not composed of experienced gamers. Half the class was self-reported novices, with 20% of survey respondents indicating that they had never played any kind of electronic or computer game, while the next 32% played any game at most "a few times a semester" (*n*=39). Just three respondents had ever played any game in the multi-game *Civilization* franchise (*n*=39). Even though half of the students were not regular gamers, all of them were frequent computer users, with 100% reporting that they used a computer one or more times per day on an average school day (*n*=39).

Total Time and Resource Investment

Four members of the teaching staff spent an additional forty-six hours in total (in addition to normal duties) proctoring sessions in the game lab and attending meetings to coordinate and plan the project. This is likely a recurring requirement. Development of the modified version of the game for class use was the most time-consuming activity, accounting for about eighty hours of development time by the instructor, and about twelve hours of time volunteered by six play testers. However, this is a one-time investment that will not need to be repeated. Firaxis Games and 2K Games donated games valued at $1470 for physical copies and $3600 in additional licenses.

The library's commitment to the project included a combination of staff time (through training, classroom setup and monitoring, and technical services work) and a monetary investment for equipment and copies of the game. For staff time, Library IT contributed a total of five hours from one of their student workers for setting up the gaming lab; purchasing and installing the gaming cluster computer; and working with the instructor and his TAs on installing and testing the game mod to ensure it worked properly. Library graduate assistants monitored the gaming lab a total of six hours/week for three weeks. Public services staff training time was negligible, as all training was conducted as part of existing regular weekly training.

The library spent approximately $800 on the gaming cluster computer, which was essentially a modified version of the standard public PC used by the library, and an additional $200 for five copies of the game (three PC and two Mac). Total staff costs (for IT student worker and graduate assistant time) are estimated at $130. Technical services staff, already developing new procedures for support of games as a unique format, spent roughly thirty hours engaged in the acquisition, cataloging, marking and processing of *CIV IV* as reserve materials. While this is several times as long as would be needed to process a print or electronic reserve request of equal size, the hope is that having invested the time and energy up front to develop the necessary procedures will allow the library to mainstream processing of games as reserve materials in the future.

Student Preferences for Playing CIV IV

Table 1 summarizes student responses for how they accessed the game during the class, based on the survey. Extrapolating from another survey question ($n = 26$), we estimate that students started new *CIV IV* games 213 times outside of class. They reported starting a mean of 5.3 games each (standard deviation 3.2 games).

Table 1: Student Self-reported Game Access Method (n = 40)	
Question from Survey	Yes
I played the game for this class in the computer lab at the Undergraduate Library	83%
I played the game for this class during discussion section.	63%
I played the game for this class on my own computer	25%
I played the game for this class at the designated computer in the Undergraduate Library (not in a computer lab)	
I played the game for this class on my friend's computer.	3%

As Table 1 shows, it was a surprise to find that students preferred library gaming even though they were offered a free copy of the game to permanently install at home (a $39 value)—only nine students of the forty survey respondents accepted the free game. Only four students (10%) reported checking out a copy of the game from the library. Anecdotal evidence suggested that the installation requirements and lack of technical support discouraged students from trying to play at home. In fact, students requested additional library lab hours after the project began. Multiplayer lab play was preferred by many students even though they were not required by the out-of-class part of the class assignments.

Finally, Table 2 shows the results of a survey question looking at future student preferences for accessing games/software like *CIV IV*. The lab option rates highly here, as with Table 1, but students also report a higher preference for using the reserve option for the game (32.5%) than they did during the class (where only 10% of students indicated they checked out a reserve copy of the game).

Table 2: Future Preference for Accessing Software Like CIV IV	
Question: If you took another class that required software like Civilization IV, what would be your preferred method to obtain it? (n=35)	
Answer	Yes
Use a computer lab on campus that has the software already.	46%
Use a library copy on reserve that I can check out.	33%
Buy my own copy at the bookstore when I buy my books.	15%

While we found that students preferred class and lab time because of the ready availability of technical support and assistance with assignments, in fact the game was quite difficult for the teaching and library staff to support, even after extensive training. The game was clearly not designed for lab use. Collecting, tracking, and distributing DVD-ROMs was time-consuming, while the startup menus for the game itself were confusing. This led many students to start multiplayer games with different settings from other players, which caused the game to crash. A typographical error in a shortcut to the game also closed the lab for one day, sending students away frustrated. This sort of frustration with technical problems was widespread, leading just 36% of students to agree in their final evaluation games like this should be used in future courses, while an additional 35% were "neutral" (*n*=39).

Educationally, the game had a polarizing effect. Those students who were drawn into the game performed exceptionally well. Their written work on the gaming assignments was far more developed than other weekly assignments, and it was often over length. Writing by these successful, engaged students often included statements like, "After a lot of early confusion as to what to do and when, I slowly began to understand a little more each time." There was also some anecdotal evidence that the game appealed to a few students that otherwise would not have encountered this kind of digital media experience at all. As one student wrote, "I have to say, I hated this game at first. I was impatient and did not understand all of the complex steps that were involved. I was the girl who could never win a video game to save her life. UNTIL NOW."

An outside expert on digital media and learning who was invited to speak at our evaluation forum, Karrie Karahalios, remarked "There is a very steep learning curve for this game," but despite the difficulties, "the [student] reflection is the most valuable deliverable you have in this project." The assignments asked students "to come up with a theory and try to test it, and that is a very valuable experience." "You have students writing amazing narratives." "You are using… this technology as a social catalyst in the class," and it is very important "that [students] have both face-to-face time and 'virtual' [interaction] time playing this game."

Analysis & Conclusion

One of the key goals of the project was to determine the viability of both including games as a long-term reserve item for the library, as well as determining and assessing the most appropriate ways that libraries can partner with instructors to provide gaming support. A key finding is that the increasingly social nature of new videogame platforms suggests an important role for libraries. Even games (like this one) that provide computer-mediated gameplay are tools that, according to our experience, are often best used by groups in public labs, not at home alone. There are many important questions for libraries to consider when entering gaming partnerships with instructors, including: Can the game be played in a stand-alone environment, or is multiplayer interaction desired? Can the game be played out of-the-box, or is modification required? How many copies of a game will need to be accessed simultaneously? Is a monitored lab environment pedagogically desirable? What system requirements does the game have? Are there licensing restrictions on how the game can be accessed?

Relative to processing traditional print and electronic reserves for classes, the model developed for supporting one game for one class involved a significantly higher upfront investment of time and resources for the library. However, a lot of this took the form of one-time, start-up efforts—determining how to set up a LAN in the library lab for gaming, devising and training staff on new methods for accessing games that were different from print and e-reserve methods, and purchasing and setting up a gaming cluster computer to access the game. Now that this work has been done, adding different games for other classes in the future should require significantly less time and resources—primarily, staff contributions from IT to set up the game in a lab environment and/or on the gaming cluster computer. As games evolve (in terms of system/graphics requirements), additional hardware may also be needed to meet the demands of games other instructors may want to place on reserve.

Maintaining hardware and providing a classroom environment for gaming are the biggest concerns that developed out of this collaboration. *CIV IV* fortunately had very low system requirements which the existing library lab computers were able to meet, but instructors wanting to use more graphic- and processor-intensive games, or games that have an audio communication component (such as *World of Warcraft*), would require significant upgrades to existing computers, at a significant cost for a lab environment of forty PCs. Additionally, the library teaching lab is primarily intended for library instruction classes and was used for this class only on a pilot basis. Long term, the ever-increasing time demands for regular library classroom instruction make this particular room a bad match for ongoing support of classroom gaming.

Possible alternatives for a lab environment include expanding the gaming cluster (including investigating options for making all library PCs dual boot), and/or partnering with campus IT in developing a classroom space that could be used specifically for gaming. This space would include computers that would function as regular PCs in an open environment when not in use (the library lab is locked when not used for teaching), and also be set up to use whatever games from the library's collection that instructors put on reserve for a given semester. *CIV IV*, like many PC games, requires that an individual, physical copy (disc) be used with each computer the game is running on, making the library an ideal environment to develop a gaming lab in, since it houses the gaming collection, and an ideal place to develop a campus center for classroom gaming support.

But even for libraries without a classroom environment, student interest in using gaming/software reserves for future classes (from Table 2) suggests that the library would remain a good partner for classroom game reserves. As with traditional reserve services, gaming reserves allow an economical way for students to access required course content. In particular with gaming reserves, however, the social nature of gaming and the inherent collaboration/competition embedded in the gameplay of many titles suggests that a group environment to play the game in is an extra value-added element for gaming reserves.

Future Directions

As noted above, one of the primary findings to emerge from this collaboration was the need for a long-term classroom facility to support instructor use of gaming technology on a campus-wide level. The library's gaming collection and experiences with reserves position it as the ideal partner to take on this role, and one of the next steps the library is investigating is how to partner at the campus IT level in order to develop a facility for gaming support that will take advantage of the availability of the library's existing gaming resources.

But even this solution is a step towards a larger goal. As with other electronic resources the library purchases (such as online article databases, e-books, digital audio and film content, etc.), libraries in general need to negotiate with game creators and vendors to develop a purchasing model which will allow for simultaneous use of preloaded or remotely stored copies of games, without requiring that a physical disc be present in each individual PC. This would allow for a gaming lab to be set up anywhere, or even for regular library PCs (or campus computer lab PCs) to be used to access games as electronic resources in a similar manner that other library online research resources are accessed. The Steam multi-game platform (on which *CIV IV* is available) may be a step in this direction, and we will watch the development of multi-game platforms closely. The biggest hurdle to this kind of purchasing/content licensing arrangement is that present generation gaming software uses a combination of physically requiring discs in machines, along with entering multiple serial number/access codes tied to individual physical copies of games, as means of copy protection and requiring purchase of copies of a game by everyone that wants to use it. The library's experience with negotiating contracts for access to online content for multiple users makes it an ideal campus partner for providing support acquisition and access to games for classroom use.

The educational results of this project were promising enough that it will be continued in the course. The library will again provide support for the next iteration of this assignment. The key goals for further research and improvement will be to better structure training about the game in class settings in order to address the steep learning curve, to conduct more extensive "preflight" computer testing to reduce technical problems in our lab, and to work to eliminate the requirement that students must use physical DVD-ROMs. These last points lead to what is ultimately the largest question for this kind of project in the future. That is: if it is hoped that there is promise in using commercial digital media for education, how can the producers of digital media be convinced that the educational market is an important destination for their products? For efforts like this one to succeed on a larger scale, we need to design both licensing arrangements and software that meet the needs of academic clients like libraries.

Notes

1. "Video Game Sales Post a Record," MSNBC, http://www.msnbc.msn.com/id/16597649/ (accessed December 14, 2007).

2. Scott Nicholson. "The Role of Gaming in the Library: Taking the Pulse," http://boardgameswithscott.com/pulse2007.pdf (accessed December 14, 2007).

3. Danielle Kane, Catherine Soehner, and Wei Wei, „Building a Collection of Video Games in Support of a Newly Created Degree Program at the University of California, Santa Cruz," *Science & Technology Libraries* 27, no. 4 (2007): 77-87.

4. "Gaming," Library Success: A Best Practices Wiki, http://www.libsuccess.org/index.php?title=Gaming (Accessed December 14, 2007).

5. Federation of American Scientists, "Harnessing the power of video games for learning," Summit on Educational Games, http://www.fas.org/gamesummit/Resources/Summit%20on%20Educational%20Games.pdf.

6. MacArthur Foundation. Digital Media, Learning, and Education. http://www.macfound.org/site/c.lkLXJ8MQKrH/b.946881/k.380D/Domestic_Grantmaking__Education.htm (accessed December 14, 2007).

7. Library of Congress, " Digital Preservation Program Makes Awards to Preserve American Creative Works," http://www.loc.gov/today/pr/2007/07-156.html (accessed December 14, 2007).

8. ALA Techsource, "ALA TechSource Gaming, Learning, and Libraries Symposium," American Library Association, http://gaming.techsource.ala.org/index.php/Main_Page (accessed December 14, 2007).

9. Lynn Sutton and H. David Womack, "Got Game? Hosting Game Night in an Academic Library," *C&RL News* 67, no. 3 (2006): 173-6.

10. University Library, "Gaming Collection," University of Illinois at Urbana-Champaign, http://www.library.uiuc.edu/gaming/ (accessed December 14, 2007).

11. Alternate titles at other universities include "Information Technology and Society," "Media, Technology, and Society," and "Information Systems and Society."

12. In the literature on active learning there is a longstanding interest in simulations dating to paper-and-pencil roleplaying. See: John P. Hertel and Barbara J. Millis, *Using Simulations to Promote Learning in Higher Education.* (Sterling, Va.: Stylus Publishing, 2002); Chet Meyers and Thomas B. Jones, *Promoting Active Learning: Strategies for the College Classroom*, (San Francisco: Jossey-Bass, 1993).

13. Jenn Shreve, "Let the Games Begin: Entertainment Meets Education," *Edutopia Magazine*, April 2005, http://www.edutopia.org/let-games-begin (accessed December 14, 2007).

14. For details of the modifications, see http://pact.uiuc.edu/innismod/ . The mod (called "InnisMod") is freely available for download, however it requires a commercial copy of the game in order to run.

15. Eszter Hargittai, "Survey Measures of Web-Oriented Digital Literacy," *Social Science Computer Review* 23, no. 3 (2005): 371-9.

16. A streaming video of this fifty minute forum, called "Serious Games: Video Games in Undergraduate Education," is archived at http://pact.uiuc.edu/innismod (under "Dissemination").

17. An elective system allowed students to choose to perform a subset of the class assignments. All students participated in the in-class sessions, however.

 CHAPTER 5

Gaming in D. H. Hill Library, NC State University
Joe M. Williams and Mary C. Chimato

Overview

The D. H. Hill Library is the centerpiece of the North Carolina State University campus with over one million annual visitors, a 24-hour schedule, and a major research collection of books, e-resources, and other media. In March 2007, the NCSU Libraries opened a new space in D. H. Hill—a Learning Commons—that is not only student-centered, but student-defined.

NCSU Libraries recognizes the rapid changes taking place in how students study and learn, and in how they socialize and communicate with those around them. The Learning Commons is designed not just to accommodate these changes, but to facilitate more change and to offer students a place that provokes their imagination. In order to remain a space rich in possibility, the technologies, the services, the facility—all aspects of the Commons—will continually be informed by the students themselves and offer new ways to communicate and to learn.

Technologies currently available to students, faculty, and staff in the Learning Commons include over one hundred Mac & ShuttlePC workstations with an extensive menu of productivity and specialty software applications; six multimedia workstations with dedicated document scanners; two numeric & geospatial data workstations; and nine digital signs that provide imagery, information, announcements, and showcase student and faculty work throughout the learning space.

The Commons also offers a Presentation Practice Room, which can be reserved by students, with overhead LCD projector and Polyvision Walk-and-Talk interactive whiteboard, and two group study rooms with 42" wall-mounted LCD monitors for laptop display purposes. NCSU patrons may bring and use their own laptops in the 100% wireless D. H. Hill Library, or they can borrow a laptop or tablet PC from the Learning Commons service desk. Other technologies loaned from the service desk include audio and video iPods, iTouch, mp3 players, digital cameras and camcorders, GPS units, graphing calculators, and videogames and controllers for the various gaming consoles available in the Commons.

Reasons for Providing Games

The Learning Commons is the result of an intensive planning process that invited and implemented numerous recommendations from university faculty and students. Those recommendations included support for digital games to accompany the variety of multimedia support already offered in the library. The library also considered research findings about the study habits of the current generation of students ("Millennials" or "Y Gen") and the educational benefits of gaming; the experiences of other libraries that have created a Learning Commons; and the fact that gaming is a growing part of the curriculum and research at NC State (for example, see the NCSU Digital Games Research Center at http://dgrc.ncsu.edu/).

The D. H. Hill Library is open twenty-four hours a day during the fall and spring semesters, and students have often expressed their desire to spend long periods of time in the library with the opportunity to take breaks and play (chess, checkers, *Cranium*, and other board games are also available) and to be able to eat and drink while studying. The majority of feedback that the Libraries continue to receive about access to games from students who use the Learning Commons has been extremely positive, both formally from students on the University Library Committee and Student Advisory Board and informally through comments to library staff.

Serious games and virtual online environments are being used for a growing range of educational purposes in many disciplines, such as those where three-dimensional visualization enables new kinds of computer-mediated learning experiences. Faculty and students at NC State are investigating the scientific, design, social, and educational challenges of creating games and game technologies. North Carolina is home to a cluster of leading game companies that offer excellent employment opportunities to graduates in these areas. The Libraries seek to showcase leading-edge research being done at NC State while helping to make students aware of related educational and career opportunities.[1]

Gaming Technology Available

D. H. Hill Library has made an enthusiastic effort to provide students with easy access to a high-tech and comfortable environment for game play. Like other library services, gaming is available during all of the library's operating hours (24 hours Sunday-Thursday, closing at 10 p.m. on Friday and Saturday nights).

During operation hours, the Learning Commons is equipped with three 48-inch LCD monitors dedicated to gaming. One gaming console is connected to each screen: a Nintendo Wii, Sony PlayStation 3, and Microsoft Xbox 360. The monitors and consoles are mounted on rolling carts, which allow students or staff to move the systems when necessary. The consoles have been secured to the carts with locks. A small number of additional gaming consoles are also kept on hand to use during special events and as needed. Multiple controllers have also been purchased for each console, to accommodate the maximum number of possible players for each console, and to serve as replacements if and when a controller breaks. See the full equipment list below for details.

Circulating Equipment

To play games in the learning commons, patrons check out games and game controllers from the Learning Commons service desk by presenting their valid NC State All Campus ID. Games and controllers are loaned for a four-hour period of in-house use only. Renewals are not allowed by the system, but staff will renew a controller or game at a patron's request if there are no other patrons waiting to use the equipment.

If the patron has not borrowed a gaming console or other device from NCSU Libraries within the last twelve months (we also loan laptops, digital cameras, camcorders, etc.), they are required to read and sign a device lending agreement before completing the transaction. These agreements are kept on file for one year by Learning Commons staff, and signing of the agreement is noted and dated in the patron's electronic borrower's record.

The Learning Commons service desk is open and staffed all the hours the library is in operation. Reference and information services are provided at this service point by professional librarians, paraprofessional staff, and graduate students. Device lending (including videogames and game controller circulation) services and tier-one desktop support duties are provided by student technical assistants.

Overdue games and gaming equipment accrue overdue fines at the rate of $10.00/hour, and patrons are notified by e-mail when their item becomes overdue. Assessing and billing fines, damages, and lost materials are handled through the ILS by full-time library staff, as are all inquiries into and petitions of device-related fees.

Game Selection and Purchasing

While the library has committed to creating a modest collection of current videogames, the preferred and encouraged model is for students to bring their own games into the Learning Commons to play. The library has cultivated a small collection of popular and/or highly-ranked games through suggestions from students and staff, and from popular videogame review sites like

Nintendo Wii:	Microsoft Xbox 360 (cont.):
Excite Truck	Gears of War
Legend of Zelda: Twilight Princess	Ghost Recon: Advance Warfighter
Pixar's Cars	Guitar Hero II
SSX Blur	Halo 2
Super Paper Mario	Halo 3
Wii Sports	Harry Potter and the Order of the Phoenix
	Madden NFL '07
Sony Playstation 3:	Major League Baseball 2K7
Madden NFL '08	NCAA College Hoops 2K7
MLB '07: The Show	NCAA Football '08
NBA Street Homecourt	NCAA March Madness '07
The Bigs: 2K Sports	Tony Hawk's Project 8
Tiger Woods PGA Tour '08	
	Microsoft Xbox:
Microsoft Xbox 360:	Dance Dance Revolution: Ultramix 4
Burnout: Battle Racing Ignited	
Call of Duty 3	Playstation 2:
Forza2 Motorsport	Guitar Hero II

Figure 1. Current List of Circulating Videogames

Video Games	
Qty.	Item Information
3	View sonic N4200w-2 LCD monitors
3	Peerless rolling plasma screen carts
2	Nintendo Wii consoles
10	Nintendo Wii-motes with Nunchuck controllers
3	Microsoft Xbox 360 consoles
15	Microsoft Xbox 360 wireless controllers
2	Sony Playstation 3 consoles
14	Sony Playstation 3 wireless controllers
2	View sonic N4200w-2 monitors
2	Peerless rolling plasma screen carts
1	Microsoft Xbox
1	Sony Playstation 2
Board Games	
Qty.	Item Information
5	Chess
1	Catch Phrase
1	Cranium
1	Taboo

Figure 2. Current List of Gaming Equipment

GameSpot, GameDaily, IGN, CNET, and MetaCritic. Some unexpected but welcomed and appreciated additions to the game collection have also been donated to the Learning Commons by NCSU students and staff.

The Library is currently investigating expansion of its collection development policy regarding videogames. Several courses on campus focus on animation and game design and require that certain game titles are accessible to students taking the course. For more information on gaming in the Libraries, at NC State, and the surrounding area, please see the gaming information at http://www.lib.ncsu.edu/learningcommons/.

Gaming-related Events

The Learning Commons opened March 12, 2007, with gaming offered as one of many new services available. The following Fall semester, two gaming-related events were hosted in D. H. Hill library in addition to ongoing game services.

Madden NFL Tournament

A *Madden NFL '08* Tournament on PlayStation 3 was held from October 8-December 13, 2007. Participants had one week to complete each round of play, to accommodate student class and study schedules. Ample time was provided so that no participant would have to forfeit a game. The weeks ran Monday-Sunday, with each new round beginning on Monday.

Participants were required to subscribe to a Tournament electronic mailing list administered by library staff, and used the list to announce their team name, select opponents for each round, and coordinate game times for each round.

Tournament play had to take place in the D. H. Hill library, and the outcome of each match was verified by library staff. When students finished a round of tournament play, they would notify staff at either the Learning Commons desk or Main Circulation Desk. The staff member would verify the final score display on-screen, then record and initial the outcome of each match in a notebook kept behind each service desk.

Game play lasted for four two-minute quarters. In the event of a tie, participants played an additional two-minute quarter, until one player scored. The first to score won the tie. This was a single-elimination tournament. Once a student lost a match, they were out of the tournament. Scores and standings were then updated and displayed on a web-based bracket linked from the Learning Commons homepage.

The Tournament winner received an NC State football signed by Coach Tom O'Brien as a grand prize, and the winner was announced on the Learning Commons web page. A total of 32 students participated in the Tournament, and library staff received much positive feedback from both players and spectators.

LAN Party

In November 2007, D. H. Hill library collaborated with the NC State Multiplayer Gaming Club (MGC), a student-run gaming organization on campus, to host the library's first LAN party.

The Club is a recognized student organization whose membership is open to all interested NC State students, faculty, and staff. The group has six officers and a core membership of 10-15 other students. The group had experience hosting LAN parties during the past two academic years in dormitories and the Student Union and provided their own games and networking equipment for these events. For more information on the MGC, see http://clubs.ncsu.edu/mgc/.

The Libraries partnered with this student group by providing a safe, comfortable, well-lit space for a LAN party. The library also provided the added attraction of our three 42" LCD monitors with popular gaming consoles and games and some light refreshments for the gamers throughout the afternoon.

The LAN party took place on Sunday, November 11, from 3:00-9:00 p.m. in D. H. Hill's West Wing. The West Wing location was chosen because it is less-populated during the weekend, so few researchers would be disrupted. The West Wing also contains plenty of long, empty table surfaces and available power outlets.

MGC officers arrived at the library at 1:00 p.m. and began setting up their equipment—a router, two servers, and each of the officers' personal computers. Four library staff members were on hand to assist with setup, to get the consoles networked and running, and to place directional signs for the event throughout the library. Prior to the event, the library's Information Technology staff had registered the MGC's router with the campus network, so that the gamers could access the internet and download game patches and upgrades if necessary.

Game play began shortly after 3:00 p.m. *StarCraft* and *Counter-Strike* were the two LAN games played, and *Halo 3* and *Madden NFL '08* were the most requested and played console games. *Halo 3* was played on two Xbox 360 consoles networked together, allowing eight students to play at one time.

Approximately thirty students attended this event, with fourteen participating in the LAN games. There were no complaints by patrons regarding noise, and student gamers were extremely pleased and satisfied with the event and venue.

Lessons Learned

NCSU Libraries has provided gaming support, services, and related events since March 2007. Our services and involvement in this area continue to evolve and already we have learned some important lessons that will help us develop future services and events, which are discussed below.

Introducing Gaming

Expect lots of questions. The presence of games and gaming in a library seems to provoke lots of questions, comments, and discussion from library patrons. Reactions from users at D. H. Hill library have been mainly positive, but we have also received a number of negative comments from both students and faculty. Most questions convey some level of surprise and confusion at the idea of providing games in a library. So, it is useful to plan for these reactions, and to make information about the gaming program readily available when the service begins.

Contain the gaming area. Introducing games into even a very social space seems to change the dynamics of the venue. If games are being played on a large screen, even the quietest game seems to attract onlookers. Space is required for the gamers themselves, but also consider providing some space for a shifting number of spectators, friends, and momentarily interested passers-by. Keeping gaming activities located in a single, defined area makes it easier for any patrons uninterested in games to avoid the activity.

Noise and space are concerns. The volume of most games can be controlled fairly easily, either through wireless headphones or the volume controls on the monitor. But, as we alluded to above, the people playing or watching the games are often the noisiest or most disruptive part of the gaming experience. There are also some games which produce distracting noises, even when the player is using headphones. Dancing games that involve lots of jumping movements, or guitar-based games that require repetitive strumming or thumping on controllers, can be distracting to nearby patrons. Wii games also require some additional space for the gamers to move.

Students like gaming. As we mentioned earlier, the response to gaming at D. H. Hill library by the students who use the service has been overwhelmingly positive. Staff have noted that many patrons frequently choose to work directly beside the crowded gaming consoles, even when other parts of the learning space are clearly quieter and unoccupied. Circulation numbers for our games are high, which also suggests popularity. Anecdotally, there is rarely a time—in this 24/5 service library—when at least one of the game consoles is not in use.

Circulating Games and Controllers

Make sure all desk staff know how to circulate and operate the gaming equipment. Issues such as getting wireless controllers to connect with 360 or PS3 consoles, or resetting the Wiimotes can cause real frustration for staff anxious to provide good service, and for patrons wanting to game for a short time between classes or study sessions.

In D. H. Hill library, we do a high volume of game and controller lending, and our overdue fines for these materials are substantial. So, it is essential that all desk staff are well-trained in the mechanics of checking in and out all the equipment.

Storing Equipment

There are a number of things to consider related to storage of game controllers. The most space-efficient and effective method of storing some controllers is to simply keep them all in a box or drawer. However, some new controllers are very sensitive to motion and turn "on" when they are jostled or come in contact with other objects, which can leave you with a drawer full of controllers losing power for long periods of time. Get to know the specifics of your controllers and plan the storage accordingly. It may be worth devoting some prime shelf storage space to keep your controllers fully charged. Some games, such as versions of *Dance Dance Revolution* and *Guitar Hero*, have controllers that are large or awkwardly-shaped for storage. Keep in mind the associated storage issues when selecting games.

We found it useful to purchase extra controllers for replacements, as some will inevitably break and replacements can take time. Many popular games have a much more limited appeal when the number of players is limited. For this same reason, we also found it useful to invest heavily in rechargeable batteries and chargers. It is useful to develop a workflow for replacing all device batteries weekly (or based on use), and also to develop workflow to continuously clean the console hard drives of saved games and settings, clean all the controllers, LCD screens, etc.

If you are using large-panel monitors for your display, mounting the screen onto an adjustable height cart has benefits both for game play and storage. Lowering the screen height makes it that much smaller to store, and patrons will appreciate being able to adjust the screen to their own height, or their preference for standing versus sitting during some games, such as *Wii Sports*.

Gaming Events

To reduce staff time and effort, we will keep future gaming tournaments short in length; ideally a one-night event that runs between four and five hours. Keeping up with a lengthy tournament was extremely labor-intensive for our staff, despite our best efforts to reduce staff involvement (e. g. mandatory mailing list for players to pair with and/or challenge each other).

Student feedback for our two major events was excellent. The tournament and mailing list provided great ways for us to meet and interact with new students. Our LAN party event helped us build new inroads with the student community. In both events, students told us that prizes were necessary to offer, but that they did not have to be elaborate at all. Local vendor and business giveaways were very appreciated as prizes.

Future gaming event ideas proposed by students include more LAN parties but on Friday or Saturday nights, a *Super Smash Brothers* tournament in collaboration with the campus' Super Smash Brothers Club, a *Guitar Hero* competition, a *Halo 3* tournament, and a chess tournament.

Notes

1. NCSU Libraries, "Gaming information," NCSU Libraries Learning Commons, http://www.lib. ncsu.edu/learningcommons/gaming.html (accessed January 15, 2008).

 CHAPTER 6

Get Game@ZSR—How We Did It And What We Learned Along The Way

H. David "Giz" Womack and Lynn Sutton, PhD

Background

The idea to conduct a pilot gaming event at the Z. Smith Reynolds Library (ZSR) of Wake Forest University was born out of a desire to reach students who were not likely to come to the library before cramming in the last week of final exams. The Library routinely conducted tours during freshman orientation but it was evident that a large number of students were not being reached. First-year men, in particular, were targeted for outreach as they are commonly referred to as the loneliest students on campus. First-year women typically receive a good deal of attention from upperclassmen, but men are less sought out. What better way to appeal to eighteen-year-old males and bring them into the library than to offer them free food and a night of video games?

Wake Forest University is a medium-sized, private university in Winston-Salem, North Carolina, with a liberal arts emphasis and strong professional schools. Freshmen are provided with a ThinkPad laptop and printer as part of their tuition and receive a new model ThinkPad in their junior year that they keep when they graduate. The Z. Smith Reynolds Library is an integral part of the university's award-winning technology program. Staff members in the Library's Information Technology Center (ITC) train faculty and students on a wide range of topics including ThinkPad management, the Blackboard course management system, mobile technology, blogging, spam filtering, Endnote, Web design and many other emerging technology issues.

Despite the Library's extensive involvement with technology, the proposal to host a game night in the Library raised a few eyebrows across campus as well as in the Library itself. Some questioned whether a serious academic support unit like the library should stoop to frivolous entertainment. Yet this sentiment ignored the growing body of evidence that gaming is both big business and can have serious academic implications. Since 2004, the gaming industry has outpaced the film industry in total sales. Gaming has affected a whole generation of users, as today's college student has been playing video games practically since birth. Gaming theory is a well-studied field of academic inquiry and is being adopted in many different disciplines—not the least of which includes information literacy and library instruction. In the last several years, a small number of pioneers in public, academic and school libraries have seen the marketing and educational value of the gaming phenomenon and embraced the movement for the sheer fun of it. Their efforts achieved a certain level of recognition when the American Library Association sponsored the first annual *Gaming, Learning and Libraries Symposium* in July, 2007.

The history of the Wake Forest experience may serve as an example of how an academic library can expand its user base, gain credibility with its least-enthusiastic users, use technology in creative ways, and have a little bit of fun. It is not necessary to have a large budget or invest in expensive, short-lived equipment. It only takes a little imagination.

Initial Planning

In the summer of 2005, Lynn Sutton, the director of the Z. Smith Reynolds Library at Wake Forest University, approached the members of the Technology Team with the idea of a video-game night sponsored by the Library. As the planning began, it soon became clear that more than Library staff would be needed to pull off the event later known as Get Game@ZSR. In addition to Library staff involvement, these events would also require student participation. The Information Systems department at Wake Forest University employs Resident Technical Advisers (RTAs). RTAs are students who live in the residence halls and assist students with the effective use of the ThinkPads issued by the University to all full-time students. The Manager of Technology Training in the Library contacted the Information Systems (IS) staff member who administered the RTA program and arranged for the Library and IS to partner on this project. IS also funded the cost of drinks, candy and paper goods for each event. The lead RTA for the 2005-2006 academic year was an avid gamer who proved himself a valuable resource in planning the first event of this series.

With three months to plan the first event, the Manager of Technology Training, the Training Specialist and the lead RTA formed a group and began by finding a name for the gaming program. Finding a name was a challenge, and it involved the collaboration of students and Library staff. Ultimately, it was the Library Director who took the list of suggestions and morphed them into the title "Get Game@ZSR." Once a catchy name was established, the group started addressing the logistics of such an event. There was no real model to follow. Some public libraries were hosting game nights, supplying the participants with library-owned game consoles and either TV or projectors for game play, but there were no academic library models that fit the requirements of Get Game@ZSR. The primary requirement focused on hosting an event without buying gaming consoles or projectors, while creating an atmosphere that would bring students out of their residence halls and into the Library with their own gaming equipment. Food, projectors, and a wide open space for gaming were the keys to drawing participants to the event!

Early meetings focused on compiling a list of questions that needed to be addressed. Once the list was created, the group began addressing those questions and as answers were identified, the format of the event began to take shape.

Questions that Had to be Addressed

Where to Hold the Event

Initially, three spaces were considered: a large, all-night study room, the student computer lab and lobby, and the Library atrium. The group chose the ZSR Library's atrium for its size and dramatic beauty.

It is a large, open space, with six floors of windows on either end. It connects the two wings of the Library and provides sixteen tables for study. Based on the size of this space, there was room for at least eight game consoles and projectors each with up to four players and plenty of room

The Z. Smith Reynolds Library atrium during a Get Game@ZSR event.

for spectators and food. The choice of this space, however, limited the potential timing of the event. Because this space is open to the entire Library and because the event was expected to be noisy, if held in the atrium it would have to be held after Library hours.

When to Hold the Event

The challenge with timing was to find a time that didn't conflict with other events on campus but that would still be practical for the staff who were working the event. Initially, options such as an overnight event or late evening event were discussed. Everyone agreed that holding the event early in the semester while new students were still looking for things to do was the best option for getting good attendance at the event. Finally, Friday evenings were selected. The Library closes at 7:00 p.m., so the event could run from 7:00-11:00 p.m. without causing an undue impact on students or staff. The idea of hosting an overnight event presented a staffing issue, and other times were tested and found to be less popular with the students.

How to Get Game Consoles

Since this was a pilot event, it didn't make sense to invest too much money in game consoles that may or may not be used again. So with no budget to purchase game consoles, and no resources or budget for renting game consoles in number, the only solution was to ask students to bring their own. As it turned out, students did not mind bringing their own game consoles, controllers and games; some even preferred it!

Can Any Game Console Be Supported

We had concerns that for our first event we should limit game consoles to the two primary consoles in the market at the time, the Sony PlayStation 2 and the Microsoft Xbox. We thought this would be necessary to support the event and ensure projectors could be connected to consoles. In retrospect, this limitation was not necessary and for future events the game nights were open to any game console, encouraging students to bring a wide variety of consoles and games.

How to Get Projectors

We knew we would need at least six LCD projectors to host an event of 24 or more students. This was a huge hurdle. Rental costs were prohibitive, and the Library only had access to one

LCD projector. The Library approached Information Systems and requested that the end-of-life LCD projectors that were being removed from electronic classrooms across campus each year be used for this project. IS had tried selling these well-used projectors, but as they were at the end of their useful life, there was no market for them. The Library had to promise to handle the disposal of these projectors as they ceased to work and to agree to take them with no promise of future tech support. This creative solution turned out to be a win-win for both parties as IS did not have to deal with the disposal of this equipment and the ZSR Library had projectors for these gaming events and other events.

How to Get Screens
Because the atrium did not have blank wall space for projection, screens needed to be procured for the event. The Library had one screen as part of our equipment available for checkout. Additionally, when cleaning out an office in the old wing of the Library, an old screen was discovered and pressed into service. For the rest, the Library rented six screens at a cost of $150 from a local video production company. Once it appeared that this would be a recurring event, four new screens were purchased from the annual budget. These screens paid for themselves in saved rental costs after three events. As a result of the success of the events, and plenty of projectors, more screens were needed over time. The group learned that makeshift screens can be created from blackout curtain liner fabric and a curtain rod, but not from standard bed sheeting.

How to Have Students Register for the Event
Fear (or at least a healthy skepticism) of the unknown dictated that we require students to register in advance for a seat. There was limited seating available based on the number of game consoles. The Library needed an idea of how many students were bringing game consoles and needed to match those consoles to other players. However, in marketing the event we made it clear that if students didn't register in advance, they were still welcome to come and participate as a spectator and enjoy the free pizza, sodas and candy. Students e-mailed the Manager of Technology Training and were sent a confirmation message that requested information on the game equipment they planned to bring if any. This information was placed on a diagram that paired students with game consoles to ensure everyone registered had a place to game. Registra-

tion remains a requirement for guaranteed seating and to ensure a smooth event with adequate numbers of game consoles for gamers.

How to Market the Event

In addition to flyers, e-mails to students, and the efforts of the Resident Technical Advisors (RTAs) to talk up the event among users, a YouTube video, a Facebook group, and even an article in the student newspaper were all used in an effort to get students to attend. Marketing the first event was a challenge and has not proved any easier over time. Getting the average college student to commit to an event, register in advance and then attend is not easy. No matter what date is selected, there were always competing events. Known for delaying decision making, the Millennials were true to form. As such, there was always a last-minute flurry of registrations just when the group began thinking no one would attend the event.

Each event had its own set of issues to address, and with each event the group running this program became more efficient in the use of resources to prepare and host these events. The specifics of each event and the key elements of each event can be found below. Two different time slots and locations have been used for Get Game@ZSR. The RTAs are listed below as attendees, as they both work the event and participate in the events. They are broken out from the total number of attendees to accurately express student attendance.

The Events:
Fall 2005
Event: Xbox and PS2 Video Game Night
Date: Friday, September 16th 2005
Time: 7-11PM
Location: ZSR Library Atrium
Total Attendees: 48 students, 12 RTAs
Staff: 7
Total Cost: $424

The first event of any program is always the most arduous. One prepares for every possibility in an effort to ensure success. In addition to the hours spent planning prior to the event, the day of the event was completely taken over picking up screens from the equipment rental company, buying extra cables, video connectors and power strips, preparing backup equipment such as extra projectors in case they needed to be pressed into service and ordering food. With the help of library staff, the atrium was repurposed in an hour, screens and projectors were in place and students began arriving. As the evening went on, we tripped two circuit breakers and had to run some extension cords, allowed in organizational space for temporary events. Additionally, there was such a run on pizza at the start of the event that we placed another order for the same amount only to discover the students had already consumed their fill of pizza for the evening. While the four Xbox consoles networked together to play an enormous game of *Halo 2*, the two PlayStation 2 consoles played *Madden 2006*. These were serious gamers who hunkered down for the evening and needed little assistance from the Library staff or RTAs. This was a very successful kick-off to these events with lots of positive feedback from the participants.

Spring 2006
>   Event: Xbox *Halo2* Tournament
>   Date: Friday, February 17th 2006
>   Time: 3-7PM
>   Location: ZSR All-Night Study Room
>   Total Attendees: 17 students, 6 RTAs
>   Staff: 6
>   Total Cost: $171

By the spring of 2006, screens were purchased, making equipment rental unnecessary. This saved the Library $150 in rental costs. *Halo 2* on the Xbox was selected as the game for the tournament. The tournament only had room for sixteen students, making it a much smaller event. Additionally, both a new venue and time were selected. The all-night study room isolated the noise from the event, making it possible to hold the event during normal library hours. Based on the survey results from the previous game night, the 3 p.m.-7 p.m. time slot was equally appealing to students. In reality, the later time slot, 7-11 p.m., has proven far more popular. The tournament was double-elimination, with each round lasting for eight minutes or twenty-

The first Get Game@ZSR Tournament Winner.

five "kills," whichever came first. This meant the tournament was completed by 6 p.m., making for a short event. However, students were very pleased with the event. A trophy was given to the winner and the student's name was added to a Get Game@ZSR perpetual plaque, which is displayed across from the circulation desk in the library.

The challenge that came from this event was how to keep tournament players around once they had been eliminated. One solution proposed was to combine an open game night and a tournament, so that gamers could stay once they were eliminated and continue playing, and those not in the tournament could still play games and attend the event. Even in this new venue, circuits were tripped and had to be reset during the tournament. Once again, pizza, sodas and candy fueled the gamers.

Fall 2006
    Event: Open Video Game Night
    Date: Friday, September 15th 2006
    Time: 7-11PM
    Location: ZSR All-Night Study Room
    Total Attendees: 11 students, 6 RTAs
    Staff: 5
    Total Cost: $167

The Fall 2006 open game night was the least successful event to date, with only eleven students attending the event. The competition of a beautiful September evening coupled with other events held by student organization on campus and community outdoor music events held downtown proved to be a more powerful draw than videogames and pizza. However, costs were kept low and were limited to pizza, sodas, candy and paper goods, and the students who did attend enjoyed the event. As the third event in this series, all the equipment required, screens, power strips, hubs, was already available and setup and breakdown of the event was quick and efficient, using as few resources as possible. After two small events in the all-night study room, everyone involved agreed that moving back to the atrium was a good idea, allowing for more space for game play, spectators, and food.

Spring 2007

Event: Open Video Game Night
Date: Friday, February 9th 2007
Time: 7-11PM
Location: ZSR Library Atrium
Total Attendees: 39 students, 3 WFU staff, 10 RTAs
Staff: 5
Total Cost: $160

In an effort to avoid the low attendance of the Fall 2006 game night, marketing efforts were intensified for the Spring 2007 Get Game@ZSR. A YouTube video was created and distributed, fliers were heavily distributed, and the RTAs were pressed to market the event among the students. Additionally the student newspaper did an article on the event. A new Nintendo Wii was the centerpiece of the evening and everyone took turns playing *Wii Sports*, with doubles tennis being the most popular game. Between the Wii, the marketing blitz and some door prizes, this was an exciting event with a diverse group of games ranging from tennis on the Wii to *Guitar Hero* and *Dance Dance Revolution* (DDR) on the PS2. The diversity of videogames created a different atmosphere that encouraged students to try a variety of games. The core of these events, our hardcore Xbox *Halo 2* gamers had their own space away from the chaos of the Wii and *DDR*. This segregation of space and game consoles made it much easier to have some children attend the event as well. It was a welcome surprise when a few Wake Forest faculty and staff attended, bringing their children to play *Wii Sports* and *DDR*. There was a distinct party feel to this event, making it unlike any previous event.

Fall 2007
    Event: Open Video Game Night
    Date: Friday, September 21ˢᵗ 2007
    Time: 7-11PM
    Location: ZSR Library Atrium
    Total Attendees: 32 students, 5 WFU staff, 10 RTAs
    Staff: 4
    Total Cost: $160

Following up on the success of the Spring 2007 event, the model changed little for the Fall 2007 Get Game@ZSR event. Door prizes were dropped based on the lukewarm response they received at the Spring event. Place cards were created so students knew exactly where to set up their equipment, and in an effort to continually update the event, party games like *Catch Phrase* were added to the event and enjoyed by some of the adults who brought children. Additionally, some remote controlled cars were brought to the event and several of the students enjoyed driving them around the large, open atrium. The party feeling of the previous event was maintained with a variety of games and game consoles, and instead of one Wii, there were three. More WFU staff and their children attended this event, and staffing for the event was scaled back to four members of the Library staff with the full cadre of RTAs.

Spring 2008
    Event: Open Video Game Night and Tournament with UNCG
    Date: Friday, January 25ᵗʰ 2008
    Time: 7-11PM
    Location: ZSR Library Atrium
    Total Attendees: 40
    Staff: 8
    Total Cost: $160

After a two-year hiatus, due to low turnout from the previous tournament, the game night tournament was held again in Spring 2008. By combining it with an open game night, it can be a larger event with more participants than a tournament alone, and participants in the open game night can also play in the tournament or be spectators. Additionally, we had hoped to team up with the Jackson Library at the University of North Carolina at Greensboro, so that students could compete across the two campuses. Unfortunately, logistical issues prevented this from occurring, though we hope to attempt it again in the future. The game of choice for the tournament is *Halo 3* for Xbox 360. The winner of the Get Game@ZSR event will receive a trophy and have their name added to the Get Game@ZSR perpetual plaque.

Lessons Learned

Over the three years Get Game@ZSR events have been hosted by the ZSR Library, many lessons have been learned. First, marketing of these events is a difficult and ever-changing proposition. There are always conflicting events such as home sporting events and pledge night and circumstances beyond one's control such as weather that can all affect the number of participants. New approaches to marketing the events must be continually implemented.

Never assume that library staff know what the students want in these events. Survey the student participants after the events to learn about various times, formats and venues that may also appeal to the students. Be sure to ask some open-ended questions to give students the chance to tell you what their other answers won't. Web survey tools like *Zoomerang* and *Survey Monkey* make surveying participants a snap. We asked questions such as "What day of the week do you prefer for these events?" and "What time of day do you prefer?" We also asked if they minded bringing their own equipment and discovered to our surprise that they liked bringing their own game console, controllers, and games to the events. This was an answer we did not expect! We also learned there was significant demand for a tournament event based on their survey responses.

Work to partner with other groups on and off campus. In addition to the RTAs sponsoring the beverages, candy and paper goods, the off-campus used book seller, Edward McKay Used Books, sponsored the perpetual plaque and individual trophy for the event. Beyond financial support, student employees in the Library help set up the atrium for the event. By finding sponsors both on campus and in the community, more people feel like they are a part of these events and they in turn discuss and market the event themselves.

Conclusion

Before the clean-up from the first event started and the gamers were packing up and leaving the Library, they began asking when we would be hosting the next event! These events become less expensive and require fewer resources as time goes on, making them an efficient Library marketing tool. Also, these events offer the Library staff a chance to meet students and learn more about the culture of gaming and even play a few games themselves. Additionally, when marketing these events, many students as well as staff at the University who are initially shocked the Library would support gaming begin to learn more about the Library and realize that new and exciting things are happening at ZSR! Students enjoy these events and they give the Library a chance to show itself as both a place for gathering and a place for learning.

 CHAPTER 7

Hosting Game Events in a Small, Liberal Arts Academic Library
Sheree Fu

Background: CUC and Libraries
The Claremont University Consortium (CUC) is the central coordinating and support organization for The Claremont Colleges, located in Southern California. The Claremont Colleges is a cluster of five undergraduate colleges and two graduate schools. Pomona College, Claremont Graduate University, Scripps College, Claremont McKenna College, Harvey Mudd College, and Pitzer College are on adjoining campuses. The Keck Graduate Institute of Applied Life Sciences is located on a nearby campus in Claremont. Originally established in 1925 as part of Claremont University Center, in July 2000, CUC incorporated as a freestanding organization. CUC is a nationally-recognized model for academic, student, and institutional support services that meet the needs of over six thousand students and over three thousand faculty and staff. Among these services are the Libraries of The Claremont Colleges.[1]

As one of the academic support services of CUC, the Libraries function in a complex and challenging environment. The Libraries are in the position also of being dependent upon the support of all of the member colleges and yet not belonging to any one. A defining concept of Claremont's consortial environment is economies of scale; that is, each of the colleges receives more in the way of resources and services than each would be able to afford on its own. The extent of the Libraries' resources and services exceed what many small, private liberal arts colleges individually are able to afford. As a central service supported financially by each of the seven institutions, the Libraries strive to provide resources and services equitably to all of the colleges. Our efforts can encounter inherent contradictions; for instance, each independent college expects to receive personalized services aligned with its special focus while at the same time it benefits from the advantages of economies of scale afforded by the consortial arrangement. Furthermore, the consortium collectively expects the Libraries to address diverse and competing interests among the seven institutions, across disciplines, and between undergraduate and graduate levels. The Libraries' challenge is to meet this complex set of expectations at the same high level of excellence for all[2].

Start: Exploratory Research Questions

This chapter addresses the origins and follows the evolution of the gaming program at the Claremont University Consortium, specifically at the Libraries of The Claremont Colleges. I explore how the library applied marketing and customer service principles in the development of a gaming program, while also suggesting additional avenues for research based on the gaming experiences inside and outside of the library.

The gaming program featured sponsored events for all types of games and gamers. Board games and puzzles were housed in a large reception hall and meeting area on the library's main

Guitar Hero Tournament in the Library, April 13, 2007

floor. The room was open to library users during operating hours and is now often referred to by students as the 'game room'. Events in the game room included weekly game nights, periodic tournaments, and videogame-related lectures. For one of these lectures, a recent graduate spoke about how his education prepared him for working in the videogame industry.

The games program grew from an inspiring conference presentation on games at Internet Librarian 2006. In her closing keynote speech, Liz Lawley stated that games "change the way people use [library] tools and think about what they want in an information environment."[3] Library program planners can learn much from games and gamers about public spaces, social services, and self-motivated learning. One particularly appealing notion mentioned in Lawley's talk described how games could help libraries create a sense of place and revitalize neglected public spaces. As a result of her presentation, one library goal was to bring students into the library, and expose them to an underused space (i.e. the game room). Other aims, some echoing Lawley's closing keynote, embraced the unique appeal of games in libraries. They consisted of expanding library services based on games as an interactive information media; reaching an underserved audience; creating immersive, social experiences; and building relationships with individuals and organizations on and off campus. In a lengthy proposal to library administration, numerous ambitious goals were stated:

1. Involve students and student groups that do not normally come to the library. This includes inviting gamers into the library and going to places where gamers frequent.
2. Provide entertainment, intellectual stimulation, and mental challenges through games and other activities
3. Encourage creativity, problem solving, and teamwork
4. Promote camaraderie, connection, and community
5. Enjoy the process/journey[4]

The proposal was accepted and the games began. During Fall 2006 study breaks, games and puzzles purchased by the library were made available so students could relax. A local game store owner was contacted by library staff to bring in some additional games and instruct players, thereby increasing the variety of games offered and depth of services to library users. As library staff watched and played, the local expert and business owner talked to students and matched their interests and time requirements to a game. Results from a survey given to the participants in these gaming activities suggested that students and visitors enjoyed the diversion, competition, and education about games. (The study and results can be found in Appendices A and B respectively.)

After the initial success and positive feedback, the library's game group, a mix of librarians and library staff, met to determine the next step. The expert gamers in the group played board games on a regular basis, most frequently on weekends. The group recognized that students are most active socially and academically in the evenings; they come to the library after normal business hours. The group decided to establish a regular, weekly game night that would feature board games during the school year, mirroring the gaming events that the expert gamers enjoyed and building on the momentum from the study breaks. Since this formula was successful in the past, we decided to continue using it. The library staff who volunteered to support a library gaming program, making it part of their daily work, included librarians, information technology staff, digital library staff, materials handling staff, instructional support staff, and facilities and central services staff, all with varying levels of expertise with respect to games but sharing a love of games and play[5]. The weekly game nights generally started at 5:00 p.m. as staff ended their work days and often lasted late into the night since the games, snacks, caffeine and camaraderie invigorated participants.

Establishing a Market

Appreciating expert knowledge is basic to marketing, customer service, and academic libraries. The Libraries conducted an environmental scan, looking for information, existing gaming clubs, and other resources. We interviewed a student who organized gaming events at his college, the owner of a local game store, and interested library staff who donated games or made suggestions about what game purchases or events students would enjoy.

Casual gamers, expert gamers, and library users and staff shared information that laid the foundation for an active gaming program. Attempts to motivate and recruit expert gamers to participate and play in the game nights coupled with Internet Librarian[6] inspiration led to several conclusions. The library should emphasize the joy of games and their social and intellectual qualities, choosing not to employ games as a means to promote other library services. These results can be achieved organically, as the librarians discovered when they were asked reference questions during the game nights.

The group focused on the process and skills of recreational gaming as a worthy end in itself. Teaching beginners how to play unfamiliar games would draw in more patrons as well as accomplish other game-centered goals. The library would share materials, skills and knowledge, focusing on what the users of all skill levels want—a satisfying gaming experience. Successful marketing, understanding what a customer needs, creating a product that will appeal to that customer, and then effectively educating the customer about that product or service, can be assisted by an environmental scan,[7] which the staff performed prior to beginning the project as well as informal, ongoing assessment, which the staff conducted by talking with gamers and conducting surveys. This continuing information gathering created a feedback loop to improve the library service.

The environmental scan answered basic questions of who, what, where, how, and why. It also prepared the staff with ideas on how to proceed with services and inform the Claremont College community about the latest games and services. As a small group in a service organization committed to serving the underserved, a focus on the ever-changing "who," the people, was key in shaping the program. Although the remaining what, where, how, and why elements are addressed below, the "who" being served and their responses heavily influenced game events; the ongoing feedback allowed us to adapt the events to gamers' requests.

Library staff recognized several overlapping subgroups. The study break showed that people in the library appreciated a temporary diversion from their studies, usually including amusement and sustenance. Casual gamers enjoyed games as entertainment but didn't want to commit to the hours of play involved with strategy games or perfecting the hand-eye coordination and exact timing required for musical games, like *Guitar Hero*. At the other end of the continuum, experienced gamers built communities on regular enjoyable experiences. To varying degrees, the subgroups appreciated fun, novelty, and competition.

The program or the "what" were based on game nights, games and their unique appeal, and validating the recreational gaming experience. The "how" or the method proposed was that the library would offer inclusive services and resources to gamers and sponsor gaming events. The new outreach service included building a community across the colleges and featuring new games weekly and instruction to beginners and special events for advanced gamers.

The services would be located in the library since we wanted to create a sense of place and bring people into the library. We examined various locations that were underutilized and available and how suitable they were for gaming events. Considerations included accessibility, furniture, lighting, refreshment storage, noise levels, and general atmosphere of the space in the effort to create a sense of place.

Lastly, what I and other staff realized was that most importantly, games are fun, despite winning or losing. Because we reap what we sow, staff recognized we had to sincerely enjoy the process and the results if we valued fun and play. Such gamer characteristics and beliefs address why we focused on games.

I have had numerous discussions and responses about the place of fun in the library's services. The majority were favorable comments such as "That's cool" and "I wish my library had videogames." Although the academic library cannot be everything to everyone, library users are engaged by games as a medium in addition to being educated and enriched by gaming experiences. Games such as chess, videogames, and sports contests not only lead to careers but can also serve as educational tools. Of course inherently, games are simply fun.

Marketing and Promotion

Once the basic questions about potential market are answered, it was time to begin marketing and promoting the gaming program. Constant innovation was a key marketing technique we chose to employ. As a result, we included new snacks and new games to continuously rejuvenate and sustain ourselves and the program. Regular innovation is critical to the program lifecycle and reaching constituents.

In the beginning, several members questioned what would be the most effective form of publicity. The decision was ultimately made to push mass marketing to the entire Claremont Colleges community of students, faculty, and staff. We customized outreach to existing or high-potential populations such as gamers by using the gaming listserv. We also reached students on the various campuses with existing gaming organizations. Word of mouth marketing was used for various special events. In informal ice-breaking conversations with game night attendees, library staff asked how they had heard about the event. Answers varied and no patterns emerged. Alternative approaches to the implemented publicity plan could be investigated in the future.

Another future question would be to assess the effectiveness of communications and community building on Facebook, the

JOE GAMES ♥ YOU   facebook

Joe Games supports gaming in libraries.

social networking site that began in a college setting. A librarian who was part of the gaming group created a Facebook profile to market games at the library using the name Joe Games. The account facilitates communication, access, advertising, and services to the Claremont Facebook community including eager incoming students who were discussing who would bring videogame consoles such as the Nintendo Wii to campus months before the start of classes. Library staff on Facebook informed them that the library hosted game nights where they could play Wii games. Some new first years promptly befriended the library staff member in order to receive future information and invitations.

Initial marketing strategies involved going to Facebook, where the students were, and engaging with them as someone who also enjoyed games. Although a formal marketing plan was never documented, the spirit of play and humor was clear in the Facebook communications and other materials such as the first user survey. Questions in the study break survey include: "Do you feel better now? (Then get back to work)" and "All answers will be kept confidential, unless there is someone behind you looking over your shoulder as you write."

The questionnaires allowed game room visitors to give feedback and for the library to promote, respond, and improve its services and collections. In general, the responses were positive and demonstrated that the library was creating goodwill among the small population that returned the survey. Two particular responses were included in other proposals to show how the program was changing perceptions and creating a sense of place. One student remarked, "it feels good to hear laughter instead of tortured whining," while a visiting parent reflected, "I can only imagine the fun it would be to spend time [in the Founders Room] with peers and professors…and the rapport/reflections that result are cemented in [the game room.] If I were a student at this place, I would frequent this room on a regular basis."[8] A third comment was also quite remarkable. In fall 2008 at an outside social organization fair, a group of students told library staff that they had *heard* of the library parties, referring to the game events where students, faculty, and staff played games and ate snacks. Library constituents clearly articulated that the library was recognized as a social place.

The anecdotal comments suggest that the outreach services and marketing had some impact on students' perception of the library. In establishing this gaming program, we made a positive impression not just on the participants but outsiders as well.

The library table at a campus-wide social organization fair

The findings from the ongoing assessment and the desire to disseminate information effectively and improve services led to establishing more tools and resources. Additional promotional components included a Web site with a calendar of events, description of the game collection, and other information[9]; a public service slideshow that aired during the summer in one campus student center; and an internal annual report that documented the program's growth and changing goals[10]. The surveys and informal assessment were deliberately continued throughout the program as staff solicited and analyzed comments regularly to understand what gamers needed and how to communicate and support their needs. Even staff not directly involved in the games provided feedback by passing on comments such as one from a student from another area college wanting to attend the weekly game nights and academic deans enjoying games in the game room before a meeting. Frequently, individuals provided informal feedback on the services and events, not on the devices or methods that led them to game nights or other offerings. Hearing and seeing that the library was meeting a need rewarded and encouraged the staff.

Marketing Lessons Learned

In hindsight, the library could have created a boilerplate to better meet clients' needs. A boilerplate is standardized text that can be reused. At times, it is attached to the end of a document for promotional purposes or serves as a legal disclaimer. A boilerplate statement for the Libraries began this case study; the first two paragraphs provided standard information about the organization and context. A marketing boilerplate for the games program would provide consistent basic information after the provocative hook of "We have games: Wii, Xbox, and *Settlers of Catan*, even *Guitar Hero*." The generic statement could also be later reused and customized for different purposes and audiences.

Clearly, the library invested time and energy in customizing services and marketing to unique populations. Based on the environmental scan and continuous feedback, staff focused on creating a specific, appropriate atmosphere for each event. A careful marketing analysis could be planned to better allocate resources to serve a diverse audience and leverage creativity and flexibility.

Customer Service

As was previously mentioned, providing knowledgeable help is critical to customer service. Expert gamers from inside and outside the library regularly attended game nights and other gaming events to lend their expertise. The library staff who participated in the events wanted to create enjoyable and popular experiences, so they kept the user's interests in mind along with the understanding that the library was building a service. Empathy and expert skills and knowledge were paired as staff and attendees both participated in coaching new players and each other, explaining the rules, and showing how one strategy was better than another. In addition to basic, small-community courtesies such as greeting people by name, we also attempted to anticipate customer needs. Some people would bring friends, and some would look for new players to play with. Therefore, experience taught that having two library staff present at game nights was optimal. One would greet and monitor and replenish refreshments, and the second would play with anyone who wanted to play or was waiting for a game. For the most part, reasonable requests for new board games and refreshments were accommodated within a semester. Players were invited to bring their own games, and the library would publicize their games to entice other players.

When mistakes were made, such as failing to communicate the consequences of being late to a tournament, staff apologized sincerely and admitted they were still learning. The library tried to be engaging, responsive, credible, and approachable, showing the gamers that they were respected and heard face to face, on Facebook, and via surveys. The staff continued to consistently keep players informed, sending out regular messages, and having events at the same time and place weekly.

At times, the social support and conversations became secondary to games and caffeinated beverages. Staff and students have discussed Asian politics and current events, their instructional experiences as students or visiting faculty, and the struggles of family, poverty, and stress of graduate students. Interested attendees were treated as if they were individuals first, not just library users or expert gamers. Such practices and habits are time-consuming at first but build loyalty and build on how many library staff enjoy working with people as individuals. Quality customer service can be sustained in an institution that wants to be recognized as a national leader in providing academic and business services.[11]

Adapting to Change

The summer brought changes to gaming events as library hours shortened and the majority of students left the campus. Weekly games nights moved out of the library building. One college agreed to share its space without charging any fees. The twenty-four-hour space the college provided was a living room with study space, numerous couches, and a self-serve espresso machine. It also led to the mail room and promised exposure to people on their way to check their mail.

New faces appeared, mainly staff, including temporary student workers who were employed on campus during the sleepy summer months, other regular staff who had time and interest, and some summer school students. The majority of these people had never before attended a gaming event in the library. Funds had not been allocated to support weekly events, and the quantity of snacks was greatly reduced. The course of events helped to test the assumption that clients only came for the food. Although attendance was considerably diminished, a core group attended regularly.

Some in library administration objected to a library event featuring library resources being held outside of the library building. In response, the games group created a statement that acknowledges the advantages of moving beyond the physical building and adds that games and services are for use and to build relationships with others.

> A congenial library presence at external locations not only creates more visibility and goodwill for the libraries, it brings additional users into a library. It introduces them to a welcoming library that values social interactions and builds relationships with its users where they are. Services can meet the users at their point of need at their convenience in person, virtually, wherever they might be whether it is in the library, another campus location, or studying abroad. One student abroad describes the games he is playing in Egypt and looks forward to attending events upon his return.
>
> **The Libraries are more than a building.** When our services travel to external locations, we not only promote the accessibility of our services, but we also help to create a social network between other college organizations in which collaboration and co-sponsorship can be mutually beneficial…[12]

During the pre-summer game events the library created an additional regular forum and space to interact with students, faculty, and staff from outside their normal spheres based on a shared passion for games. In moving to an outside location, some new attendees asked who was sponsoring the event and heard about the library and its game program. Mostly, they seemed to appreciate the opportunity to socialize, play, and relax. Some were favorably surprised. Unquestionably, the summer weekly game nights attracted new players. The events moved beyond promoting the library as a space and towards better service to new library clients and building relationships with other colleges, sharing their space that also served students. The program was now about serving the community at large and supporting nomadic gamers with library resources.

Another summer trend, more noticeably, was the increased involvement of staff and their families. Generations of family and friends of the Claremont College community had attended previous events. Library staff would bring their children to the library for game night and their children would enthusiastically beat or coach college students and their parents at games after work. Some youths were also rumored to have bragged to their peers about their accomplishments. Some were also taught how to set up videogame consoles, boosting their confidence by learning new skills.

The spring semester trend continued into summer as the offspring of staff participated in the game events under their parents' supervision. During the summer months, another staff person and her daughter who was attending college the next year regularly taught Mahjong to the summer students, staff, and their family. The summer games encouraged interaction among people of different generations. It exposed how smaller communities, such as families or groups of friends could strengthen their own ties and participate in a larger gaming community, one that was intergenerational, did not come just for the food, and was motivated by playing games.

Another summer project involved mapping the library mission statement to games. The additions described how library services can expand into the gaming environment and how games fit into library traditions. The mission statement, with additions italicized, reads as follows:

> The Libraries are partners with The Claremont Colleges in learning, teaching, and research. *Games create opportunities to strengthen existing partnerships and form new relationships.* We are committed to fostering intellectual discovery, critical thinking, and life-long learning. *Games inherently support intellectual discovery, critical thinking, and life-long learning.*
>
> Accordingly, the Libraries tie our academic community to varied cultural and scholarly traditions *(games are both a cultural and scholarly subject)* by offering user-centered services *(students, staff, and faculty play games)*, building collections *(library is building a game collection)*, developing innovative technologies *(video games are the innovative technology and media for recent generations)*, and providing an inviting environment for study, collaboration, and reflection *(staff who facilitate game events create such an environment inside and outside the library as games require one to be fully present to play)*.[13]

Not all library missions need to be centered on games, although the gaming perspective can exemplify how the library is a growing organism. As the initial goals of serving an underserved community, promoting the library as a social place, and using games as method to engage students developed into providing services to gamers outside of the building, strengthening communities, and offering a more inclusive picture of a growing library, the program changed.

Summer Lessons Learned

The summer changes as well as the prior gaming experiences beginning in Fall 2006 led to a few significant lessons about how to sustain an outreach program.

In the summer, library staff learned that the library's presence can cross traditional boundaries and media. Though moving game nights outside of the library was controversial, the continued support of gamers ultimately justified this decision. The new influx of participating staff and their family members changed the nature of the events from individual students to micro-communities of staff and families.

It became obvious that the library staff supported and responded to requests, rather than empowering the community it served. Although we worked closely with individual students and users and did anticipate needs, staff initiated programming and library users, for the most part, either played limited creative roles or only attended events. In the future, encouraging gamers who do not work at the library to be actively involved may further their education and create unique opportunities for them to explore their interests as well as create additional allies. Creating internships or short-term projects could expand the base of support while providing useful experience to students.

Conclusions and Future

In short, we observed the environment, followed successful examples, practiced continuous improvement, and adapted to change. The goals of bringing an underserved population into the game room evolved into serving families and other communities and reinterpreting the library mission to include games

The library also employed continuous, informal feedback to guide the games program, emphasizing gamers. In addition to attendance statistics, qualitative descriptions and images show how a library can support and engage library users. From reflections on the accolades and gathered information, customer service staff recognized not only the needs of gamers, but also involved experts. Library principles that highlight non-judgmental material use and the library as a growing organization may nurture future gaming research, success, and innovation. The development of a gaming program may encourage future research on effective publicity and marketing for the audience, the impact of a social networking tool on user involvement (e.g., use of Facebook), and determining who uses library services such as game nights and why. Testing and improving the timesaver checklist below for a gaming program could also help future generations.

1. Continuous communication and feedback with constituents to ensure one
    a. provides relevant and growing services and
    b. understands the changing environment and core values
2. Record key statistics such as number of attendees and comments
3. Build personal relationships and value allies
4. Give back to the community
5. Have fun

Gamers and gaming libraries seem to benefit from the social relationships and a sense of community created by gaming events. As growing individuals and institutions exercise their ability to learn and determine their future through games and programs respectively, basic needs are met and community identities affirmed. I hope our informal examples, experiences, and preliminary analysis can serve to recommend a games program to academic libraries.

Notes

1. Libraries of The Claremont Colleges, "Executive Summary: Introduction," *Self Study Portfolio*, September 8, 2003, http://libraries.claremont.edu/selfstudy/execsum1.html.
2. Ibid.
3. Elizabeth Lane Lawley, "All the world's a game… and all the men and women are merely players" (presented at the Internet Librarian 2006, Monterey, CA, October 25, 2006), http://www.infotoday.com/il2006/wednesday.shtml#endnote.
4. Sheree Fu, "Proposal2Game," e-mail message, November 20, 2006.
5. Games team includes: David Bolinger, Sheree Fu, Allegra Gonzalez, Josh Kline and Rory Reiff,

6. Lawley, "All the world's a game… and all the men and women are merely players."
7. Susan Webreck Alman, *Crash Course in Marketing for Libraries* (Westport, Conn: Libraries Unlimited, 2007), 2.
8. Fu, "Proposal2Game."
9. Libraries of The Claremont Colleges, "Games at the Libraries," *Games Home*, February 18, 2008, http://libraries.claremont.edu/games/
10. Sheree Fu, "Games Statistics and Evidence in a Library Context," e-mail message, August 1, 2007
11. Robert Walton, "Claremont University Consortium Values," February 19, 2008.
12. Rory Reiff, Allegra Gonzalez, and Sheree Fu, "Regarding the use of Library Game's Hardware," e-mail message, June 15, 2007
13. Fu, "Games Statistics and Evidence in a Library Context."

Appendix A
Study

Break at the Library
Official Gamers Survey
December 3–9, 2006

Was this event beneficial? (Why?)

What game(s) did you play?

Did you win?

Did you cheat? *

What was your favorite game? (Why?)

What was your least favorite game? (Why?)

Was there a game you didn't get to play? (Why?)

Was there a game you thought should have been included but wasn't here?

Would you like to see games in the library for use anytime?

Do you feel better now? (Then get back to work)

* All answers will be kept confidential, unless there is someone behind you looking over your shoulder as you write.

Appendix B
Survey Results

Twelve surveys were returned. Many questions were not answered. Respondents also gave additional comments as well. They are included at the end. The following tongue in cheek survey was designed entertainment as well as feedback purposes. It was customized to people who play games and have a sense of humor, not necessarily intended for scientific research and scholarly publication.

The numbers after the responses indicate how many people had that response. If no number appears, there was only one response.

Was this event beneficial? (Why?)
Yes: 9
No, because there are no more snacks

Comments for yes:
Gave me a much needed break
Great!
Help me relax,
No more free food after snacks. And man, it feels good to hear laughter instead of tortured whining.
So beneficial!

What game(s) did you play?
None: 4
Uno: 2
Bluff
Checkers
Chutes and Ladders
Mind Bender
Seven

Did you win?
Yes: 2
No: 2
I didn't finish
Sometimes

Did you cheat?
Yes
No: 4

What was your favorite game? (Why?)
Apples to Apples
Scrabble
Chutes and Ladders
Sudoko

What was your least favorite game? (Why?)
Mind Bender

Was there a game you didn't get to play? (Why?)
No
Mancala

Was there a game you thought should have been included but wasn't here?
Mancala
Operator
Set

Would you like to see games in the library for use anytime?
Yes: 6
Comments:

And snacks
For taking a break
If it is kept in one place, so people can be loud

Do you feel better now? (Then get back to work)
Yes: 6
No, because I didn't get any snacks

Additional comments written on the surveys:

Can you keep the coffee out over the semester too? Coffee+games=fun

Caffeine+food+break=refreshing but the coffee ran out

I liked snacks

Thank you

Put some cups out so I can actually drink

I am a visiting parent, with a student interviewing, a senior in high school. I am favorably impressed by this room, the games and puzzles and though I visit on a quiet Friday morning in December and it is deserted, I can only imagine the fun it would be to spend time here with peers and professor… and the rapport/reflections that result, are cemented in this room. If I were a student at this place, I would frequent this room on a regular basis. Delightful! Kudos2U

CHAPTER 8

Shaking Up the Library: How *Quake* Introduced Students to the Library

Vanessa Earp and Paul Earp

Introduction

Jernigan Library is the primary library for Texas A&M University-Kingsville, and its director in 2004-05, Dr. Ortego, was always seeking ways to improve and expand the relationship of the library with faculty, staff, and students. To build on that goal and increase student/library interaction, the director actively sought out additional activities for students to improve the student/library relationship, always exploring ways to be 'friendlier'. Having kept current on trends in libraries in higher education and libraries in general, the director was aware of cutting-edge ideas and had an open mind to suggestions from library faculty and staff that aligned with those trends.

A concern of most libraries has been that they are seen as antiquated by students and young adults. To gain an accurate grasp of student perceptions, Jernigan Library performed a voluntary and simplified survey of students to measure perceptions and satisfaction with services rendered. The survey was not scientific in design, as the results were not intended for viewing outside of the library.

To keep the survey brief, only a limited number of short multiple-choice questions were asked. Questions similar to the ones below were asked in an attempt to ascertain student perceptions.

- What is your most frequent purpose when entering the Library?
- How often do you come to the Library?
- Have you ever participated in a class requiring Bibliographic (Research) Instruction?
- Please rate your satisfaction with the overall services you have received at the Library.

This survey confirmed that students were unaware of most of the services available, and for the most part only used the building for individual or group study, and for the open computer lab. Student employees asking students walking into the library lobby to participate in the survey reported frequently that the participants were unaware of many library services.

Once this information was obtained, it was clear that changes needed to be made. A review of existing outreach was conducted, and department heads were instructed to find ways to get the students' attention and participation. Outreach programs that were in place, such as liaison programs with the colleges, were improved with better communication and more collaboration. All handouts and direct student outreach (including freshman and graduate orientation packages) were reviewed and improved to stand out more and catch the students' attention. The library also began participating in campus events, having both faculty and student employees staff booths with the new handouts.

Of all these activities, the most popular with the students was the Finals Blow Out. This was a gaming event that allowed students to de-stress by playing first-person games that were locally networked within the library.

Opportunity Knocks

At the end of fall and spring semesters, when the library would become a tomb of silence while students crammed for finals, one of the student clubs on the campus would provide punch and homemade snacks to students in the student lounge. As the lounge was not centrally located, the offering was not as big a success as one would hope. A lackluster response may have led to the discontinuation of this program. This opening provided an opportunity to try something new and, at the time, cutting edge.

The Network Manager was an avid computer gaming fan, and in a previous position on the campus would offer the reward of a gaming session on the last night of school for his student employees. This would involve setting up multiple computers on an isolated network, with one computer as the game server, and the rest as game stations for the students. A free-for-all bash would occur, with free pizza and soda provided by the technical staff. It was the talk of the student employees for the entire semester.

The Network Manager shared this with the Library Director and suggested that this could be a tool to accomplish some of the goals she had set in improving the public/student perception of the library. However, as an academic library, care would need to be taken in the administration of the game so that students wouldn't be tempted to play instead of studying for exams.

Policies and rules would also need to be developed and refined, permission and buy-in obtained from the University Administration, and the legality of any financial expenditures and the accounts that would fund them had to be determined. Because of the complexity of issues, a committee was named to explore, develop, and manage the project. The committee consisted of the Director, the Network Manager to offer technical and security recommendations, two senior librarians and the head of circulation (all faculty), and was simply called the Game Committee.

With support from the Library Director and assistance from faculty, the process of working out all the details began. The following questions needed to be addressed before the Administration could be approached for their support and permission:

- How would this benefit the library, university, and student body?
- What was the library's goal in offering this event?
- What were possible negative results, and what could be done to prevent them?
- What would be the cost both fiscally and in man-hours?
- What department and fund would cover the costs?

The answers were carefully researched, thought out, and prepared for the Library Director to present to the Administration, and the Administration was supportive and encouraged by the enthusiasm of the library staff and faculty.

In the case of this particular library and university, the following answers were sufficient, but may not work well for other organizations. The benefit to the Library was the positive perception created among the students. The benefit to the university and student body was the opportunity for students to de-stress without the involvement of alcohol, drugs, or other dangerous activities. The library's goal was to show that it was a valid and willing participant in new media and even embraced it as a tool to help in the education process.

The last three questions were more difficult to answer. It is not always easy to predict what questions and concerns an administration may have in pursuing new student outreach programs. In this case, their concerns were dealt with by the policy and rules that were outlined for the event. The Business Office determined that if the funds were from a private donor account there would be no legal concerns, but that University budget funds could not be used because the event was not tied to the educational mission of the university. Likewise, staff time could not be fully committed to the event because it was not specifically tied to the educational needs of the student body, and thus did not fall within appropriate use of employee time and energies. The attitude from the Administration was supportive, but only if it did not cost the university any time or money.

The faculty and staff involved in this effort volunteered to use non-work time to get the event off the ground. Some even volunteered to donate funds to help cover any costs that might occur. With these accommodations, the green light was given to continue.

Game Proposal

The committee began in earnest developing the rules, policies, and procedures needed to ensure a smooth event would take place. A debate also began on what type of game would be played, first-person interactive or online role-play.

The following is a summary of the rules and guidelines that were created for the gaming event. It was determined that "policies" was too strong a term, so "guidelines" was adopted in its stead.

- Students must have completed all their finals. Each student was asked and taken at their word prior to being admitted to the game room.
- A three-hour time limit per student, with a minimum break of three hours between sessions, tracked by a sign-in sheet.
- Access for participation is on a first-come basis. The three-hour game limit created opportunities for those waiting.
- Valid student ID required.
- Offensive language, horseplay, physical contact between participants, and inappropriate conduct (as determined by the monitor) would result in immediate removal from the game, and future access would be denied.

The one factor that overruled the majority consensus that students would want to play some form of role-playing game was the issue of time restrictions. Many role-playing games require a participant to have a pre-existing profile or a considerable amount of time to build such a profile. The committee did not want to have the game room monopolized by a few participants.

A second key factor that played a role in the decision to move forward with a role-playing game was the requirement for it to work off a server located on the Internet. It had been determined by the Network Manager and Library Director that students working on final projects, faculty working on continuing projects, and staff doing their daily duties were far more important uses of the existing bandwidth than the game. With a first-person action game, the segment of the network of those computers could be physically removed from the LAN by simply disconnecting a single backbone uplink. The first-person action game server typically is a part of the game itself and can be run independent of Internet access as long as the computers have static IP addresses.

Of the many first-person action games available, *Quake III* was chosen primarily due to the Network Manager's familiarity with the game server that is part of the game CD. The game server could be set for several styles of play: Capture the Flag, where two teams would attempt to protect their own flag while simultaneously attempting to capture the other team's flag to win the session, or Free-for-All, where each player is on his own, and the game is either timed or set to a high score. The player with the highest score wins in the timed session, and the player that first reaches a specific score would win in a high-score session. Since there were time limits, the committee decided on a timed session of Free-for-All.

Licensing

Having chosen the type of game and the game itself, finances and obtaining valid licensing quickly became an issue. The game could be purchased at the time for roughly $40 a license. None of the local stores had any information on volume licensing—no one had ever looked into volume licensing before for games like *Quake* or *Doom*. To complicate matters more, the purchases would have to be made from multiple locations and through multiple online vendors to get twenty-four copies, since no one vendor had more than two or three copies available. The cost with shipping was easily over $1000 to obtain twenty-four legal copies.

Using funds donated for the purchase of books and periodicals was a serious ethical concern. Finding that much money from donors for a game session did not look promising and finding it in just a few days was unlikely. It appeared the experiment would fail.

On a whim, the Network Manager went to the *Quake* Web site to look for a way to contact the company. The Network Manager e-mailed the company, described the dilemma, and asked if there was any type of discount pricing for direct purchase in bulk from the vendors themselves, after describing the intended use of the game during these end of semester events.

Much to everyone's surprise and joy, the vendor, after a couple more e-mails of explanation, gave written permission to use the single copy owned by the Network Manager for three or four days at no extra cost. This speaks highly of the company president, who answered the original e-mail.

The understanding was that the game would only be used at the end of fall and spring semesters, that we would share any positive feedback from the participants (the survey), and that we would take photos of the event and e-mail them to the company for their possible use in advertisement. Therefore, the licensing issues were resolved at no cost to the library.

Location

The Director agreed early on to allow the use of the Bibliographic Instruction Computer Lab for this event. This lab was in an ideal location and configuration for the game. The entrance to the lab was located away from any study areas that might be disturbed by noise that the games frequently incite. The door would stay closed, with appropriate posting of hours, rules, and requirements, to act as a sound barrier.

The room itself was large enough to be comfortable, and the computers were set up along three of the four walls. Originally it was planned that a single game server would be set up on the more powerful instructor's computer and that the remaining twenty-three student computers would simply be clients. The plan did not go well, as the game's built-in server would not host more than seven clients.

Fortunately, each wall had at least seven computers, so each wall became a single game. The server was set to time out as close to three hours as possible, and with a few student employee volunteers, the setup was tested. We found that having three separate games could be beneficial, since the games could be started every hour to accommodate staggered student entry.

We decided that each game should be played on a different level of game terrain. There were more than three levels, so each day a game row was put on a different level to avoid giving experienced participants an advantage over those who were playing *Quake* for the first time.

Implementation

We bought two additional copies of the game so that each of the three session servers would have the CD. For the game to work successfully over the network, each client station requires a valid CD, just as the servers do. We used a shareware software program that allowed us to fool the client stations into believing that they each had a CD running. This required temporarily copying the CD onto the computer hard drive. To comply with the use agreement with the vendor, we ensured that the software was completely uninstalled and all related folders and files were deleted after the semester ended.

The three sessions were tested and worked with very few adjustments required. Over the course of the actual game week, there were occasional crashes, but the volunteers were capable of handling the few problems that arose.

Advertising

Having started this rather late in the semester, the entire project was very rushed. Once all the details of the game, location, setup and licensing was completed, we needed a way to get the word out. At the time, the campus supplied e-mail accounts for all students, but they were not mandated for official use. As a result, much of the student population did not check the accounts frequently, and there was a substantial number that did not use the accounts at all. Personal e-mail accounts were documented with the two or three departments on campus that needed them but working through the red tape to get access to them was impossible on such short notice.

Media Services created several different eye-catching flyers that were posted all over the campus and in the dorms. They also created posters that were placed in the Student Union and the Library. Unfortunately, this was the week before finals, and they were not as effective as they would have been with earlier placement.

Student employees did more to get the word out than the posters. They e-mailed their friends and asked that they contact others. Since many of the volunteers were avid gamers, there was more excitement from them, and this was shared with their friends in the campus gaming community.

The intent of the committee was to advertise to the entire campus community, so everyone would have an opportunity to participate. Since the event was ultimately marketed mostly to gamers, we did not meet our original advertising goal. The event still had a good deal of success, just not as much as was initially hoped.

Volunteers

There was such enthusiasm from the student employees, staff, and faculty directly involved that finding volunteers to staff the event was no problem. It was determined that the Network

Manager, who worked the day shift, and the Computer Support Technician, who worked the evening shift, would check in on the event every hour or so as work permitted. This worked out well, and very few actual man-hours were used during the event.

Media Services personnel would come down every so often and take photographs, and the participants were asked to fill out a short survey on their way in and out of the event.

Game Day

With the beginning of finals week, the Game Room was opened. At first there were very few participants, as finals were just getting rolling. The first day averaged around four to five players at a time throughout the day, and in the evening at least two full sessions were going. There may have been some who misled the volunteers staffing the room on whether or not they were finished with all their finals, but our policy indicated that students would be taken at their word.

With the room decorated with homemade posters, store-bought posters on loan from students, and the lights dimmed, the atmosphere was one of fun and laughter.

By the end of the week, the participation grew as more students finished their finals. There was considerable laughter and camaraderie in the game room, and it appeared to be successful in alleviating the stress of finals.

Conclusion

Informal feedback from students indicated that they enjoyed the game, and that they would be likely to use the library's resources and services in the future. Student employees who had volunteered their time were receiving all types of positive feedback through the break and were frequently asked questions from friends and classmates. A persistent question was "would there be another game session?" The Director's office, Reference, and Media Services were all receiving inquiries.

The students that participated in the event were excited about the prospect of another session at the end of the semester and wanted to know if it would occur at the end of each semester. The event was successful in the goal helping to reduce student stress. The positive feedback on the event was welcome as part of the overall effort to improve the image of the library with the campus community.

 CHAPTER 9

Games in the Library: Creating an Awareness of Library Resources for Lifelong Library Users

Sharon Mazure and Amy Hughes

Students' awareness and knowledge of library resources, including the role of an academic librarian as a resource was lacking at Fairmont State University. Student feedback through library instruction evaluations, informal surveys and word-of-mouth indicated that we needed to promote our roles. In order to improve our students' awareness and use of library resources, we wanted to try a different approach and needed to investigate different ways of being involved with our students. Our goal was to make students aware of library resources, but we also wanted to convey a message that the library is a great place to be. We were hopeful that by increasing student awareness of library resources, the likelihood of their success in school would also increase. Gaming became our strategy and marketing tool.

Using rudimentary qualitative methods, we assessed our current student population to gauge the interests of incoming students. Games in the library emerged as a popular theme, and we decided that gaming was an approach worth trying in order to encourage students to visit the library and use its resources. We decided to try both physical on-site activities and an online, virtual game station.

Our Strategy

We planned a three-pronged approach in which one aspect, purchasing a Nintendo Wii, would become a permanent part of the library, and the other two were one-day events that would provide a snapshot of our services and help familiarize students with areas of the library, including general information such as where to ask for reserve materials and the location of labs and multimedia rooms. The single-day events were held a few months apart, at the beginning and middle of the semester. While one took place during the day, when classes were held, the other took place on a Saturday evening. The time between the two events provided valuable marketing time, and we hoped that offering the events only a few months apart would keep the library in the minds of students.

We chose the themes for the single-day events because we felt that those were the right types of games for our student population. West Virginia is a small state, and local fairs and small town carnivals are a mainstay. Therefore, a small carnival with food and games fit in well with the culture of West Virginia. The murder mystery event also worked for our student population for several reasons. Like small-town carnivals, folklore is an important part of West Virginia culture, and we were able to capitalize on the library's history since it is named after a prominent West Virginia folklorist, Ruth Ann Musick, and houses a considerable folklore collection.

A Gaming Station: Nintendo Wii

At the suggestion of our director, we invested in a large high-definition flat-screen television, a Nintendo Wii system, and two game bundles which consisted of six different games in April 2007. Purchasing the television would not only serve as a permanent gaming station for the Wii but would also allow us to view breaking news stories in an area that would accommodate a large number of people. The library's student lounge was an ideal location for the Wii. Previously the lounge held a few couches and coffee tables; the addition of the television helped to create a more welcoming and comfortable atmosphere. Moreover, the Wii quickly became a signature feature of the library for prospective students who have been pleasantly surprised to learn that Wii games are available for student use.

The Wii is popular among students and continues to be checked out on a daily basis. It is housed with reserve materials at the circulation desk. Students are able to check out the gaming system for a three-hour period and can renew the system if no one else is waiting to check it out. In order to check out the Wii, users are asked to read and sign a one-page agreement in which the student agrees to assume responsibility for the games and its components. The student must also have a current university ID.

Wii pieces are labeled, tagged and housed in a plastic storage container. On the lid of the container is a contents list so that the circulation staff can quickly check to make sure all of the pieces are included inside the box when it is issued and when it is returned. When students want to check out the Wii, they must check out the entire box. To date, we have not had major complications with the procedure.

The Wii has been a marketing tool for freshman seminar courses, facilitating group co-hesiveness, or serving as an ice breaker. Additionally, it is popular among our international students who are unable to travel during holidays. We promote use of the Wii for snow days, exam breaks, during evening hours, and on the weekends. Since we purchased the Wii, several students have requested different games, and the student gaming club has requested use of the student lounge for meeting purposes. Other clubs have also shown an interest in using the Wii system as an activity for their group.

Purchasing the Wii before the start of the fall semester gave the library an exciting new feature to talk about as faculty and students returned to campus. And we were able to mention the Wii when we started marketing the library carnival. The purpose of both the purchase of the Wii and the special events was to use fun to get students to visit the library and see what it has to offer. We hoped the variety of approaches would attract different types of students to the library.

Library Carnival

Planning for the carnival began in the spring semester of 2007. Our primary purpose for host-ing the carnival was to increase student awareness of the library. We wanted students to be aware of the location of the library, both the physical resources and the online resources, and we wanted to convey that the library was a friendly, helpful place. Initial planning meetings consisted of making lists, determining what resources were available, and brainstorming ideas for activities.

Deciding on a time and date became the first objective. We decided that the second Tuesday of classes during the first full week of school was the best date, and since we have a lot of traffic in the library during lunch hours, we agreed on a four-hour carnival from 10:00 a.m.–2:00 p.m. The second step was to identify available resources and draft a preliminary budget.

Again, we agreed that our volunteers, mostly library staff members, were the most valuable resource. We informed the staff of the carnival immediately so that they knew what we were planning. An e-mail invitation was sent to library staff members two months prior to the event. After discussing the event, we estimated that we would need a minimum of eleven volunteers. We learned that keeping them informed helped to maintain interest, and the staff members were excited and more than willing to help. In the time leading up to the event, we sent two additional e-mails which served as reminders and sustained enthusiasm for the event. The day before the carnival, we gave instructions to each of the staff members about their duties. Since our school colors are maroon and white, we asked that the volunteers wear a maroon-colored shirt and jeans. We provided drinks and snacks in the library lounge for volunteers.

In addition to the library staff, student athletes volunteered to help with the games. We sent an e-mail to our athletic coaches and asked if any of their athletes would be able to help at the library carnival. Several coaches responded, and we had several student volunteers from the men's football and basketball teams. While the student volunteers were not necessary to manage the games, they did help to generate interest, and they stepped in when library staff volunteers wanted to take a break. More importantly, the student athletes were a big help with marketing the event as they spread the news via word-of-mouth. Other student groups such as freshman counselors also helped spread the news.

Our initial marketing strategy was to focus on a target audience. Freshman seminar classes were targeted because we wanted to establish long-term relationships both with students and the instructors of the freshman seminar courses. We attended a meeting for the instructors of the freshman seminar classes to inform them of library resources and our services. At this meeting, we invited them to bring their classes to the library during the carnival. It was suggested that instead of offering a more traditional library tour, the library carnival would be an engaging way to introduce students to our library services.

In addition to contacting freshman seminar instructors, resident assistants and freshman counselors also were contacted and asked to attend the carnival with new students. A library student worker hung posters in the dorms, student union, and in the library. We were able to get large banners from the Pepsi-Cola Corporation for free because our university has an account with them. We merely asked our contact at Pepsi, and they were happy to provide the banner. These banners were hung outside the library the week prior to the event.

Although the target audience was new students, we sent an e-mail announcement to all students and invited them to attend. We placed an advertisement on the televised network in the university's student union and submitted the same advertisement to the student paper. Lastly, we contacted the university's public service representative and requested coverage on the university web site. This last contact increased our coverage, and a local television reporter attended the carnival. A story about the event was aired later that night. Much to our surprise, we had the most success with telephone calls, whether we were calling businesses or vendors for donations, or contacting instructors to invite them to the carnival. Similarly, news spread via word-of-mouth proved to be more effective than e-mail announcements.

Drafting a budget required some research into carnival games, decorations, food, and prizes. We proposed that the initial cost of the carnival would be $1200. This start-up cost included purchasing promotional materials, games, prizes, food, and a popcorn machine. The majority of the budget was spent on prizes, which included an iPod and three MP3 players as well as several other donated gift certificates, candy, and trinkets such as key chains. We requested small prizes from many of the library's database vendors and had a good response from them. In return, we listed their names on the game sheet next to each game. Local businesses donated prizes and gift certificates for this event, and the university's bookstore made a donation as well. We sent thank you notes to our donors after the event.

We spent approximately three hundred fifty dollars on both the games and materials for the games. Inexpensive game parts such as colored cones and bean bags were purchased through a party supply company catalog. The company offered premade, inexpensive games and materials. A volunteer offered to help build a Plinko board and a large tic-tac-toe board. Other materials were gathered from supplies we had in the library.

On the day of the event, several staff members helped to decorate the library with balloons and streamers, posted directional signs to the games, and helped stage the gaming areas. While students were playing the game, or watching their peers, they were simultaneously being exposed to the layout of the library and the resources that we offer. Large signs with prominent arrows directed the students to the various games. For instance, a Frisbee game was located near the print journal collection. While students were playing the game, the staff member mentioned that most of our journals were online, available from the library's Web site, and that the print collection was only a small portion of what the library offers.

Many suggestions for improvements were made by the volunteers who helped with individual game stations. One suggestion was to include music, which we previously decided against due to budget restrictions. Another suggestion was to change the date of the event. Since our target audience was new students who lived in on-campus housing, it was suggested that we host the event during freshman orientation week rather than during the first week of school. This would also help to keep the carnival within a reasonable budget. Hosting it during the school day was confusing for some students and library staff members, who felt overwhelmed by trying to accomplish multiple tasks among such a large crowd of students. Another idea presented at our evaluation meeting was a redemption center. Instead of having prizes at each gaming booth, tickets could be awarded and then redeemed at a centralized prize table. It was agreed that the drawing for grand prizes would be retained.

In addition to a carnival for students, we are planning a carnival day for faculty and staff. We think that this would be a unique way to work with our department liaisons and would be a fun activity to host during faculty development week.

Game Structure

We strategically set up nine different games on all three floors of the library near a point of interest, such as the reference desk, the DVD collection, and the student lounge. In order to be eligible for one of the grand prize drawings, students had to play every game. Upon entering the library, students were greeted by the smell of freshly popped popcorn and directed towards the circulation desk by the "ringmaster." The game sheet that each student received had nine blocks and within each block was the name of a game. We worked database names into the titles of the carnival games so that students would recognize these product names on the library Web site, such as the OVID Bean Bag Toss. After participating in the game, the student would have their game card initialed by the carnival volunteer who was assigned to that game station.

On the ground floor of the library, there is a lengthy hallway which was a perfect fit for the egg and spoon race. Colorful miniature traffic cones were set up in two zigzagging rows so a pair of students could maneuver through the barriers holding a wooden egg in a matching colored spoon in each hand. The winner of the race received a small prize, and both participants had their game cards signed.

Students proceeded up the marble staircase to the middle floor of the library and were greeted by five more carnival games in progress. The plate spinning game consisted of a plastic plate with an indentation in the middle and a wooden stick tapered to a rounded point. The object of the game was to get the plate spinning on the stick in less than one minute. A bonus prize was awarded if the plate remained spinning for more than one minute. It is more difficult than it sounds. A hula hoop was attached to a large metal coat rack for the Frisbee launch.

Each student had three chances to get a disk through the hoop while standing behind a tape line about twenty-five feet away.

In the nearby student lounge, two players could compete against each other in a game of tic-tac-toe. Players stood about fifteen feet away from the board and each held five large bean bags of the same color. Another game, Plinko, was modeled on a game similar to that seen on *The Price is Right*, but on a much smaller scale, using a 4' x 6' piece of peg board and nearly 300 small wooden pegs. Large metal washers, about 1 ½ inches in diameter, worked well. Plinko is a game of luck. Each student was given five chips (metal washers) and was instructed to place them anywhere on the top row. When the chip was released, it would zigzag erratically down the game board and land in a tray at the bottom. Three trays were marked as "win" trays, and winners received a small prize.

A dice rolling game was situated near the Video/DVD collection. Large foam dice were purchased, and a large square using blue painter's tape was marked out on the floor. Only dice landing inside the target square counted. Four of a kind, three of a kind, two pair, and any straight were prize winners.

On the third floor of the library, we placed the last three games, the ring toss and the baseball bean bag toss. The ring toss game consisted of five pegs fastened to five star-shaped stands. The rings were circles of rope. Students stood behind a line about twelve feet away and pitched all five rope rings toward the pegs. The baseball bean bag toss proved to be the most difficult. The game board was colorful and inviting, but the five "prize" holes were much too small. Most baseball-shaped bean bags could not be pitched into these holes successfully. A larger version will be constructed for the next carnival.

"Hula Hoopla" was a really popular game. Students won a prize if they could keep the hula hoop moving around their waists for at least fifteen seconds. We plan to use a stopwatch the next time and award larger prizes to those having the top three longest periods of continuous hula hooping.

According to the feedback that we received from students, course instructors, and staff, the carnival event was a success. We learned that certain details for the event were essential, such as providing food and drinks for staff and volunteers, and a assigning a "ring-master" to answer general questions about the event. And the success of the carnival helped motivate us as we planned for the murder mystery event.

Murder Mystery Event

We started planning for the murder mystery event in the last week of September 2007. We researched and read articles dealing with library mystery tours, library murder mysteries, and even short mystery plays presented to students in a library setting. Since our goal was to increase student interaction with the library and its resources, we wanted our students to be involved in the mystery instead of being merely passive viewers. We decided on an interactive game in which participants would solve eight different clues using our library resources. These library clues would then be part of a larger puzzle used to solve a mystery.

We held frequent impromptu meetings which were less time consuming and helped keep us on track. Originally, the event was designed without a budget. We utilized basic office supplies, materials from home, and items in the library for props and game materials. However, the library director decided to provide light refreshments for the participants, and we served finger sandwiches, cookies, and cider after the mystery was solved.

In our game, the mystery was to identify a victim, who was represented as a chalk outline drawn on the floor in front of the reference desk. The clues were developed so that the participants had to use the catalog, an atlas, a dictionary, an electronic book, a database, the study rooms, the photocopier, and the reserves area. Each team would begin with the use of the catalog, but thereafter would receive a unique clue in order to avoid a bottleneck at any one area in the library. This seemed to create competition among the groups as they rushed to find the clue and worked similarly to a scavenger hunt. Several days before the event, we did a run-through of all the clues to estimate the amount of time it would take to complete the mystery. We determined that two hours was enough time for the game.

The murder mystery event was held after the library closed on the last Saturday in the month October of 2007, from seven to nine o'clock. Since the event was held at the end of the month, it was already dark outside. Most of the lights were extinguished and the emergency lights, which remained on, helped to create an eerie atmosphere. Cobweb decorations, battery-powered candles, and a few props added to the atmosphere. Four staff members, three reference librarians and the library director helped host the event, and we dressed in ghoulish costumes. From our CD collection, we used various recordings of music and sound effects to play while the teams were searching for clues. All of the participants received a small goody bag at the end of the night. We gave away the candy that was left over from the library carnival. The winning team members received dinner-for-two coupons donated by a local restaurant.

Marketing the event was compressed into a two-week time span. We felt that too much prior notice might allow initial interest to wane, and we wanted to take advantage of participant curiosity. We sent out two campus-wide e-mails to students. Since there were several steps involved, we capped the event at forty participants. The e-mail was an advertisement and invitation, asking students to help solve the mystery. It alluded to a murder mystery event and was purposefully brief and open-ended. This drew a lot of interest, as several students responded. In addition to the e-mail, we hung posters in buildings on campus, including the dormitories, two weeks prior to the event. Two different advertisements were delivered to the student newspaper in the beginning of October. The first article was an announcement of the event, and the second article contained a registration form. The chalk outline of a body on the library floor generated interest as well.

The sign-up sheet for the event was located at the reference desk, which is prominently located on the ground floor of the library. We scheduled ten days for students to sign up for the event. Registering for the event was closed on the Wednesday before, so that we knew how many people would attend. Two days before the event, we sent an e-mail reminder to the students who had registered.

Game Structure

As students entered the library on the evening of the mystery event, they were greeted by a librarian and given a color tag—as opposed to a name tag. There were eight different teams each represented by a different color. Attributing a color to the teams allowed for those students who signed up with a friend to be in the same group. The teams also had names corresponding to famous murderers: Jeffrey Dahmer, Lizzy Borden, Ted Bundy, the Unabomber, James Earl Ray, Jack the Ripper, the Zodiac Killer, and Charles Manson.

Once everyone had arrived and was sitting with their group, the rules were presented. Each team was given a flashlight and a packet that contained the starting clue, a pencil, a small notepad, and a dime. Everyone started at the same time. Since the first clue required participants to use the library catalog, all of the teams logged on to the nearest computer to access it. Once the answer was located they had to check-in at the reference desk. A librarian at the reference desk checked to make sure the answer was correct, and, if so, the group was given their second clue. This method forced students to check in at the reference desk after each task.

At the circulation desk, the librarian had a color-coded folder for each team, a master sheet of clue answers, and a spreadsheet. Each team folder had eight puzzle pieces and clues two through eight. The spreadsheet had a team color column and columns for each of the eight clues, so that it was easy to keep track of which team had correctly answered a clue.

Clue #1: The murderer was using this very library to research murder and death! Your team will do a catalog search for two book titles. Write down the call numbers of the two books you find. Locate the two books on the library's shelves, and then bring them to the circulation desk for check-out. You will then receive a puzzle piece and your next clue. Search for *In Cold Blood* and *Death Grows on You*. (Each team had different book titles.)

Clues #2-8: The dictionary clue required that each team visit the student lounge, locate the table holding an unabridged dictionary, and look up the definition of a murder-related term. Each dictionary clue was different, using words such as asphyxiate and massacre. Students were instructed to write down the definition and the page number on which it was found. When this information was correctly reported to the reference desk, another puzzle piece and another clue would be issued. Another clue asked students to search for book titles in each of the four group study rooms. A number of books containing folktales and ghost stories were in each room. Students had to search in each room and in each book to locate a specific story, then make note of the book, author and page number. A third clue involved locating the reserve materials, which are located behind the circulation desk. Other clues required students to locate and use an atlas, log on to a computer and use NetLibrary to search the text of a specific book, access a specific online database to search for a journal, and make a photocopy using the dime we provided in the group folder. All of the clues related to the lives or crimes of the serial killers who names we had selected for each team. For instance, the Charles Manson team was asked to search the electronic database to find the names of his victims.

It was fun to see students running through the library, laughing and whispering strategies. A few teams struggled with finding the answers to some of the clues, but overall the teams worked well together and were energetic about solving the mystery. Once we had a winning team, we notified all the other teams, and we adjourned to the main lobby of the library for refreshments, awarded the grand prize, and listened to a dramatic reading of one of Ruth Ann

Musick's ghost tales. We continued to receive positive feedback from students for weeks afterwards, many students commented on the details, and we are looking forward to hosting this event in 2008. Overall, we felt that the event should not last more than two hours, allowing one hour to complete the puzzle, and thirty to sixty minutes for students to mingle.

We felt that all three types of games—the Wii, the Carnival, and the Murder Mystery—were a fun way for students to experience the library, and the students and faculty responded positively to the events. The murder mystery event, which had fewer participants, generated the most thorough feedback. We even heard positive feedback from a parent of one of the participants. After each of the events, we posted pictures on the Web site.

The Future

We are anxious to host these games in the library for the 2008/2009 academic year because we believe that there will be an even greater interest. At this time we are planning two library carnivals, one for new students and a second for faculty members. Both carnivals will be hosted the week before students arrive. The combination of the carnival, the Wii, and the October murder mystery event all helped to generate awareness of the library. We wanted our students to feel comfortable in the library, and we believe that these gaming events have helped to create an environment that is welcoming to students and faculty.

 CHAPTER 10

Geocaching
Linda Musser

Introduction to Geocaching

Geocaching is essentially a treasure hunting game using Global Positioning System (GPS) technology. The "treasure" generally consists of a hidden container holding a log book and some trinkets. The GPS coordinates and clues to the container's location are posted to a central geocaching Web page, http://www.geocaching.com, which lists basic information about the cache.

The first geocache was hidden near Portland, Oregon in May 2000 following the U. S. government's unscrambling of GPS satellite signals.[1] Clues to its location were publicized via the Internet, some people accepted the challenge to find it, and geocaching was born. Since that time, the popularity of geocaching has grown and the number of caches has multiplied to over 200,000 active caches in 218 countries. Geocaches are registered at http://www.geocaching.com, which provides indexed access to geocaches by location (country, state, latitude/longitude, zip code, etc.), keyword, waypoint (a code name for a specific cache), type, and owner.

A standard cache contains a logbook, pen or pencil for finders to write comments, and tokens such as small toys, CDs, books, tickets, and coupons. Finders are encouraged to write a comment, take a token, and leave something in exchange. The one firm rule is no food. Since most geocaches are hidden outdoors, it is important that the cache not attract local wildlife. Also frowned upon is propaganda or suggestive material; geocaching is very much a family activity and cache owners are expected to make their caches appropriate for all ages. Cache owners are also expected to obtain permission to hide their cache if not placing it on their own property and to use common sense about where to place the cache. For example, hidden containers at an airport would cause anxiety. Locations that are dangerous to reach such as highway medians are also not recommended.

Finding the cache begins with logging on to the geocaching Web site and selecting a cache to locate. Each geocache is described by a Web page that gives latitude/longitude coordinates, a description of the type of cache, clues to its location, a difficulty rating, terrain rating, and a map of the local area. The difficulty rating reflects factors such as how long it will take to locate the cache and if specialized equipment is required. The terrain rating reflects physical factors such as wheelchair accessibility or trail steepness. Also included on the Web page are links to nearby caches, landmarks, hiking trails, etc. Finally, it provides an opportunity for enthusiasts to record their comments about the cache and even upload photos of their hunt.

Types of Caches

Caches are quite varied. A traditional cache is about the size of a one quart container, large enough to contain a log book and trinkets. The cache can be larger although that makes it

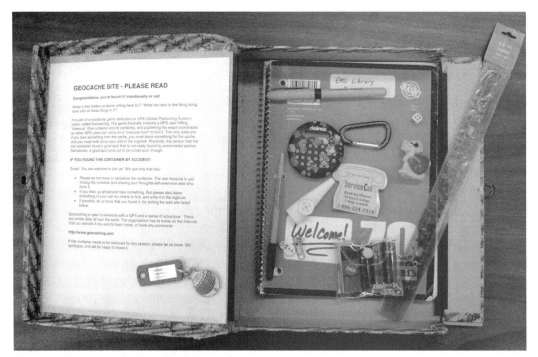

Figure 1. Contents of a Standard Geocache

more difficult to hide. A microcache is about the size of a 35 mm film canister. A typical cache is hidden (behind a rock, under a bush, etc.) and requires only the GPS coordinates and sharp eyes to locate. Depending on the make and model, the accuracy of GPS units range from 6 feet to 100 feet so finding the cache is frequently difficult! One variant is the letterbox cache which contains a rubber stamp that the searcher can use to stamp their geocaching 'passport'. Enthusiasts try to collect as many geocaching stamps as possible.

Unlike the traditional cache, a multicache involves several steps. The initial GPS coordinates take the searcher to a location from which they follow multiple clues or steps to locate the cache. A mystery cache is a type of multicache that requires users to solve a mystery to find the cache. An offset cache will commonly start at a historic marker. A puzzle cache starts with a puzzle which must be solved to gain the requisite clues.

Another type of cache is the virtual cache. A virtual cache is itself a landmark or similar place. The successful searcher must answer questions to prove that they located the cache. New virtual caches are no longer accepted at the geocaching Web site; rather, posters are encouraged to register virtual caches at http://waymarking.com, which is devoted to this type of cache. Another variant is the earthcache, which is an educational virtual cache that features an interesting geological feature. Earthcaches are formally approved by the Geological Society of America and are commonly located in state and national parks.[2] There are even event caches where enthusiasts can meet and discuss geocaching.

Locations of Caches

The vast majority of caches are located outdoors since many GPS units have limited capability indoors. Cache owners may place their cache near a favorite outdoor location or landmark, as a way of sharing their top picks for local hikes or interesting locations. Caches are located in remote and populated locations, urban and suburban, rural and remote. There are geocaches on every continent including Antarctica (22 caches as of 2007). A search of the geocaching Web site identified over sixty-eight hundred geocaches in the Chicago, Illinois, zip code of 60611 alone.

Cache Contents

As previously stated, a standard cache contains a log book, a writing tool, and some trinkets.

Other items that are frequently found in caches include travel bugs and geocoins. A travel bug is a trackable item consisting usually of a trinket or other item attached to a dog tag with the travel bug's unique identification number. The purpose of the travel bug is to travel (the finder notes the identification number and location on the geocaching Website and the owner tracks its movements). The travel bug owner places the travel bug in a cache and cache finders are encouraged to move the bug to another cache and log its new location. Many travel bug owners include specific requests about where they would like to see their bug travel. A recent travel bug arrived in our library's geocache as part of its owners request that

Figure 2. Example of a Travel Bug

the bug visit all the universities in the Big Ten athletic conference! Geocoins are similar to travel bugs in that they are trackable items but are specifically designed for individuals or groups as unique, signature items. Examples include state designs (similar to the U.S. Mint's state quarters series) as well as topical and organizational designs (e.g., Christmas geocoins and Scouting geocoins).

Geocaches and Libraries

Why should libraries care about geocaching? Libraries are, after all, indoor environments. At the least, geocaching as a new, popular activity deserves a place in our collections. Indeed, the first book on geocaching was published in 2003. More importantly, geocaching provides a way for the library to become more involved in the local community by becoming an active contributor to a popular recreational activity. Geocaching also provides a vehicle to publicize the library's resources to a broader audience and alter the public's perceptions about what the library is and the services it provides. Ultimately, geocaching is a low- (almost no-) cost method to bring

Figure 3. EMS Library Geocache on the Library Shelf

people to the library, particularly non-traditional users. As users increasingly visit the library online, geocaching provides a creative way to bring them back to the physical library.

The EMS Library Geocache

The Earth and Mineral Sciences (EMS) Library at Penn State University is an academic science library and part of the University Libraries system. "By George", the EMS Library's geocache, is a multicache that is hidden in the library[3]. The cache container is shaped like a book and shelved in the library stacks. The cache was first hidden in October of 2005 as a way of making the library more fun to our users as well as attracting more folks to our library. Outreach is part of the library's mission and that was one way of trying to do something for the non-scholarly audience.

The GPS coordinates from the Web site lead to the front of the library building where an interesting geological formation is on display. Following clues[4] the searcher is led to the library, where they need to find a secondary clue sheet which is hidden on the bust of George Deike, near the front of the library. (The clue sheet contains some basic information about the library, then asks the user to do some clue finding and basic math to calculate the call number for the geocache—GV1200—the official Library of Congress classification number for geocaching. The user then goes to the stacks to locate the cache. In the process of gathering the clues, the searcher is introduced to the library's art collection and other resources.

Responses to the EMSL geocache have been extremely positive. Most enthusiasts are intrigued by the uniqueness of the cache and indicated that they enjoyed the hunt. Many comment that they have frequently passed our building but never stopped before; others mention that they have seen our collections for the first time. A sampling of comments from the geocache log book include the following:

- "This was a really neat cache! "
- "Man that cache was fun! Great hide and great box."

- "Not only did I experience a truly unique caching adventure, but I learned something as well. That's crazy!"
- "Thanks for bringing me here."
- "It's about time we found this cache…since we work in the [nearby] building. Anyway, this is definitely an awesome cache idea. I never would have thought of it myself. It's funny, because we found the cache with tons of people around and nobody was the wiser."
- "This was a great find. A lot of fun doing some detective work on this one."

From the point of view of the library staff, they are pleased to be in on the fun and enjoy watching visitors, both students and non-students, as they search for the cache. Many geocachers stop to chat and ask questions about the library and the university. A recurring theme is pleasant surprise that a stuffy 'academic' organization would be involved in something that is just—fun.

The geocache concept has been adapted for other purposes as well. In the fall of each year, the University Libraries host an open house for all new students. A recent theme was sports, and each library was asked to tailor their open house activities around that theme. The EMS Library chose to feature geocaching as our sports theme and decided to incorporate a special geocache into our activities, separate from the "By George" geocache. The clues were designed to introduce students to the Library of Congress classification system and to lead them into our stacks so they could become familiar with the layout of the library. Since participation in the geocache activity was optional, we offered incentives in the form of inexpensive prizes (bandanas, Mardi Gras beads, etc.) to those students who chose to participate. Students working alone or in groups were asked to read a brief description of the classification system, do a range of activities to determine the call number for the cache, then use the call number to find the cache in the library stacks. The cache itself includes a certificate for students to turn in for one of the prizes. Student responses were very positive, and we have since repeated the activity annually in addition to maintaining our regular geocache. Although the activities have varied somewhat over the years, generally they have included looking up a book using the library's online catalog, checking the library's Web site for hours or other information, answering a question that requires the students to explore particular locations or collections in the library, and sometimes using an online database.

Geocaching has now spread to include other Penn State libraries, particularly those at campus locations. The Pennsylvania State University has over twenty campuses scattered throughout the state, and each campus library has as part of their mission to support and engage their local communities. Geocaching is seen as one way to achieve that mission. Other libraries are also hopping on the geocaching bandwagon. I have been contacted for advice on establishing geocaches by academic and public librarians from across the United States.

Conclusions

Libraries can capitalize on the popularity of geocaching in several ways. Most obviously, geocaching is a way to introduce people to your library. It brings new people to the library and exposes them to resources of which they may have been unaware. A creatively designed multicache can double as a library tour. Clues can be imbedded in the online catalog or in database records as a way to highlight these resources and can even be used to explain your library's classification system. Geocaching can bring some fun into your library and support your outreach mission by contributing to recreational opportunities in the local area.

On the educational side, recent studies by OCLC and the Council on Library and Information Resources[5] report changing usage patterns and expectations of students for libraries. Students increasingly want academic libraries to not only be places for studying and learning but to provide recreation and relaxation opportunities as well. Geocaching is one way to contribute to that transformation. As stated by Margot Kelley, "…the geocaching community as a social grouping… offers insights into what might come in the near future as people struggle to live well in both the physical and virtual worlds."[6] To remain vital, libraries need to pay attention and participate in these new social groupings.

Notes

1. Groundspeak Inc., "The History of Geocaching," http://www.geocaching.com/about/history.aspx (Accessed January 15, 2008).
2. Geological Society of America, "Earthcache," Boulder, CO: GSA, 2004 http://www.geosociety.org/earthcache/ (Accessed January 15, 2008).
3. Groundspeak Inc., "Geocaching.com," 2005 (Accessed January 15, 2008). Use waypoint GCQXJR

to access "By George" webpage or http://www.geocaching.com/seek/cache_details.aspx?wp=GCQX JR&Submit6=Find

4. Once the searcher has found the geologic formation, the clues state, "From this location, you will see a date. Multiply this date by 2, divide by 30, then subtract from the result the number of letters in the English alphabet. The resulting room number is where you need to go and visit "By George" for the next clue!" For those who have difficulty with either their math or with finding the next clue, there is an encrypted hint on the webpage that states, "There is a bust of George Deike near the north entrance to the Fletcher L. Byrom Earth and Mineral Sciences Library."

5. Council on Library and Information Resources, "Library as Place: Rethinking Roles, Rethinking Space," http://www.clir.org/pubs/abstract/pub129abst.html (Accessed January 15, 2008); OCLC, "2003 OCLC Environmental Scan: Pattern Recognition," http://www.oclc.org/reports/escan/ (Accessed January 15, 2008).

6. Margot Anne Kelley, *Local Treasures: Geocaching Across America*, (Santa Fe, New Mexico: Center for American Places, 2006).

CHAPTER 11

Your Library Instruction is in Another Castle: Developing Information Literacy-Based Videogames at Carnegie Mellon University

Donna Beck, Rachel Callison, John Fudrow, and Dan Hood

Introduction

Being part of an institution possessing a world-renowned computer science school and a reputation for developing innovative new technologies, the University Libraries at Carnegie Mellon were motivated to explore a new method of information literacy instruction. This method was to be the creation of a web-based videogame. Through a $50,000 grant from the Buhl Foundation, awarded in the Spring of 2006, the University Libraries began developing a series of "web-based instructional modules."[1] The University Libraries soon formed a representative group of three librarians, self-dubbed the Library Arcade (LA) Committee, to help define how to best transmute the goals of traditional information literacy instruction into a videogame format. The committee began this process by investigating the past and current trends in videogame culture.

Gaming and Culture

Over the past 50 years, gaming has grown exponentially due to technological innovations and found a broad audience. Gaming technology was greeted enthusiastically by those ready for entertainment that would not only challenge their problem-solving skills and hand/eye coordination but keep them coming back for more. Arcades provided a social space for a shared activity with gaming as its center. As computer games became more complex, and the quality of the graphics improved, they were able to encompass detailed narrative stories with unforgettable characters.

Gaming culture shifted from the arcades into the home as console systems became accessible by a larger portion of the population. Just as previous generations vied for playground sports supremacy, many children spent vast amounts of time challenging each other at their favorite videogame. Opportunities for players to experience gaming in an online environment increased with the advancement of Internet technologies. These developments allowed game manufacturers to spread their titles via the Web and for players to interact in new virtual worlds across global networks. The current appeal of massive multiplayer online role-playing games (MMORPGs) and the inclusion of online connectivity as a standard feature on next-generation game consoles give evidence to the social role that gaming has adopted. Many gamers develop complex social networks and utilize information literacy-related skills when playing these immersive games.

The use of videogames in libraries is a fairly new concept, and a librarian having an influence on their creation is equally novel. Games are a large portion of the popular culture, and libraries recognize them as an attractive method to engage young adults in library activities. Gaming can provide avenues for exploration and experimentation through which players pursue goals and take risks without the fear of permanent failure. Gaming environments allow students to try playing a game multiple times, and, in doing so, alleviate the pressure of getting it exactly right the first time.

We also know from observation and the professional literature that our undergraduate students are digital natives and for the most part grew up playing videogames. Having an audience that is familiar with modern gaming opens any library game to the risk of falling victim to the "lame-factor" which plagues most educational gaming initiatives. Designing an engaging library instruction session is challenging in itself, but creating a videogame that attempts to translate the information literacy goals of the library might be viewed by students as lame. The LA Committee knew that if we were to make successful use of these facts, we would need to enlist the expertise of those beyond the library realm.

Advantage of Having the ETC

The work that goes into producing a modern online game is extremely diverse. Various talents and experts are often utilized, including artists, producers, writers, programmers, and animators. Game design, a complex discipline in its own right, was not an expertise that members of the LA Committee inherently possessed. However, we were fortunate to have access to the experience and services of the Entertainment Technology Center (ETC) at Carnegie Mellon. The ETC awards a Masters of Entertainment Technology degree, which combines an understanding of the arts and technology through which the graduates are able to create the next-generation of digital entertainment. The ETC curriculum is experiential and project-based, rather than course-based, and "students devote most of their energy (and do most of their learning) as members of inter-disciplinary teams completing projects in lieu of taking traditional classes."[2] These semester-long projects are typically overseen by an ETC faculty advisor. The five ETC students, who would become the iLit team, possessed varied backgrounds: computer science, electronics and communication, fine art, psychology and journalism. By working together, the two groups were able to produce design documents for an interactive, web-based information literacy computer game which resulted in the completion of two playable stand-alone modules. Without the ETC, the majority of activities involved in the creation of these games—design, programming, user testing and maintenance—would not have been possible to accomplish in-house (within University Libraries) alongside the existing duties and responsibilities of the LA Committee members.

As students would be directly involved with the game's production, the project timeline was based upon an academic calendar. Initially, considerable time was spent brainstorming with the ETC faculty member who would oversee the project to coordinate student involvement and address any additional programming or outsourcing needs. The deliverable product was to be completed in about a year's time and ultimately uploaded to the University Library Web servers.

Where Do You Press Start?

Before the LA Committee was established in 2006, the University Libraries Administration approached the Science Librarians to help create a specific concept for a prototype. Engineering, specifically sustainable engineering, was initially considered a game theme that would fit well within Carnegie Mellon's interdisciplinary environment. Creating a centralized repository to hold resources on sustainable engineering was appealing, with the game serving as a modern "pathfinder." This concept raised concerns about copyright authorization due to the anticipated amount of work that would be needed to obtain permission from authors to allow their articles to be placed in a repository. Much work would also be needed to maintain the timeliness, accuracy and relevancy of the data for future users. If a repository starts to grow, and at a later time other students have access to the repository, would the students be motivated to play the game if what they needed was already gathered? Since our goal was to improve undergraduate research skills using a videogame interface, and not to build a large-scale set of data that might quickly become hard to manage, we focused on creating something that would aid in sharpening the skills of an individual. Although it was decided not to have data collection integrated into the playing of the game itself, having it as an addendum to the end product was left on the table for future discussion. The LA Committee revisited one of the original grant proposal goals as a guide, "Developing, testing, evaluating, and refining educational modules that will be lively and attractive, as well as intellectually sound."[3] Thus, at the start of the fall 2006 semester, the project was still somewhat of a 'blank slate' when the aforementioned ETC iLit team joined the development process. As the client, the LA Committee needed to provide answers to several questions: What is our motivation? What would motivate students to play or interact with our final product?

The Playability Challenge

We quickly realized that some of our original plans were not going to be workable within the constraints of the game design environment. The experts at the ETC explained that if we started out with very specific ideas, directed at too narrow of an audience or for only one course, then the game would not be adaptable to different subject modules. Decentralizing the focus away from 'sustainable engineering'—i.e. opening the game up to other subject disciplines—would better position us in creating a game that would be broader in its playability. Another clarification we made was to redefine our target audience from "upper-level undergraduate" to "higher education student." The "what do we want?" phase soon flowed into an active "how do we do this?" phase with the start of the spring term, 2007. Every few weeks the iLit team met face-to-face with the LA Committee. Initially, a shared document manager was set up; however, in-person meetings presented the best opportunity to brainstorm. The students started to address the problems of the playability involved in designing a game by acknowledging the following questions, commonly posed before beginning the design of any game: How will we fake the real world? How will the game be scored? Will the act of collecting data be rewarded? How much time should it take to play the game? How can skills be gained, but at the player's own pace? The teams then decided to develop several mini-games that would be placed within the context of a single narrative storyline.

Would Finding it on Google Count?

In order to clarify what the University Libraries wanted to accomplish with an educational videogame, the committee conducted a review of the Association of College and Research Libraries' (ACRL) Information Literacy Competency Standards for Higher Education. With the overarching aim of imparting life-long learning skills to our students, the committee was united by the belief that the sources where the player might find information within the game should include, but not be limited to, subscription databases. Other relevant "sources" of information could include their colleagues, professors, a Web site or a printed encyclopedia. Through this reflection came the discussion point: "Is the way or means by which students seek information as important as the information itself?" Do we penalize them in the game setting if they were to use, for example, Google to find information?

Information Literacy: Standards, Accreditation, Assessment & Measurable Objectives

The LA Committee wanted the final product, eventually named *Library Arcade*, to be a convenient venue for incorporating an information literacy assessment tool. With accrediting agencies such as Middle States focusing more on assessment in their evaluations, the *Library Arcade* could become an increasingly useful asset. Measurable learning outcomes on which to base in-game assessments would need to be outlined. The LA Committee began using the learning objectives from the ACRL Information Literacy Competency Standards for Higher Education.[4] These standards served to focus both the librarians' efforts on providing content for the game as well as deepen the iLit team's understanding of information literacy as an educational goal. As the two groups met and hammered out the structure of the games, we decided to focus on one ACRL information literacy standard per mini-game. It was crucial that the learning outcomes were identified before any assessment was built into the game design, otherwise the team could run the risk of getting off track in the game's design and/or ultimately creating a game with immeasurable outcomes. The games' learning outcomes are as follows:

Mini-Game 1: Learning how information is organized and categorized using the Library of Congress Classification System
ACRL Standard # 2.3.b

Standard 2.3. The information literate student retrieves information online or in person using a variety of methods.

Outcomes Include:
(b) Uses various classification schemes and other systems (e.g., call number systems or indexes) to locate information resources within the library or to identify specific sites for physical exploration

Mini-Game 2: Discerning the relevancy of information
ACRL Standard # 1.2.c,d:

Standard 1.2. The information literate student identifies a variety of types and formats of potential sources for information.

Outcomes Include:
(c) Identifies the value and differences of potential resources in a variety of formats (e.g., multimedia, database, Web site, data set, audio/visual, book)
(d) Identifies the purpose and audience of potential resources (e.g., popular vs. scholarly, current vs. historical)

In coming up with learning outcomes for each mini-game, the team discussed outcomes on a spectrum very similar to Bloom's Taxonomy.[5] For example, with mini-game 1, our most basic outcome was, "[the information literate student will] recognize that the books are arranged on the shelf in a logical order." The official, measurable learning outcome 2.3.b was chosen because mini-game 1 deals with the Library of Congress Classification System and the student's ability to apply what he/she learns about the LCC through the game play of arranging books on a shelf. Even though nearly all libraries discourage patrons from re-shelving books, the student should come away from this game with a better understanding of exactly how the books on the shelf are arranged. As another example, mini-game 2's most basic outcome was "[the information literate student will] recognize that there are a variety of information sources," while the more measurable outcome is 1.2.d, the identification of a resource's purpose and audience. Each mini-game was to have primary measurable learning outcomes in addition to underlying informal outcomes.

Performance measurements varied by mini-game. For example, the completion of the three levels in mini-game 1 is the only satisfactory performance indicator for this game. Mini-game 2, however, would use points to determine the player's level of performance. The scoring rubric for mini-game 2 is still in development. The overall performance measurement for the entire game is not yet complete, but will likely combine the player's performance on each game and apply it to a scale devised by the librarians. This could ultimately make the games playable on "easy, medium, or hard" levels to facilitate implementation in K-20 environments.

Librarians Collaborate with Students

As the semester got underway, the LA Committee communicated regularly with the iLit team to provide them with advice and direction. We expressed how we wanted something decidedly different from a typical library instruction module, i.e., a product that would not be "tutorial" in nature. Before the iLit team was sent off to work on 'story' ideas, we agreed to some basics. The product would make use of Adobe Flash technology; the games would be short, make use of a single player, feature more images than text, would be re-playable, interactive and (of course) entertaining. The LA Committee also wanted to assure the iLit team that the artistic creation of the product was in their hands. We did not want have a negative influence on their creativity but hoped to provide constructive feedback when asked.

Storyboard Emerges

The iLit team presented their preliminary story ideas, concept art, and the basic game mechanics to the LA Committee in February 2007. The game's story featured the character of a typical college student named 'Max'. We discussed the possibility of allowing players to choose between several main character avatars, but this feature would have increased the amount of programming that was possible during the time allotted. Having received an "F" on a paper, 'Max' is presented with the opportunity to go back in time in order to improve his research methods with the help of a "Father Time" character. Each mini-game would progress Max through the storyline and highlight different research skills. Themes for the individual games were labeled: Classification Concepts, Appropriate Finding Tools, Evaluation of Resources Sources, Information Ethics/Plagiarism, Brainstorming for a Research Paper, and Assessment. Ideally, the game design would support them being played in a progressive sequence but would also allow them to function independently of each other.

The iLit team expected to outsource most of the programming needs for the deliverable product. Although much of the design had already been outlined, time constraints prevented finishing all six mini-games at once. The teams then focused on the first two games in the story. Game 1 would focus on Classification Concepts, while Game 2 would address Appropriate Finding Tools.

Baffled by Game 1

The LA Committee was disappointed that the first mini-game was set in a virtual library and involved putting books in order. We reasserted our desire to the iLit team that the games forgo "library themes" and that simply knowing how to shelve a book was not important to information literacy. Instead of dismissing the work that iLit team had already started, we gave suggestions to direct the learning goal away from putting numbers in order and more towards an understanding of classifications and an introduction to subject headings. We thought that the story would still work if Max could somehow learn how to use the online catalog to begin searching for information on his subject. We debated the use of a timer, but were finally swayed by the argument that timing a player is common to most games. Furthermore, the iLit team needed a way to score a player's progress through the levels.

We had to agree with the mindset that we should not worry too much about players failing because they will eventually "get it"—this is the appeal of playing a game. During development, feedback was solicited by some informal testing, and the LA Committee continued to suggest ways to edit the look and feel of the mini-games and help with the wording, especially on the "Hint" pop-ups.

Creating Questions for Game 2

Mini-game 2 was designed to depict the physical space of a library. Again, we expressed disappointment with the choice of setting, as we had emphasized to the iLit team that libraries provide a wealth of information electronically; suggesting that students do not necessarily need to physically visit the library to use its resources. The iLit team reassured us by describing the plans for mini-game 3 to be set in a virtual "campus" setting, complete with a dorm room, a professor's office, a classroom, as well as a library. However, once these additional variables were added, the amount of time to fully design and implement mini-game 3 far exceeded the allotted project time line. With that realization, the teams set out to create the content for mini-game 2.

The LA committee was asked to script the questions and answers for mini-game 2. Since a minimum of 60 research questions were needed, we appealed to our colleague liaison librarians, who command a variety of subject specialties, to help generate questions. Their assistance was greatly appreciated, and many of the submissions were based on actual questions received at our reference desks.

The flow for the game mechanics was to depict Max visiting other students in the library and helping them with their research. For example, when Max receives the question "Do video games make kids violent?" these choices are presented: PsycINFO database, the American Psychological Association (APA) Web site, a Time magazine article, or a monograph titled, *Game Producer's Handbook*. Points are assigned depending on what he chooses. The resources are evaluated in terms of "best," "good," "not that useful," and "not useful at all." Comparing "best" versus "good" seemed especially difficult to measure since the questions could not be too long in length, and, of course, one source might be better than the other depending on the need and circumstance involved in the research. As the semester was rapidly ending in April 2007, mini-game 2 was completed without explanation to the player about why the resource they may have chosen was not considered the "best." Expanding on the "hint" function would be a desired feature to an updated mini-game 2. The hint would encourage the player to "think again" about the resource that was picked by posing a hint like, "If you picked a reference book, maybe it is not relevant because it has information on many topics and just a little information on your topic?" Keeping in mind that the games learning objective deals with the awareness of a variety of sources, these hints could also be perceived as supplemental to the already instructive game play. Since the iLit team finished their semester's project, with a few of its members graduating, future work on the game would need additional funding and new team members. After some additional programming was completed by ETC, we were ready to share the games with the Carnegie Mellon community.

Making the Arcade Our Own

The final versions of the games were reviewed by the committee in mid-June of 2007. Those present shared their thoughts on the application and execution of each game. The committee added another member to act as an expert analyst on gaming and to market the games to the student community. The most pressing question that arose in our initial marketing discussions was how to best name and package them. Within the originally envisioned unified game experience, each mini-game would be a stage, not necessarily requiring a name. Now that the tasks comprised individual games, finding appropriate names became more pertinent. We agreed that leaving library jargon out of the naming would be a main goal. It was thought that students would shy away from even trying a game if the name featured "Information Literacy" or "Library" or "Classification." To this end, the members of the assembled committee brainstormed a series of related terms and concepts for each game.

For the game in which the player re-shelves books in Library of Congress Classification order, the concepts hovered around such things as shelving, order, arrangement, and classification. The final concept was "Within Range," which directly refers to the library term "call number range" but manages to remain similar to other more popular gaming titles. The title also encompassed the actions the player would take as they attempted to find the proper location for their title by scanning the surrounding numbers in a search-like manner. The logo was designed to mimic the rows of books found in the game. Title letters were designed to be slightly off center horizontally, to provide a sense of movement.

The item retrieval game was more complex in nature and consequently created some challenges in finding an appropriate title. With the many actions found within this game, the concepts discussed ranged from finding, deciding, evaluating and locating. In the end, we settled on "I'll Get It!". This not only represents the actions of the protagonist, as he eagerly retrieves items for the library patrons, but a reference to the abilities gained by the player. By exercising their ability to evaluate resources and choose question-specific item types, the players will begin recognizing the role of evaluation as it relates to information literacy. The graphic design of this logo incorporates the main protagonist and shows him performing the actions in the game.

Going Live

To present the games to our audience, the committee decided to create a page hosted on our library Web site (http://www.library.cmu.edu/Libraries/etc/index.html). This page would serve as not only an entry portal to the games themselves, but as a secondary information source for users to find out more about the concepts of information literacy and how other libraries are approaching gaming. Initial design concept was to use the title logos in rectangular button forms to act as a clickable button link. This design proved to be adequate, but not overly engaging. To that end, two early arcade-era boxes were created to display not only the title logo panel, but also a screen capture of the game in play. This design featured a large Nintendo-styled "Play" button on the face of the arcade box. Users were instructed to hit play, but in the event that this instruction was not clearly understood, the entire image was made to be the clickable link. The original page layout placed these game boxes side-by-side underneath a short introduction to the library arcade project.

Figure 1. Original Page Layout

The page also featured a short explanation of the parties involved in the making of the game. Below this text, several links highlighting other academic gaming initiatives were featured. In the final right portion of the page a feedback section was featured. The means of feedback were through a group e-mail link and a general survey (see Appendix). This survey featured questions inquiring as to the users gaming experience, reaction to our games, and direct input for future modifications. During the initial release of the games, no public marketing was created. Being that this was the unfinished version of the library arcade, the power of viral marketing was thought to be sufficient in spreading the word of the games. In short, the committee hoped that the audiences reached through social networking channels would be able to offer opinions on their previous gaming and library experiences. The page did not initially contain any instructions as to how to play the games or what skills they were designed to strengthen. Due to the inherent exploratory nature of videogames, we felt that players would be curious as to what they could click and how they would interact with the virtual environment.

The *Library Arcade* Web page was unveiled on September 18, 2007. A link to the arcade page was placed on the Carnegie Mellon University Libraries main Web page, and an announcement was sent to all library personnel via internal e-mail lists. The ETC announced the live version of the games on their web site shortly thereafter. The games were featured on a blog, *The Extensible Librarian* (http://johnfudrow.wordpress.com) and soon other library bloggers began to share the *Library Arcade* with their audiences. Over the next few weeks, comments on the games could be found on a range of Web sites including library-related blogs, online videogame sites and several Web discussion forums.

Player Reactions

A large portion of the initial players seemed unsure of how each game functioned. Their comments and questions framed the evaluation of what type of descriptions should accompany the games at their entry points. Based on the number of comments requesting guidance, the LA Committee decided to draft a set of short instructions for each game. Not wanting to walk the player through the entire experience, the instructions both outline the concept of the games and the basic interactions with which the user can engage the games. To facilitate the display of the instructions on the Web page, a design incorporating images of library catalog cards was created. Placed beside a scaled down version of the videogame boxes, the catalog cards display the title, description, and a fictional library call number for each game. The page was updated to feature a longer introduction, encouraging users to leave feedback for ways to add to the game experience.

The various reactions to the game intrigued the committee members and provided fuel for the planning of future revisions. Though many of the comments focused on the game being set in a library, others focused on the applicability of the games to their own experiences. "Within Range" was described as well crafted but somewhat unclear as to what information was to be taken away from the completion of the tasks. We received several comments from school librarians wanting to use a modified Dewey Decimal version of "Within Range" to train their students and staff. As can be seen in other collected comments, many players began to reflect on how they used libraries as well as the profession of librarianship. Because several players immediately recognized the adaptation of the popular Web game "Diner Dash," we decided that "I'll Get It" should become the lead game for any future marketing campaigns. After further refinement, both games are set to be released in a final version.

From This Point On

The Library Arcade project is being developed as freeware so that anyone can download the mini-games and customize the content to fit users' skill levels or interest, whether their audiences are K-12 students, college students, or adult learners. We believe that the final product could be easily incorporated into any course. Many universities have a required library/computer skills course for incoming freshman that would be well suited to feature the games. At Carnegie Mellon, twenty percent of the incoming freshmen matriculate from Pennsylvania and fifty-one percent come from the Middle States of Delaware, the District of Columbia, Maryland, New Jersey, New York, Ohio, Pennsylvania, and West Virginia.[6] As such, Carnegie Mellon University Libraries has a vested interest in starting and maintaining information literacy outreach with local K-12 institutions. By supporting such initiatives, the University increases its chances of enrolling students equipped with information literacy skills.

We feel that the project was successful though it was not without the difficulties found in producing any type of digital project. Having more than one semester to collaborate with the same student team would have allowed more time to apply the revisions suggested by user testing and survey responses. Alternately, we realized that a better understanding of the client/developer relationship could have allowed the clear communication of our project vision. With this in mind, the desire to not make these games a library simulation may have been realized sooner in development. Overall, Carnegie Mellon University Libraries benefited from a product that will provide the greater community with a unique vehicle in which to challenge their information literacy skills.

Notes

1. Carnegie Mellon University Libraries, Proposal to the Buhl Foundation for "Information Literacy Web Tutorials" (grant proposal, 2005).
2. Carnegie Mellon University, Entertainment Technology Center, "The Entertainment Technology Curriculum," Carnegie Mellon University, http://www.etc.cmu.edu/curriculum/index.html (accessed January 3, 2008).
3. Carnegie Mellon University Libraries, Proposal to the Buhl Foundation for "Information Literacy Web Tutorials" (grant proposal, 2005).
4. Association of College and Research Libraries, "Information Literacy Competency Standards for Higher Education," American Library Association, http://www.ala.org/ala/acrl/acrlstandards/informationliteracycompetency.cfm (accessed January 3, 2008).
5. Benjamin Samuel Bloom, *Taxonomy of Educational Objectives the classification of educational goals*, vol. 1, *Cognitive domain.* (New York: McKay, 1956).
6. Carnegie Mellon Office of Institutional Research & Analysis. "Carnegie Mellon Factbook 2006-2007," Carnegie Mellon University, http://www.cmu.edu/ira/ (accessed January 3, 2008).

CHAPTER 12

The Fletcher Library Game Project
Bee Gallegos and Tammy Allgood

The Millennial Generation

Games are exceptionally prevalent in our society. Board games, cards, crossword puzzles, video games, and MMORPGs (Massive Multiplayer Online Role Playing Games) are just a few of the different types of games that are widespread. Games are especially popular with Millennials. A 2003 Gallup Poll reported 69% of teenagers play video games every week.[1]

Because of this popularity, many researchers have been looking at the learning potential of games. Prensky stated that computer games have the ability to create a new learning culture that matches the habits and interests of students.[2] Based on his research, James Paul Gee in 2003 stated his belief that gaming technologies for instruction will increase and eventually become pervasive.[3]

Today's high school students and incoming first year college students are part of the Millennial generation that cannot remember a time when technology did not play a prominent role in their lives. The Millennial generation, composed of those born between 1980 and 2000, has specific characteristics that identify and distinguish it from previous generations. Generally, Millennials are very social, collaborative and prefer to work in groups. Many of them prefer structure and organization. This preference is mainly due to the involvement of "helicopter parents" in organizing their children's lives.[4] They also want activities that engage them so that they can learn by doing. Multitasking comes naturally for Millennials. They often do homework while listening to music, watching television, text messaging friends or being on the computer.[5]

ASU at the West Campus

Arizona State University (ASU) at the West campus is a community-focused metropolitan campus located in the western area of metropolitan Phoenix. The campus, founded in 1984 as an upper-division campus, is one of four campuses of ASU. During the early years of the campus, junior, senior and selected master's degree programs were offered. In fall 2001, the initial freshmen class of 251 students was admitted. In fall 2006, the number of first-time freshmen was 539, an average annual increase of 17 percent from 2001 to 2006.[6]

Using the West campus Library's *Information Competencies*, developed in the early 1990s as the foundation, in 2001 the Library's Lower Division Implementation Team defined and developed a list of information competencies for first-year students.[7] This list, known as the *Information Skills Outcomes for First Year Students*, forms the framework for a library curriculum emphasizing three levels of competency in the areas of library services, research processes, online catalog, database search techniques, evaluation, attribution and citation. The competencies link concepts and skills to specific courses within the first year English curriculum providing a sequenced approach and guiding the Library's development of instructional content to be offered.

Lower-Division Instruction Program

In 2003, the Lower-Division Instruction program was created to focus on providing instruction for freshmen students. The Lower-Division Instruction Team was charged with the development and delivery of instruction to students enrolled in first-year English Composition classes and Learning Communities.

In early 2004, the team began a concerted effort to revamp existing instruction for freshmen. After researching Millennials, it was determined that interactive group work and hands-on activities were the most effective means for delivering instruction. Educational gaming was an option that was determined to be viable and, in fact, held great promise. Game-based learning offers students an opportunity to learn in a non-threatening, fun, approachable and interactive environment that engages them.

A library tour exercise previously used with English 101 students was an early target for change. Students and librarians alike complained about this exercise because it was labor intensive to complete and grade. The idea of creating an online version that could be administered and graded automatically surfaced routinely. This thinking led to the idea of creating an exercise or game that could be used to engage students while teaching them about detailed, complex and, for students, very boring information processes.

Serious discussion regarding a game began in early 2005 with the team targeting completion of the project by the start of the fall 2005 semester; however, the Game Project team was naïve in its estimation of this timeline. After exploring online games, it quickly became evident that the project was much too big to complete in a short few months. The decision was made to design and pilot a board game to serve as a prototype for a computer-based game that would be readied for fall 2006. The project plan included evaluation and assessment of the board game's potential as a computer-based game.

In order to develop an interactive instructional tool, the Lower-Division Team recruited another librarian with the technology skills needed to complete the project. In addition to the technology librarian, the Game Project team consisted of the lower-division program coordinator, two library staff who at that time were in the process of earning MLS degrees, and a new library graduate hired in a split reference/instruction position. Midway through the project in 2006, the reference/instruction librarian left the project to pursue a position out of state.

The Board Game

In the summer of 2005 with an online game as the expected end result, the team began the process of learning more about games, gaming and gameplay. Several weeks were spent playing different kinds of games: board games such as *Clue* and *Trivial Pursuit*, games on DVD, Massive Multiplayer Online Games (MMOGs) and online Flash games. At the same time, educational gaming literature was reviewed across multiple disciplines.

Several approaches were reviewed as a context for the game, including scenarios that generated urgency in solving a dilemma and involved identifying, locating and evaluating information as an aspect of solving a problem. It was decided a game with action elements reflecting a problem-based approach was appropriate for an online game but not workable for a board game. Instead, the board game would follow the typical manner of gameplay for a board game. While a board game required less time and money to create and was attainable by the deadline, it was a large undertaking.

Although it did not serve as a prototype for an online game, the board game has been successfully used in the classroom with positive and enthusiastic feedback from students and instructors.[8] The game involves students in interactive learning, incorporates chance, penalties and rewards and allows non-librarians to deliver the instruction. Students learn about library services and types of resources while being engaged in a team-based game. Experience with the board game confirmed for the project team that game-based learning was an innovative and viable teaching method. In terms of a large project, it also gave the team a preview of what was to come in developing the online game.

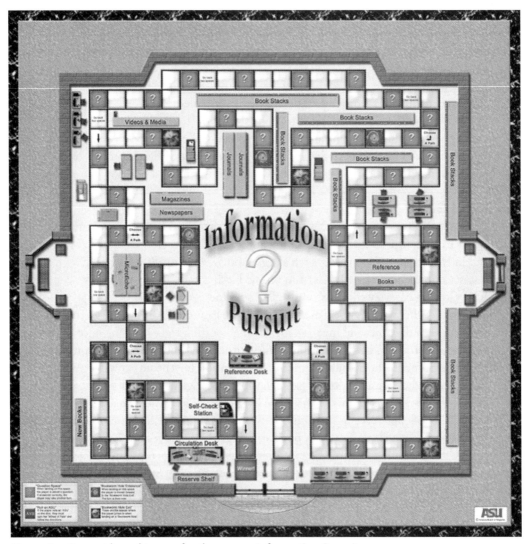

Figure 1—Current board image for the game, Information Pursuit.

Online Game

The Game Project Team found the book *Andrew Rollings and Ernest Adams on Game Design* to be an invaluable source of information during development of the online game. The authors recommend a process for developing a game. They suggest three different documents to guide the development: a High Concept document which contains an overview of the game and serves primarily as a marketing tool; a Game Treatment document that identifies and describes the characters, provides highlights of the storyline, including the back story or context for the game, lists hardware and software requirements, shares the budget and includes the High Concept document; and lastly, a Game Script that details the game plot, decision trees, and gameplay elements. While these are listed as separate documents there is some overlap and a level of duplication within the documents. The Game Treatment document serves as a bridge between the shorter High Concept document used for marketing that provides a quick overview for interested individuals and the Game Script document that outlines the storyline in detail including the characters' words and actions.[9]

The team decided a single-player game was the best approach for the initial version due to the complexities of multi-player games and the inexperience of the team in game development. A tile-based game in which the underlying game surface was laid out on a grid would simplify programming and revisions.

The team chose Flash as the development platform to enable delivery via the web and to avoid responsibility for client-side developments and updates. Identifying a programmer was somewhat more involved. Advertisements were posted to local technology listservs and an international Flash game programming wiki. Two Flash companies with advertisements on the web were also contacted. Following review of each applicant's online portfolio, a copy of the Game Script document was sent to the top three candidates along with a nondisclosure agreement. Each programmer then responded with a price quote for the project. The programmer selected for the project had the most educational gaming experience and worked in the local area. He subcontracted graphic work to a designer he had worked with in the past.

Project management texts and the Rollings book helped the team identify the necessary aspects of the project plan. Visio software was used to develop a timeline and track progress for the project. The original timeline for development of the online game allowed one year for creation of both the board game and the online game. In reality, development took approximately five months longer than anticipated. An early difficulty with the plan was realizing the board game was too distinct from the online game for it to serve as a prototype. By spring 2006, it quickly became obvious that the team was running behind schedule and could not design a game, hire a programmer, conduct usability studies with students and make needed revisions prior to the start of the Fall 2006 semester in mid-August. Team members possessed gameplay and project management experience, and instructional and technology expertise, but inexperience with game design and dissatisfaction with design elements were contributing factors that had an impact on the timeline. Throughout the various phases of the project, the team reviewed the progress being made, adjusted the workload and updated the timeline. Team commitment to the project was high making its completion a priority. Team willingness to be reasonable and flexible about the timeline and meeting benchmarks set weeks prior allowed the work to flow more smoothly. Compatibility within the team, the shared vision and the commitment to open communication were contributing factors as well.

Each team member developed at least one story line and from the array of scenarios, the team members voted on their favorite game plot. The resulting scenario was a mix of aspects from several plots created and suggested by members. A requirement of any plot was to create a problem that could be resolved by identifying, evaluating and using information sources. A second requirement was the alignment of educational concepts with those associated with English 101 in the *Information Skills Outcomes for First Year Students* document. Checking this alignment was ongoing throughout the process.

The project team established a regular one-hour meeting time each week but was flexible in adding meetings as needed. For example, in order to finalize the game script, team members committed to meeting every day for a short time period. Creating scenarios and characters for the storyline turned out to be an enormous endeavor, because a storyline needs to flow and the character's actions must be believable and compatible with previous actions. As the team worked through the initial game script, it discovered the storyline needed major revisions because previous words and actions did not flow well. As the team continued to identify contradictions that needed resolution, there was a continuing worry that each change would introduce further problems. The script needed to be finished and present a cohesive story because everything that followed was dependent on it.

Meetings, especially those with the programmer, were documented, identifying decisions, agreements and next steps. These proved invaluable as the project progressed and work with the programmer intensified. Having meeting minutes helped team members remember decisions made, document group and individual action items and provide a mechanism for relaying and recording communications with the programmer.

Although the team's vision of the game characters, including their roles in the story and their general design look was agreed upon and documented in the early game documents, the design stage of developing the game took much longer than anticipated. While the team was in agreement, there was difficulty in translating the vision into the graphic designs. Direct contact between the team and the graphic artist would have made this aspect of the project move more smoothly. An example of the disconnect between the team, the programmer, and the artist was the stereotypical first design of the librarian (Figure 2). To further complicate the design stage, each character required two designs: a head-shot used for interactions with the main character and a full-length design when viewing the character's actions.

Figure 2. Stereotypical first design of the librarian

Figure 3. Final librarian design

Figure 4. Full-length design of the librarian

In addition to the characters, the campus map, exterior and interior views of buildings, building icon rollovers and the online catalog, database and Web site layouts were designed (Figure 5).

Another crucial design was the game logo. The team felt the game's name *Quarantined: Axl Wise and the Information Outbreak* needed to portray a certain look that related to aspects of the game's storyline. The programmer's initial design of this was on target and only needed minor

Figure 5. Campus Map

changes in font style, size and background color. The design aspect of the logo was relatively easy compared to deciding on the game's name. To assist the team in generating ideas and making a decision, the team ran a contest among library staff with the winner receiving a gift certificate to the campus bookstore. Library administration agreed to support this endeavor and later agreed to an additional gift certificate when aspects of several suggestions were used in the final name. Not only did this contest assist the team in deciding the name, it generated excitement and created support and buy-in among staff about the project.

After working with the programmer for five months, the team was ready to begin testing. The process for testing and fixing bugs within the game was complex. As the team began playing the game, they found there were so many bugs it was difficult to track them. To simplify the process, an online bug tracking system was created to list the bugs identified and track their solutions. The list of bugs was sent to the programmer regularly, but, as one bug was fixed, it often created a new bug.

After the majority of bugs were fixed, the game was tested with the library's student workers. This proved to be invaluable since at this point in the process, the team had lost its ability to be objective. Student workers helped the team identify additional bugs and made suggestions for changes. Across the board, the students complained about the amount of text they needed to read in the help screens, in the introduction to the game, and in the interactions between the game's main character, Axl, and the other characters. As a result the game's introduction with the storyline, the character's interactions were edited to approximately half their original length. The edits were made and bugs fixed prior to the start of the spring 2007 semester when the online game was first used as an instructional tool in the freshmen English classes.

The first instructional session brought a mix of excitement and apprehension since there was no way to know how students would react to the game. By the end of the semester, six out of seven English 101 classes in spring 2007 had played the game. The game was set with a thirty-minute time limit allowing the remaining forty-five minutes of class time for instructor announcements, pre-game instruction by librarians, the pre-test, post-test, class discussion and an online evaluation on *Survey Monkey*. At the start of each class, a team member offered approximately fifteen minutes of instruction on accessing the library Web site and completing simple searches in the catalog and a database prior to having them play the game. In addition to this instruction, students were required to complete a pre-test designed to assess their knowledge of the concepts and skills embedded in the game. Although the mini-lecture demonstration was prefaced with a statement about its relevance to successful gameplay, students struggled with finding and using the appropriate information sources within the game. Logging into the password-protected game was also problematic because students failed to listen and follow instructions. Though guided instruction was provided, students demonstrated difficulty in maneuvering characters, reading and following instructions, using the help screens and understanding the purpose of the task. This confirmed Gee's suggestion that Millennials or "digital natives" have no interest or patience for reading instructions or long explanations. Their preference is to experiment and ask only when necessary.[10] Library instructors spent time in every session monitoring student progress, providing clues as to gameplay and recording observations. The notes gathered during these classes established the basis for discussion about a revised version of the game.

A number of changes to improve game playability were identified. Some changes resulted from suggestions and requests for features from students while others came from direct observations of the difficulties students had while playing. The changes were organized, discussed and prioritized. Those that were fairly easy to incorporate into the game or were necessary for continued use of the game were identified for inclusion in version 1.1 of the game, which was implemented in the fall of 2007. Those that seemed more involved were set aside for inclusion in a future version. Examples of immediate changes included such things as adding the ability to cut and paste text within the game, a "mission status" screen with hints for completing missions, fixing the "stuck in the library" bug, moveable windows for the backpack and PDA and flashing interactive hotspots.

As previously stated, after one semester of use, minor modifications to the game were made in the summer of 2007. The goals of version 1.1 upgrades were to enhance game play and align it with computer games familiar to students. Because the original programmer was unavailable, the team had to identify and hire a new programmer. Having been through the process before, the team quickly found a replacement using *CraigsList* (http://craigslist.org). Although the team was familiar with the process, hiring the new programmer posed some unique problems due to the fact that the programmer had a company in the U.S. but was physically based in India. The company charged a very reasonable cost per hour, however, and understood what was needed. The programmer worked quickly and was able to complete the updates in less than one month.

One enhancement made was the inclusion of a mission screen that allows students to check progress within game play and offers assistance with expected game tasks. Adding the ability to cut and paste text incorporated a task familiar to students and allowed them to move more quickly through the game. Being able to move the pop-up windows of the PDA and backpack also made game play easier for students. Lastly, adding flashing interactive hotspots helped players find where they needed to be on the screen.

Another modification was the creation and inclusion of three one-minute tutorials developed in Adobe *Captivate* to assist students during game play. They demonstrate searching the online catalog and database that are used in the game. The catalog and database used in the game were created from scratch and pull from xml files to ensure full control over search results. A third tutorial was created to discuss citations. Any of these can be accessed during game play as students need help or as standalone products.

The instructional methods used with the introduction of the game in the classroom changed as well during the second semester of its use. Based on observations from Spring 2007 classes, students now play the game in teams rather than individually as originally planned. This builds on experience with the board game and the preference of Millennial students to interact and learn as a peer activity and minimizes the anxiety some students display about computer games. As an added benefit, this allowed more students to complete the game within the class period while actively engaging them in peer-to-peer learning.

Results

The reception from faculty and students has been overwhelmingly positive to this unique instructional tool. Faculty support is evidenced by promotion of the game within their classes. The following student comments indicate they enjoyed learning new skills in a fun way:

- "It was very different and the graphics were cool. A very good learning tool."
- "It helped us to learn how to use library resources in a creative way."
- "I thought it was a well designed game for helping people learn how to look for books and articles."
- "It was actually very helpful with reading citations, some articles I thought were journals were books, and vice versa. It was interesting!"
- "The game was better than a boring lecture about the fascinating world of research process."

Because of the high investment costs, the team was unable to embed assessment within the game. Instead, a pre/post-test was developed in *Survey Monkey* for use in assessing student learning. The pre/post-test looked at a student's ability to compare types of citations, identify parts of a citation, determine when to do a keyword search, decide where to search for books and articles, and use Library of Congress call numbers. The team gathered assessment statistics the first semester the game was used (Spring 2007) but decided that the game needed slight modifications before solid conclusions could be drawn about the game's value. The results of the assessment discussed are from version 1.1 of the game, introduced in Fall 2007.

The pre/post test results indicate an increase in learning in most areas after playing the game. Assessment indicates there was improvement in their understanding of library service desks (Table 1), in the areas related to understanding call numbers (Table 2), and in the multiple aspects of searching the online catalog (Table 3). In the future, it would be interesting to compare these results to matching data sets that assess improvement when only traditional educational styles are employed.

Table 1. Understanding Library Service Desks
Question 6: Where should you go to find a book that an instructor has placed on reserve?

Answers:	In the Stacks At the Reference Desk **At the Circulation/Reserve Desk**		
Percent Correct—Fall 2007			
	Pre-test	Post-test	% change
	85.9	94.2	9.66%

Table 2. Understanding Call Numbers
Question 10: What do the letters at the beginning of a call number mean?

Answers:	They stand for the author's initials They indicate the book's subject **They indicate when the book was received**		
Percent Correct—Fall 2007			
	Pre-test	Post-test	% change
	48.8	59.7	22.34%

Table 3. Searching the Online Catalog Question 4: Generally the best way to begin a search for books on a topic in the library online catalog is:			
Answers:	Title Search Subject Search **Keyword Search**		
Percent Correct—Fall 2007			
	Pre-test	Post-test	% change
	41.2	46.1	11.89%

Table 4. Identification of Citation Components Question 3: What is the title of the journal in this citation? Richards, T. S. (2006). Student motivation. College Teaching 54 (2), 43-52.			
Answers:	Student Motivation College Teaching **Richards**		
Percent Correct—Fall 2007			
	Pre-test	Post-test	% change
	68.2	63.6	-6.74%

Students had issues understanding what a citation was as well as identifying the components of a citation (Table 4). A notable decrease from pre-test to post-test was found when measuring the ability to define a citation. In the 2007 fall semester, the students' ability to define a citation decreased by 16% in the post-test. It is unclear what is responsible for this decrease.

Recommendations

Despite the issues inherent in any large project such as this, the team is satisfied with the resulting game. The team succeeded in completing an enormous project and learned invaluable skills and lessons in the process. Without the support of library administration, including the finances needed to produce the board game and pay a programmer for the online game, this kind of project would have been virtually impossible. Buy-in from administrators who allow an atmosphere of experimentation to flourish and provide members with the time to focus was crucial in successfully completing this project. For anyone anticipating a similar project, here are some guidelines the team found useful:

- Get buy-in from supervisors and administrators.
- Keep the project team fairly small.
- Recruit team members with varied backgrounds and expertise, but a shared vision.
- Meet and communicate regularly and openly.
- Document everything.
- Be committed, flexible and willing to think in different ways and take chances—even though it may not feel comfortable.
- Understand that the process is time consuming and members should be prepared mentally to face the challenges incumbent in such a project.
- Agree upon the goals and set a timeline that is reasonable. Provide adequate time for project completion and routinely check on progress. Holding the team as well as the programmer to deadlines is a crucial aspect of the success of the project.
- Plan and prepare as much as possible down to the smallest detail but understand it is a process that may change as the project progresses.
- Realize that everyone will not agree about everything; carefully pick those issues to stand firm about and be prepared with a sound assessment or alternative to what is being proposed when there are differing points of view. Operating by consensus is a good approach for this type of project.
- Lastly, be committed but don't take everything too seriously. Instead, laugh, see the humor and seek opportunities to have fun. Encourage team members and recognize and celebrate milestones as they are accomplished.

Notes

1. The Gallup Poll, "Grand Theft of Innocence? Teens and Video Games, " Gallup Poll, http://www.gallup.com/poll/9253/Grand-Theft-Innocence-Teens-Video-Games.aspx (accessed December 15, 2007).
2. Marc Prensky, *Digital Game-based Learning* (New York: McGraw-Hill, 2001).

3. James P Gee, *What Video Games Have to Teach Us About Learning and Literacy* (New York: Palgrave Macmillan, 2003).

4. Lydia Lum, "Handling 'Helicopter Parents," *Diverse Issues in Higher Education* 23, no. 20 (2006): 40.

5. Diane Oblinger, "Boomers, Gen-Xers, & Millennials: Understanding the New Students," *EDUCAUSE Review* 38, no. 4 (2003): 40

6. Arizona State University at the West campus, Office of Institutional Planning & Research, *Enrollment at the West campus: Student Profile* (ASU: Fall 2006).

7. Fletcher Library, "Information Competencies," Arizona State University at the West campus, http://library.west.asu.edu/aboutus/libdocs/infocomp.html (accessed December 15, 2007).

8. Bee Gallegos and others, "Let the Games Begin! Changing our Instruction to Reach Millennials!" in *Moving Targets: Understanding our Changing Landscape*, edited by Teresa Valko and Brad Sietz. (Paper, Thirty-fourth LOEX Conference, College Park, Md, May 5, 2006).

9. Andrew Rollings and Ernest Adams, *Andrew Rollings and Ernest Adams on Game Design* (Indianapolis: New Riders, 2003).

10. Scott Jaschk, "When 'digital natives' Go to the Library," *Inside Higher Education*, June 25, 2007, http://insidehighered.com/news/2007/06/25/games.

CHAPTER 13

Bioterrorism at UF: Exploring and Developing a Library Instruction Game for New Students

Sara Russell Gonzalez, Valrie Davis, Chelsea Dinsmore, Cynthia Frey, Carrie Newsom, Laurie Taylor

Introduction

Educational computer games emerged out of the larger class of educational entertainment materials, also known as edutainment, and were soon dubbed edugames. Because of the many problems with edutainment and edugames, the most recent movement has rebranded itself under the classification of "serious games"[1] Serious games seek to model complex situations and then test players' ability to reason through the simulated process. Simulations have been used for military, medical, and emergency training, testing, therapeutic treatment of anxiety, and legal scenarios, many of which have been expanded into serious games to allow users a greater deal of interaction with each of the component variables underlying the simulated systems.[2] Serious games, like simulations, facilitate active learning of complex and contextualized information by requiring users to both process and apply their new knowledge. Ian Bogost has argued that videogames enact a "procedural rhetoric," meaning that games present their content within and through a system with its internal rules and options for use.[3] Serious games take advantage of gaming's ability to create simulations that allow users to learn, test, and refine their actions within certain parameters. Mainstream videogames construct fictive worlds for players to explore in the same manner, but their emphasis is on the entertainment value of the fictive game worlds rather than teaching or training, which serious games emphasize. Serious games thus present a shift in emphasis but not in the method for the creation and application of the game world. Because popular and serious games are parallel in terms of their underlying logic, methods for popular game design are also applicable for serious game development.

As exploratory research spaces, libraries have experimented with using various non-electronic games like word puzzles based on clues found in the stacks and scavenger hunts designed to teach library technologies through the hunt for information. The University of Florida regularly holds library learning scavenger hunts based on themes like pirates and crime. In more recent years, libraries have expanded into board games and electronic games in order to interest patrons and to present the many complicated and interrelated technologies available.[4]

Motivation

A conversation between two University of Florida librarians who both enjoy playing a wide variety of games provided the impetus for developing *Bioactive*, a library game designed to teach research skills to undergraduate students. Both librarians recognized the importance of library instruction and were frustrated over the lack of student interest during instruction sessions. Additionally, one class period designated for library instruction was never enough time to cover the technical issues associated with accessing the library, much less more advanced research topics. A new instructional strategy to teach basic technical skills in an interactive environment that allowed students to learn on their own time was needed.

The "game team" developed gradually as different people expressed an interest in the project. Team members work in all areas of the library, some with more experience in instruction, others in reference, and others as teachers bringing students to library instruction classes. Electronic gaming background is similarly varied, with some playing games only intermittently since childhood and others regular gamers. The common tie between members is a feeling that an educational game might be a possible instructional solution given the growing student interest in games and a turn towards interactivity in library instruction.

Information Gathering: Impressions of Other Games and Interviews

Prior to game development, we undertook an information gathering process that included an examination of serious games currently available and interviews with academic institutions who were designing their own library games. This research revealed many common obstructions in game production, introduced us to the various styles of games we could create, and gave recommendations on how best to approach our game design.

It was important to explore the serious games currently available, since our previous gaming experiences were with entertainment-based games containing complex graphics and systems. Below is a list of games that were either a strong influence on the development of

Bioactive, in their approach to game play, or demonstrate what we envision for future versions of *Bioactive*.

ECON201: Principles of Microeconomics was presented at an Educause Learning Initiative by Jeffrey Sarbaum, Assistant Professor at the University of North Carolina at Greensboro. The game, which is being offered as an economics course by the University, is full of small puzzles that teach the player the theories of microeconomics. ECON201 was created using Flash, a possible solution for keeping game creation in-house, and was a collaborative effort of storywriters, faculty, artists, designers, and coders from various University departments.[5] This game dissects the various learning objectives and separates them into different games within the larger game system.

A group at Arizona State University, mainly librarians, began to investigate the viability of providing virtual library instruction.[6] The team determined that educational gaming had the most potential for delivering virtual library instruction and in the spring of 2006, they created *Quarantined: Axl Wise and the Information Outbreak*. *Quarantined* is a first-person adventure game in which players are given the task of virtually utilizing library resources to conduct research that will enable them to save the world from a deadly viral outbreak.

University of Michigan's School of Information released a game, *The Defense of Hidgeon: The Plague Years*, designed to teach information literacy to new undergraduates.[7] *The Defense of Hidgeon* was created to address what the team perceived as a problem with lack of context for research in online environments. It instructs undergraduates in the steps for conducting research utilizing a general to specific research model. The team calls *The Defense of Hidgeon* a board game for the Web and coined the term storygame to describe the game.

Two years prior to our interview, American University began planning a game to teach upper-level criminal justice students how to use JSTOR, Bureau of Justice Statistics, and LexisNexis. This game was targeted to one department which led to collaborative work between the library, game developers, faculty within that department, and the curriculum committee. Due to many concerns, American University librarians decided to "get out of the game business" and instead create Adobe Captivate tutorials for instructional needs. Their concerns included: lack of an in-house programmer and an already over-taxed systems department, revision of the curriculum of their focus department; difficulty of including tutorials within the game, alternate technology was available for developing interactive library instruction (e.g. many populated classrooms already used Clicker technology), and lack of resources due to the decision to avoid grant writing.

George Washington University (GW) developed a Massive Multiplayer Online Role-Playing Game (MMORPG) similar in design to the popular online role-playing game *Everquest*. The development of their "muckraking" game involved three librarians and one staff member. They hired a programmer, a PhD student in their Computer Science department, who was interested in "serious" games and paid for artwork. One member felt strongly that tutorials no longer suffice, as there is never one right answer to library research.[8] The GW librarians wanted to ensure the game allowed exploratory learning and would be played a few days before the first library instruction. Two constraints in developing their graphic-heavy MMORPG were people and money. The three librarians developed the dialogue, the design, the tasks, and the plot. The single programmer created the game in Flash 8, but work halted as programmers left the project. At the time of the interview, the game cost was up to $15,000. Although it was close to being finished, it was not functioning at the time of the interview.

These case examples underscored the importance of administrative support, including release time for game development and funds to hire a programmer, and limiting the scope of the project to our skill level. We were not prepared to begin a project that required a majority of our time due to already tight staffing and the abundance of responsibilities of the team members. We also could not take on a project requiring excessive financial support given the state of our University's budget. Our solution was to explore game options that would not require funding, excessive time or hiring a programmer.

Choice of Game Development Software

There is a tremendous amount of commercial and non-commercial game development software available online. Unfortunately, mainstream commercial game design is too expensive and resource intensive for most educational projects.[9] Aside from price, there were a number of other constraints we needed to take into consideration while searching for a development platform. Mainly, we needed an open source and freely available game development platform that produced a game which could run on any operating system. The development system also needed to be well-documented, with ample support for new users since most of the group are novice programmers. The software could not require expensive add-ons to produce a quality game, and the game would ideally be playable via a Web browser and independent of operating system. If this game was assigned by a teacher or recommended to an incoming group of students, we wanted it to be available to as many students using their own computers as possible.

The students' perception of the game was another factor in deciding upon a software package. Due to complex 3-D games that are created for popular gaming systems, expectations for graphic quality and game effects are high. It is not possible for a group of new programmers to equal such games and we needed to be realistic about the style of game that was achievable. We wanted to develop a game that was enjoyable for the students but did not highlight its deficiencies.

The game development system we converged upon is interactive fiction (IF). IF is characterized by a predominantly text-based game where the player, acting as the main character, navigates through a world using textual commands to explore regions and solve puzzles. The history of IF extends back to the late 1970's with the first games of *Adventure* and *Zork* developed for mainframe computers.[10] While IF games are no longer viewed as commercially marketable, there is a strong Internet community devoted to the continued play and development of old and new IF games. Interactive fiction has a comparatively simple development process and has been used extensively for various educational projects.[11] Interactive fiction games can also easily be played through a Web browser. Unlike the original IF games, you can now incorporate images into the game but support for video and sound remains limited.

Recently, a new system for creating interactive fiction, Inform 7, reinvented the way these games are programmed. In keeping with the nature of text games, Inform 7 uses natural language in English to describe the game world, actions, in-world objects, and rules.[12] While there is a strict set of rules underlying the programming environment, the game code is very understandable even for a novice programmer. The software is freely available and runs in both Windows and Mac OSX. Inform 7's documentation is extensive and includes numerous examples. Additionally, the community support is considerable with an active forum on the rec.arts.int-fiction newsgroup willing to answer basic programming questions and freely contributed extensions to add more functionality.

Several of the librarians had played IF many years ago and were familiar with its unique language and game structure. With this background knowledge, it was a logical decision to select Inform 7 as the programming environment for the game. Initially there was concern about Inform's minimal support for graphics and the resulting impact upon students' interest in the game, however we decided to proceed with IF since many students are used to playing retro games on their cell phones and other mobile devices. The entire group downloaded the development software onto their work computers and very quickly created a sample game world. Since the IF game is playable as soon as the world parameters are specified, we could program in our world, comprised of the library and its five floors, even before the game plot was developed. While the basic game world was swiftly programmed, we quickly realized the sheer amounts of description necessary for the world to be believable and decided to limit the play to just the Marston Science Library rather than the entire campus or all the libraries.

Learning Objectives
We developed the learning objectives for the game in consultation with the ACRL Information Literacy Competency Standards for Higher Education.[13] Each objective corresponds to an understanding with an associated set of knowledge and skills. Structuring the learning objectives as understandings ensured we focused on the "big ideas" we wanted students to understand while the knowledge and skills sections provided a way to measure the understandings. For example, one of our objectives was to make sure students *understood* that the catalog contains materials (books, journals, videos, etc.) that are available electronically or at various libraries on campus. We wanted students to *know* that call numbers organize materials by subject and indicate the physical placement of materials and to *demonstrate* how the catalog can lead you to library materials.

During programming we found it impossible to have learning stay completely within the game play due to the difficulty of mimicking complex library tools via text and the changes constantly happening within the library research environment (e.g. interface changes, a new catalog, and updated subject guides). We were also concerned students would not recognize skills they learned within the game as applicable to the real world environment of library resources. Research using *alternative or augmented reality games* (ARGs) supported combining the game with external, real world components.[14] So we developed the game to take advantage of multiple windows. Students play the game in one window and use actual library resources outside of the game in another window. The answers found are used inside the game to solve the game puzzle.

Game Plot

A significant challenge for the development team was conceiving a plot that was engaging to the students yet allowed us to incorporate the learning objectives in a believable manner. Brainstorming the background story took several sessions as we discussed numerous potential scenarios that would hopefully pique the students' interest. From the beginning, the group leaned towards a disaster scenario that involved the UF campus and researchers. We considered various science-related plots because we decided to limit the libraries in the game world to just the Marston Science Library and many of the game team were science librarians.

One of the early topics we discussed was bioterrorism, but the group initially shied from it due to the sensitive nature of bioterrorism at a university campus. However, we ultimately decided it would be feasible if we interjected the story with humor and biologically unrealistic ingredients. This plot story was quickly developed with tasks included to meet the learning objectives described above.

Three of the four game tasks require the player to utilize library resources outside of the game. Players must open a browser window and search the library catalog, the database Academic Search Premier, and locate a subject guide. Although game play might be smoother if everything was incorporated within a single window, having players jump into library resources prevents the game from quickly becoming obsolete and ensures the player develops expertise with the actual resources. The fourth task requires the player to use a call number to locate a book within the virtual library. The virtual library is a mirror of the real science library so the player gains a familiarity with the layout and location while learning how to use call numbers. The game ending is triggered when the student solves all four game tasks and is fairly short since the bulk of the game play is spent using the library resources to solve the tasks.

Programming

All programming for the game took place in the Inform 7 programming environment. The display consists of a split window with one side containing the game code and the other side showing documentation or the compiled game to play. The game files were in a shared folder on the library system, however, each team member interested in programming had to install the programming software on their computer. There is no way to "check out" the game when you are programming, so group members relied on e-mails to communicate that the game file was in use. Without this communication it would be possible for multiple versions of the game to be developed simultaneously—each programmer wiping out changes made by the others.

Initially, two group members expanded the game plot into detailed steps, two began programming, and one took photographs for the game. The programmers transformed the storyline into a working game that consisted of the basics, but lacked many objects, descriptions and synonyms. After the game was fully playable, much work was necessary to add descriptions and synonyms for all objects in the game. At this point, everyone on the team was encouraged to help with programming and progress was detailed using a shared Google Documents file.

Once the game was sufficiently developed for outside players, we presented the project at the UF Libraries' Journal Club and sent out an e-mail to all library staff requesting volunteer beta testers. Each tester was asked to download the game and send a transcript of the entire game play with an estimate of the time spent and any comments or suggestions. The response was tremendous and it was invaluable to see the game from different perspectives. In addition to library staff, some testers recruited their student workers and children to play, and one group member asked her *World of Warcraft* guildmates to test the game. Several aspects of game play proved extremely challenging for the testers and will require modification before release to the general UF community. Through the beta-testing process, we found users are willing to use help pages, and that the pages provided seemed thorough enough for inexperienced gamers.

Web Site Development

We designed the game Web site (http://www.uflib.ufl.edu/games/bioactive) to be a link to the game executable and to provide tutorials and help documentation for the library resources used in the game play. The Web site complements *Bioactive*'s text-based personality through the use of a fixed width font and page layout with minimal graphics. The Web site serves not only for background and promotion of the game, but also as documentation on the project and as a contact point for others interested in learning from our or sharing their game development experience.

Promotion and Integration into Classes

Many schools may face difficulty promoting or integrating games into classes. However, the University of Florida has several well-established and easily-accessible communication lines and media venues for promotion. A weekly aggregated e-mail newsletter containing announcements from students, staff, and campus organizations, "The Gator Times," is one of the more guaranteed methods for communicating with students. *The Alligator,* an independent student newspaper on the University of Florida campus, is printed every weekday and widely read by students. The campus and city of Gainesville is served by *The Gainesville Sun* newspaper. We plan to contact these media outlets to gain UF faculty and student awareness about *Bioactive.*

In addition to promoting the game through standard news avenues, the University of Florida Libraries teach a number of library orientation classes each semester, including first-year writing classes, the first-year orientation class "First Year Florida," honors research courses, and others. Each of these classes is taught by a librarian and covers searching the literature in a research library. *Bioactive* was developed for use in these classes, and that use will in turn promote *Bioactive* to the students and instructors.

Challenges and Advice in Developing a Game

Integrating the skills, experience and work of six team members to successfully create *Bioactive* was a huge challenge. Each member came into the project with unique skills and gaming experience. Early on, the team subdivided the work into areas, and members volunteered for the tasks based on their interests and skills. The varied abilities and interests of team members worked in our favor because developing the game required a wide range of skills (e.g. programming, writing and design). The range of team member's experience with interactive fiction, from those unfamiliar with the genre to experienced players, provided constructive perspectives in creating the game for players of all experience levels. Although the members worked in the same library, coordination and preventing duplication of work was difficult. We tried shared folders, a group e-mail account, and meetings, but the final solution was to create a shared document in Google Documents that all members could edit and record their progress.

Including all possible synonyms and actions a player may try to use when playing the game is a challenge in writing any IF game. Our development group alone could not conceive of the unexpected actions and words players would try to use while playing the game. The beta-testing process was crucial for making us aware of additional actions and responses we need to include in the released version.

In today's graphic and visual world, it is important to choose every word with care in a game that is all text. We needed to capture the player's attention swiftly and did not want to overwhelm them with a wall of text. Word choice was also a primary concern when referring to library resources. This is one area in which having a diverse team was not always beneficial, since uniformity of terminology is less confusing for players and is necessary for Inform to function properly. Beta testing proved helpful in identifying some conflicts with terminology.

Another issue the team encountered while creating *Bioactive* was ensuring the results of puzzles were relevant and significant. There was a delicate balance between creating a vibrant game world with idiosyncrasies and humor that engaged the player and a game world that frustrated or distracted players from the learning objectives due to conundrums.

Game projects that begin with a defined need and audience are more likely to succeed. Established time allocations and a ready set of beta testers are especially helpful. Additionally, beginning game development after a solid storyline and learning objectives are established speeds the process. In game development, like software development, each significant change adds exponentially to the requirements for time and resources.

Future Plans

As exhibited by the number of articles and conference presentations about games in libraries, many libraries are interested in using games for library instruction. Unfortunately, most libraries do not have much money or time to invest in game projects. Once the IF version of *Bioactive* is fully tested, it will be offered to other academic institutions for local customization. The Inform 7 development environment is easy to learn, so it is anticipated interested libraries will not have to invest many resources in creating a workable IF game. They will only need to update the pictures and text to reflect their own institution.

Though initial beta-testing with library staff is complete, we plan to include play of *Bioactive* as an activity in several library instruction sessions in Fall 2008. This will allow us to collect feedback from students, gauge general interest in the game, and determine its effectiveness as a tool for teaching library searching skills. Assuming positive feedback we will apply for funding to develop a more graphic intensive and complete version of *Bioactive*, again with the goal of releasing the revised game to other academic institutions.

Notes

1. Justin Peters. "World of Borecraft: The Trouble with Serious Games," *Slate* (June 27, 2007) http://

www.slate.com/id/2169019/ (accessed January 2, 2008); Ian Bogost. "Persuasive Games: Why We Need More Boring Games," *Gamasutra* (May 21, 2007), http://www.gamasutra.com/view/feature/1417/persuasive_games_why_we.php (accessed January 2, 2008).

2. Richard E. Ferdig, ed. *Handbook of Research on Effective Electronic Gaming in Education* (Hershey, PA: Information Science Reference, 2008).

3. Ian Bogost. *Persuasive Games: the Expressive Power of Videogames* (Cambridge, MA: MIT Press, 2007).

4. Ameet Doshi. "How Gaming Could Improve Information Literacy," *Computers in Libraries* 26, no. 5 (2006).

5. Jeff Sarbaum. "ECON201: Principles of Microeconomics," University of North Carolina at Greensboro, http://www.uncg.edu/bae/people/sarbaum/webpage/click_index_file_to_view_content/ (accessed January 2, 2008).

6. Tammy Allgood. "Quarantined: Axl wise and the information outbreak in Arizona State University," Arizona State University, http://www.west.asu.edu/libcontrib/game/website/ (accessed January 2, 2008).

7. Karen Markey. "Storygame Project," University of Michigan, http://www.si.umich.edu/%7Eylime/storygame.html (accessed January 2, 2008).

8. Ann, P. Ceccarini Brown and C. Eisenhower. "Muckrakers: Engaging Students in the Research Process Through an Online Game," in *13th National Conference Proceedings* (Baltimore, MD: 2007).

9. Edward Castronova. "Arden Slows Down, Takes Breather," *Terra Nova Blog*, http://terranova.blogs.com/terra_nova/2007/10/arden-slows-dow.html#more (accessed February 1, 2008).

10. Nick Montfort. *Twisty Little Passages: An Approach to Interactive Fiction* (Cambridge, MA: MIT Press, 2003).

11. Ibid, 225.

12. *Inform 7: A Design System for Interactive Fiction* (2006), http://www.inform-fiction.org (accessed January 2, 2008).

13. Association of College & Research Libraries. "ACRL Information Literacy Competency Standards," American Library Association, http://www.ala.org/ala/acrl/acrlstandards/informationliteracycompetency.cfm (accessed January 2, 2008).

14. "Developing the Ultimate Urban Adventure Game for Middle School Girls," in *Proceedings of Women in Games* (June 10-11, 2005), http://upclose.lrdc.pitt.edu/publications/pdfs/WIG%20Click2005.doc (accessed January 2, 2008).

CHAPTER 14

Education on a Shoestring: Creating an Online Information Literacy Game University of North Carolina Greensboro

Scott Rice

Gaming has gotten attention in the wider world for the ways in which it can foster interest and facilitate learning. The Summit on Education Games hosted by the Federation of American Scientists reported that "Given the digital natives' affinity for digital technologies, digital games for learning could be potentially powerful tools for teaching them the skills they will need to succeed."[1] Richard Van Eck, in the Educause Review, noted that "Several reviews of the literature on gaming over the last forty years … have consistently found that games promote learning and/or reduce instructional time across multiple disciplines and ages."[2] Libraries have begun to hop aboard this bandwagon, seeing gaming as a way of introducing library content while engaging students with an activity that is familiar to them as "digital natives."

The University of North Carolina at Greensboro is a doctoral-granting institution of 16,000 students with a Carnegie classification of "high research." The University Libraries reaches first-year students through required courses such as English 101, Communication 105, and freshmen seminars. The First-Year Instruction Coordinator teaches approximately ninety instruction sessions each academic year. These instruction sessions are the typical one-shot introductions to the library and its services, with little chance for follow up or reinforcing concepts. We were looking for a way to engage students with the information presented during these sessions and provide a casual, fun review in order to improve retention.

In 2006, we started a collaboration between the reference department and the library's IT department. Amy Harris, the First Year Instruction Coordinator and Scott Rice, the Networked Information Services Librarian, were both interested in introducing gaming to the library. Along with a once-a-semester Game Night for students, we wanted to actually incorporate gaming into instruction. We envisioned a computer game that could be used as a complement to library instruction, not a replacement. If there was a fun way to reinforce library concepts outside of class, or break the ice in an instruction session, then a game seemed the right way to go about it.

Goals

The first goal of the project was that the game should be simple to use. We wanted to produce a game that would be fairly self-explanatory and allow students to dive right in and get started. This was one of several reasons that the game ended up in the board game format. A board game format, specifically one involving answering questions while moving around a board, is a very familiar game format, popularized by such games as *Trivial Pursuit*. Students would not need extensive instruction to play; they would just "get it" right away. The rules presented on the Web site for the game reflect this philosophy as they are just a few short paragraphs intended to get across the basics of game play and the icons used in the game.

The second goal of the project was that the game, inasmuch as was possible given our backgrounds as librarians and not game designers, should be engaging and fun. This goal affected several design decisions throughout the creation of the game. We specifically wanted to avoid the "lame factor" often referred to in discussions of educational games. The special squares on the board reflect efforts toward engagement, by throwing in random game elements, adding an element of chance to offset the simple question-answer format. For this reason, a whimsical approach was taken when faced with several game design choices, such as the icons that players select to represent themselves in the game. We also felt this added personality to the game.

Portability and easy adaptability was the third goal of the project. We wanted other librarians to be able to use the game. In order for the greatest number of people to use the game, the technology bar had to be significantly lowered, so that librarians with relatively little technical ability would be able to set up and modify the game to accomplish their own educational goals. This was accomplished through our design choices, including what technologies we used to create the game, the amount of documentation provided, and the amount of support we provide to those wishing to adopt the game.

Usability was the fourth goal of the project. Not only did we want librarians of all backgrounds to be able to set up the game, but we wanted as large a variety of people as possible to be able to play the game. A number of steps were taken to realize this goal, including the choice of technologies used to implement the game, the physical layout of the board and questions, compatibility with screen-reading software and the availability of either mouse or keyboard input to accomplish game tasks.

The fifth goal was that the game should meet the requirements of at least a few of the ACRL information literacy standards, in order to be viable as an educational tool. This goal was mainly met in the categories and styles of questions that were asked. This was also one of the driving reasons behind the web evaluation exercises in the game.

Technology

AJAX (Asynchronous JavaScript and XML) was chosen as the technology to implement the game, for a number of reasons. One of the most important reasons was that as the person who would be doing the programming, I already knew some JavaScript. JavaScript also does not involve any server-side programming, which meant that the resultant game could be implemented much more widely, because adopting the game would not involve talking any Tech departments into installing software on a server. As a JavaScript program, the game could simply be placed in a Web space like any other HTML page, and it would work.

XML also had several advantages, in that it would be easy to edit. Originally, it was thought that all configuration and question sets would be placed in XML files, but a small JavaScript file which was heavily documented ended up being implemented as it was easier to program that way. The question sets were in XML both for the ease of editing the questions and for the utility of reducing the downloading overhead by breaking up the content into pieces. This would make the game easier to access for off-campus students or anyone with a slow Internet connection.

ADA Compliance

One of the most important goals in designing and programming the game was to be as ADA compliant as possible. Several steps were taken to render the game as playable as possible for differently abled patrons.

Sound cues were added to the game for on-screen events like getting an answer right or wrong, or rolling the dice. Also, a tone sounds at the end of every player's turn to let the next player know it is their turn. The game is screen reader compatible and was tested with the use of the JAWS software in UNCG's accessibility lab. On the way to making the game usable by screen reader, the game board and text areas had to be swapped, as initially the game board was on the left and questions were presented on the right hand side. This arrangement made it so the screen reader would first read the names of players in the game before it would read the questions and answers.

The game will accept either keyboard or mouse input from the user. Every mouse click has a corresponding keyboard activity that will achieve the same outcome. This was done to eliminate any reliance on one form of input device over another, for those users who may be limited to one.

After input from a co-worker, the game was changed slightly to accommodate those users with color blindness. After a player gets a wrong answer, the correct answer was highlighted in a red font. This was changed by adding a dotted underline to the correct answer, so that colorblind players could easily detect the difference.

To make it possible for those with sight difficulties to resize the game and typeface without adversely affecting playability, the game was changed so that it did not need to be opened in a fixed-size window. The game also automatically shifts the game board and pieces whenever the window is resized.

Rules of the Game

The game is in a question and answer format. First, players are presented with a screen where players are asked to input their name and select a character icon to represent them. Originally, the plan was to create icons such as might be seen on a Monopoly board. But I learned of the existence of an animated Web show called Odd Job Jack that was releasing all of its images under a Creative Commons License. There were a great number of images of various characters, some famous, that could be selected from. Sixteen of the characters were selected and used for the icons in the game.

After the icons are selected and names entered, the game begins. The players take turns rolling the die by clicking on it or pressing the 'D' key. There are four different colored squares that represent four categories of questions. There are exclamation point, light bulb and question mark icons which represent special spaces. Game play involves rolling the die and moving around the board answering questions in order to get a circle (referred to as a "light") of each color. Once this is accomplished, the player is set on an inner track, where he or she must again answer one question correctly from each of the four categories to win the game. After a player wins the game, a web page is presented with statistics of the game session showing what percentage of questions were given and answered correctly in each category. This will allow both students and teachers to have some idea where deficiencies in the player's knowledge might be and further instruction can be amended to address these.

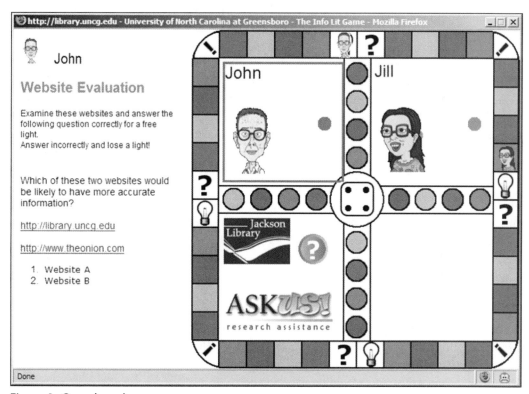

Figure 1. Gameboard

The questions are in four categories, represented by the four colors on the game board, red, green, blue, and purple. The categories are: Choose Your Resource, which gives an information need and asks the player to identify the best source (book, magazine, Web site, or scholarly journal) to meet that need; Searching and Using Databases, which asks players questions about database concepts such as Boolean operators, keywords, and truncation; Cite Your Sources and Avoid Plagiarism, which asks players to ask questions about APA/MLA formatting and recognizing the importance and means of avoiding plagiarism; and Library Wild Card, which gave players a mix of questions, many of which had to do with specific information about UNCG's library.

The light bulb space represents a different type of question. These are Web evaluation exercises that ask the player to look at either one or two Web sites. Links to Web sites open up in a new window when clicked on. The computer randomly chooses whether one or two Web sites are to be used. If one Web site is examined, then the player is asked to identify some information about the Web site, such as the author, how often it has been updated, or the presence of contact information. If two Web sites are to be examined, then the player is asked to compare the two with regard to considerations such as currency, bias, or trustworthiness. The Web evaluation exercises provide the most active learning experiences in the game.

An exclamation point space sits in each corner, which is meant to introduce a random element to the game, hopefully making it more fun. The computer randomly chooses one of a number of things that can happen when a player lands on one of these spaces. The player can lose a turn, or select another play to lose a turn. The player can be sent backward or forward on the board anywhere from 1 to 5 spaces. The player can also gain or lose a 'light.'

The solo version of the game allows one player to play against a time clock while answering questions. Twenty seconds are allowed for questions to be answered and an X is given if time runs out or the question is answered incorrectly. The fifth X ends the game. The Web evaluation exercises are not timed, as this would not be practical. These exercises are meant to produce more reflective thought on the player's part and also involve some detective work, and putting that under a time constraint would be self-defeating.

Addressing Information Competency Standards

Three of the four question categories in the game address a part of the ACRL Information Literacy Competency Standards for Higher Education.[3]

Choose Your Resource category
> Standard 1, "The information literate student determines the nature and extent of the information needed"

Searching and Using Databases
> Standard 2, "The information literate student accesses needed information effectively and efficiently"

Cite Your Sources and Avoid Plagiarism
> Standard 5, "The information literate student acknowledges the use of information sources in communicating the product or performance"

The Web evaluation exercises are there to meet Standard 3, "The information literate student evaluates information and its sources critically and incorporates selected information into his or her knowledge base and value system." These exercises are one of the most valuable parts of the game for addressing information literacy competency, as players are required to demonstrate both the skill to find the needed information on the Web sites as well as the understanding to answer the question.

Testing and Feedback

Testing was performed on the game before roll-out. Student workers in the library were asked to play the game and provide feedback on its playability, ease of use, and any other factors that came to mind. Library staff were also asked to play the game and provide feedback. As a result of comments made, a few tweaks were made to the game. One of the changes was the addition of the dotted underline to correct answers mentioned earlier. Another change was the amount of time allotted to answer questions in the solo version of the game. The original amount of time allowed was ten seconds. Player feedback quickly made it clear that this was not long enough for a player to read the question, comprehend it, read all the answers, and choose the correct one. The time was changed to fifteen seconds, and then to the current twenty seconds. A planned improvement for the game will allow adopters of the game to choose the amount of time that solo players can take to answer questions.

Feedback is also solicited through a voluntary survey that is presented on the statistics screen presented after the game ends. Three statements are presented for the survey, and the respondent is asked to what degree he or she agrees or disagrees with the statement.

Statement 1: The game was challenging

Statement 2: The game was fun to play

Statement 3: I learned something new

We limited the survey to these three simple statements to try to encourage participation. Responses collected after a six month time period are reflected in the following graphs:

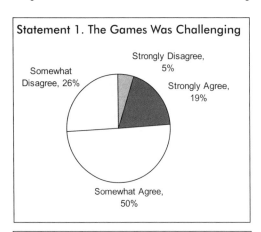

Statement 1. The Games Was Challenging

Strongly Disagree, 5%
Somewhat Disagree, 26%
Strongly Agree, 19%
Somewhat Agree, 50%

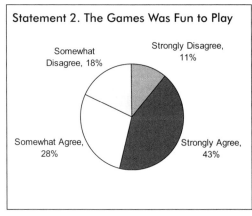

Statement 2. The Games Was Fun to Play

Somewhat Disagree, 18%
Strongly Disagree, 11%
Somewhat Agree, 28%
Strongly Agree, 43%

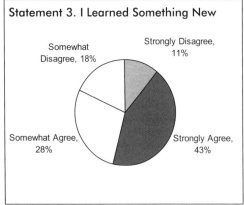

Statement 3. I Learned Something New

Somewhat Disagree, 18%
Strongly Disagree, 11%
Somewhat Agree, 28%
Strongly Agree, 43%

Roll-out

The game was officially rolled out to students in Fall 2007. The game was completed in January, which would have made a spring roll-out possible. However, we decided to wait until the beginning of the fall semester because the majority of English 101 and other first-year courses are taught during this time. Before the fall semester began, the first-year instruction librarian showed the game to new teaching assistants during their orientation, in order to facilitate introduction to first-year students. The game was also included on each class's customized subject guide page and mentioned to students during the library instruction session.

Information about the game, as well as the URL, was also placed in the textbook for UNCG's University Studies 101 classes. This class is a one-hour university acculturation class where students visit various important locations across campus, including the library. Students were encouraged through the textbook to play the game as a follow-up to their reading of the chapter and visit to the library.

The game has also been marketed directly to students on the library's Web site and through Blackboard, UNCG's course management software.

What Can Be Changed?

As the creators of the game, we urge anyone with an interest to download the game files and modify them to make your own version of the game. Many of the features of the game can be customized easily for use in other institutions. A short list of the easily modifiable features includes the following:

- Board game image
- Dice images
- Character images
- Questions
- Sounds
- Solo or no-solo play
- Help File
- Results Screen
- Library information and links
- Use of web evaluation questions
- Game messages
- Markers for correct questions

Most of these options can be changed simply by using any text editor to change the config. js file. Changing sounds requires slightly more expertise, at it involves knowing which parts of a few lines of JavaScript to change. Directions for all changes are found in a text file included with the game, and are also present in the config file itself, which is heavily commented to make it more understandable.

Institutions Adopting the Game

Following is a list of just some of the institutions that are modifying their own version of the Information Literacy Game for use.

- Brigham Young University—Hawaii
- Carroll College
- Forsyth Technical Community College
- Humboldt State University
- Ivy Tech Community College
- Las Vegas-Clark County Library District
- Moses Cone Health System Medical Library
- Tidewater Community College
- Truman State University
- University of Portsmouth
- University of Wales
- University of Waterloo
- University of Wisconsin—LaCrosse
- Washburn University
- Western Illinois University

Game Improvements

There have been a number of improvements to the game since its release in Spring 2007. The possibility of creating several different question sets for use with different classes or different patron groups was added in to the game. In the configuration file, any number of different combinations of question sets can be set up. To access the different set, the URL used to link to the game would have an added parameter pointing to the correct set. Also, a parameter identifying a particular group taking the questions can be added on to the URL. This identifier could be any string, so individual games as well as groups could be tracked.

A version of the game that uses JSON (JavaScript Object Notation) instead of XML was also released after reports from some adopters that they could not get their game to retrieve the questions properly in the XML format. JSON files are served as text files and seem to produce fewer server-side troubles. The JSON format is at least as easy as the XML format is to understand and edit. Again, all that is needed to change questions is a text editor. Looking at the file it is obvious what needs to be changed and what format to put questions in.

Another improvement was the addition of a different picture of the board itself and the dice graphics. Both the old and the new graphic sets are included with the game files and adopters are free to use any, all, or none of the above in any combination. I know of at least one library that has created their own graphics for the "lights" which denote correct answers.

The original game opened up in a window of fixed size, which was quickly perceived to be a problem, both because some adopters did not know how to link to the game properly to open the window in the right size, and because players who wished to change the font size would quickly find the information unreadable in the small size window. So the game was corrected to allow running in a window of any size, and the board and pieces would move to fit. Resizing is also possible after the window is open and the game will shift pieces around correctly.

Future improvements will include more options for configuration, such as being able to set the time for questions in solo play. Also, another set of player icons to choose from would be a worthwhile addition. A generic version of the game will also be introduced, with UNCG-specific questions removed or altered. In this way, we hope to make it even easier for other librarians to implement the game. They would simply need to grab the file, unzip it, upload it to their Web server, and start playing.

Lessons Learned

- Keep it simple
- If you program it yourself, do as little original programming as possible
- Have a plan for assessment and marketing
- Playtesting is critical
- We could build it ourselves
- The game has wider application than libraries

Keep it Simple

The more complexity you add to the game, the harder it will be to program, to write the content for, to work out the bugs, etc. A simple game is often a game that can be implemented simply. This does not reflect its educational value or playability. Our game shows that a great deal of content can be packed into a simple package. Some extremely simple games are very playable as well, such as Tetris. The combination of the two is definitely the hard part.

If you Program it Yourself, do as Little Original Programming as Possible

This piece of advice is one I wished I had when embarking on this project. There are many ways to cut down on the amount of programming you have to perform. One of these (if you are programming in JavaScript) is to use a JavaScript framework, such as jQuery, Script.acul. ous, or mooTools. A JavaScript framework already comes with a number of tools that can save you hours of your own programming time. In developing another game, I used the mooTools framework and saved an incredible amount of programming time very easily. I was able to use effects that I would not have been able to program myself, at least not easily, which made it possible to concentrate more on the actual game development rather than the mechanics of making it happen on-screen.

Another way of making programming easier is to start with a game that has already been created. There are many open source games available for modification on the Internet, as well as commercial games that can be modified to fit educational goals. Games such as *Civilization*, *Neverwinter Nights*, and *X* have already been successfully modified and used as educational games in other contexts, and it should be possible to do so in a library context as well.

Have a Plan for Assessment and Marketing

For our game, assessment is possible through the game itself, by collecting the statistics of players who have completed the game. We also included a voluntary survey that was made available on the Web page that is presented when a game has been completed, and we have received a great deal of feedback that way as well. But further assessment is needed to show the educational value of the game. Pre- and post-testing would make a stronger case for the presence of gaming in instruction in general, and the usefulness of this particular game in library instruction in particular. Also, the educational value of a tool is greatly diminished if no one knows anything about it. In future projects of this nature, a strong plan for publicizing the game will be a high priority.

Playtesting is Critical

When creating this game, we played it ourselves hundreds of times, we wrote the questions, and found the Web sites to be evaluated. As such, we had little idea of how easy or hard it would be for the average first-year student to answer the questions or evaluate the Web sites. Playtesting made it possible for us to have a certain measure of confidence that the game that we were creating would accomplish our educational goals. Playtesting revealed that there was some ambiguity in the questions that asked a player to pick out what the best source for a given type of information is, and also showed us that the players of the solo game required much more time to read and understand the questions and answers than they were currently given.

We Could Build it Ourselves

When embarking on the project, we thought it important to create something useful without needing to go into advance planning, grant writing, committees, and the other accompaniments of significant projects. We wanted to see if we could create a usable computer game on our own, in addition to our regular duties. And we wanted to do it quickly, with our original timeline for the project a slim three months. The first version of the game was complete in approximately seven months, and our desire to do playtesting and time the release of the game to the academic year expanded our schedule.

The Game has Wider Application than Libraries

Up through the point at which we started publicizing the availability of the game to the larger library world, we were under the impression that only librarians would be interested in it. We soon found, however, that educators in a variety of settings saw some value in the game as an educational tool. We had received feedback from a K-12 teacher that she would be using the game in her class. A professor teaching elementary education explained that she would be assigning the game to her students for them to use as an educational tool in their classes. We have also had interest from public libraries and special libraries as well. It quickly became apparent that the setup of the game made it possible for it to be used for nearly any audience and educational material, and changes to the game since that time have only made it more usable in a wider variety of situations.

The Information Literacy Game has undergone a number of changes even during its brief time out of the development phase. I hope to continue to refine the game and have plans to continue to refine the code and add on new functionality. In addition, I continue to provide support for those people wishing to adopt the game for their own institutions. The Information Literacy Game has proven itself to be adaptable to a wide variety of contexts and be usable enough that people with very little in the way of technology skills can create their own version.

Notes

1. Federation of American Scientists, "*Harnessing the Power of Video Games for Learning*," Report of The Summit on Educational Games (Washington D.C.: October 2006), http://www.fas.org/gamesummit/Resources/Summit on Educational Games.pdf (accessed January 15, 2008).
2. Richard Van Eck. "Digital Game-Based Learning: It's not just the Digital Natives who are Restless," *Educause Review* 41 (2006):16-30.
3. Association of College and Research Libraries, "*Information Literacy Competency Standards for Higher Education*," American Library Association, http://www.ala.org/ala/acrl/acrlstandards/information-literacycompetency.cfm (accessed January 15, 2008).

 CHAPTER 15

The 'Blood on the Stacks' ARG: Immersive Marketing Meets Library New Student Orientation
Jeremy Donald

Introduction

What is the single best thing you can teach new users about your library, and who are the most powerful role models of library use? When the staff at the Coates Library at Trinity University asked themselves these questions, we found that our answers were as follows: we most wanted new users to feel comfortable with library resources and staff, and returning students are the most influential role models of library-related attitudes, opinions, and behaviors.

Luckily, the goal of promoting comfort with campus places, people, and behaviors among new students was shared by the very people we had in mind: the New Student Orientation planning team in the office of Campus and Community Involvement, which designs the campus-wide orientation for new students. This group consisted of both full-time professionals and student residential life staff members known as Resident Mentors (RMs). To update, expand, and improve our traditional library scavenger hunt orientation, the librarians of Trinity University chose to adapt the model of the alternate reality game (ARG) to create a dynamic multimedia library orientation that would fully engage library staff, new students, and Resident Mentors.

Background

Trinity University is a private master's-level university in San Antonio, Texas, with 2,467 full time undergraduate students in the 2006–2007 school year. There were 656 new first-year students in the fall of 2006, 70% of whom were from Texas. Living in on-campus residence halls is required for three years prior to graduation. The Coates Library plays a central role in the daily lives of students, with a popular coffee shop and 140 general use computers spread over two floors. Despite the popularity of the library as a place to work, socialize, and study, anecdotal evidence from library instructors working with senior seminars suggested that many experienced students were not well-acquainted with many of the ever-increasing number of library services and resources. The arrival of a new information literacy coordinator in 2003 resulted in a substantial increase in the number of library instruction classes taught to lower-division students, but concerns remained about the best way to encourage new students to engage more fully with library staff and services in their first weeks on campus.

Moving from a scavenger hunt model which had used popular movies as themes for a fun and lively orientation to major library places and service points, the librarians took up the University Librarian's charge to adopt a mystery tour model incorporating digital media and non-librarians as participants. A group of two librarians and a member of the teaching faculty with an expertise in online gaming formed a committee to explore this idea. The theme of ancient Egypt was chosen, and the gaming expert suggested the ARG as a model for the orientation.

What is an ARG?

According to CNET, an alternate reality game is a "young medium…that blends real-life treasure hunting, interactive storytelling, video games and online community and may, incidentally, be one of the most powerful guerrilla marketing mechanisms ever invented." [1] The distinctive characteristic of an ARG is the immersion players experience because elements of the game world and the real world overlap. Fictional events may involve real world people and places; players meet in real time, under instructions from game characters who communicate by e-mail and cell phone; clues may appear in newspapers, on television, or movie posters. The extent to which an ARG's status as a game is evident in the game's content varies. The lack of self-identification as a game is referred to as This Is Not a Game, or TINAG. A recent trend in ARGs has been to downplay this element, with many games openly announcing their status as a game, their rules, and the locations of initial clues. [2]

Academic Libraries, Gaming, and Orientations

The use of games as platforms for library orientations is only recently being discussed in the professional literature, though the literature on library orientations in general is plentiful. [3] In seeking evidence of game- and mystery-based orientations, especially those that combine the elements of marketing with goals related to raising patron comfort levels, a number of examples emerge. Real-time treasure/scavenger hunts, themed activity-centered events, and online games with varying amounts of real-world interaction comprise the examples discussed below.

Marcus & Beck assert that orientation tours raise the comfort level of new students in the library.[4] They found that students completing a self-guided orientation based on a treasure hunt had higher satisfaction ratings regarding the library resources and staff than students who completed a traditional library tour. Students completing the self-guided treasure hunt also scored slightly better than the control group on a post-test designed to test their knowledge of library resources.[5] Cahoy and Bichel identified "students' fear of using the library" as the primary target of their library's luau-themed self-guided tour.[6] A mystery tour was used to introduce first-year students to the library as a "first step in a continuum of information literacy instruction for undergraduates" at the Niagara University Library, with success in meeting learning objectives including improved familiarity with the resources, services, and physical layout of the library.[7] The Brill Science Library at Miami University found that a large majority of attendees of a themed orientation involving elements of information literacy and outreach reported feelings of comfort and understanding with library services, and indicated they knew whom to contact for research help.[8]

Recent examples of gaming in library orientation and instruction include an online interactive game called "Head Hunt: The Game," designed to orient new first-year students to The Ohio State University libraries before arriving on campus, which went live in Summer 2007. The game uses a map of campus as a starting point for players to learn about libraries and play games and find clues in the process, ultimately using the clues to find the mystery location of the missing head of the OSU mascot.[9] In the fall of 2007, a fully-realized alternate reality game called "Help Me Solve a Mystery," designed to teach information literacy and critical thinking skills, was launched by educators at Western Washington University.[10]

While the literature has yet to discuss the implications of this trend in applying games to library orientation, information literacy instruction, and marketing efforts, the literature that is currently extant offers a positive appraisal of creative and fun-oriented efforts like those described above.

Campus Role Models

Our experience of past library orientations consistently underscored the powerful role of the Resident Mentors (RMs)—returning students who serve as paraprofessional student life staff and support small groups of new students throughout their first year on campus.[11] Informal observations made it clear that when a resident mentor showed little or no enthusiasm for the library orientation, the members of her group were likely to have a negative response to the activities. Likewise, when an RM was actively engaged in the orientation as a leader and as a participant, the students in that group would have a positive first experience in the library and come away with a lasting impression of the library as a fun and helpful place.

There is ample evidence to suggest that upper-division students are dependable role models for new students. The discourse surrounding student learning communities highlights the role of undergraduate mentors in both residential and classroom contexts. Benjamin notes the high degree of satisfaction new students experienced with residential and classroom mentors of both genders in a study at Iowa State University, and reviews the theory of challenge and support which she suggests may explain students' experience of satisfaction with their peer mentors.[12] New students at Portland State University report their peer mentors have significant impacts on their level of comfort and success at the university.[13] At Trinity University, RMs are positioned to have maximum contact with new students, notably during New Student Orientation, a campus-wide, week-long series of programs and events designed to acclimate new arrivals to the campus community.[14]

Little of the literature surveyed discussed the role of upper-division and/or residential life-employed students in helping orienting new students to the library. Kuh and Gonyea, considering the potential of libraries to achieve campus-wide information literacy, emphasized collaboration with the rest of campus, including student affairs professionals.[15] A library peer mentoring program at Utah State University which employed upper-division students to offer library services at the reference desk and in the classroom met with positive results.[16] Informal discussions of orientations with librarians from other institutions highlight the valuable contributions student library employees have made to orientation planning and preparation, and this has been true for past orientations at Trinity University.

Designing the Outcomes

To accomplish the goal of improving the comfort level of students in the library, the librarians involved began by convening focus groups of students, including first-year students, library work-study employees, and upper-division residence life staff and resident mentors. The first goal of these focus groups was to identify the most intimidating or conceptually challenging aspects of the library, in order to create a list of goals for the orientation. A second goal was to come up with ideas for making the game fun and engaging for new students.

Focus group participants identified a number of resources, skills, services, behaviors, and concepts they considered a barrier to optimal library use and comfort, and resoundingly stated that they had found the library intimidating as new users. The most popular recommendations from the group emphasized promoting familiarity with the library homepage, scholarly database interfaces, the library printer system, and the experience of getting help from a librarian or staff member (no ranking implied). To improve the game's appeal, respondents strongly supported the element of competition between RM groups, with a point system in place to encourage effort at every stage of the game. Marketing the game to the RMs and educating them as "insider" participants were major concerns, and an awareness campaign integrated into the week of RM training was strongly suggested.

Librarians and staff provided their own perspective by performing a review of current library usage trends. An early consideration was information from our Web site usage statistics, which indicated that our campus users were visiting the library Web site in high numbers both during operating hours and overnight while the building was closed. Usability studies had led to improvements in the design and content of the library Web site and had also indicated a surprising level of challenge faced by all students in navigating the vast number of pages and resources included on the library's Web site. This led us to place a high degree of emphasis on orienting students to the library Web site as a 'library environment' on par with the physical space.

A second consideration had to do with social trends in library use. Many of our recent decisions in terms of designing and furnishing library spaces focused on supporting group work. Our Information Commons space is frequently the site of both planned and impromptu student collaboration, as are the many comfortable seating areas throughout the building. Moreover, the anecdotal evidence reported by the public service librarians pointed to increased group work among students, impacting use of group study spaces and even the nature of reference desk transactions and research appointments. Yet our orientations had in the past focused on cultivating awareness of the physical layout of the building in individual new students. Though students had completed the scavenger hunt in small groups, the space to which we sought to orient them was intended for individual task completion rather than collective, collaborative effort.

Lastly, it was agreed that a library orientation was too brief and de-centered to accomplish any substantial information literacy instruction. However, the orientation must remain consistent with the principles of information literacy and with the information literate behaviors the library promotes throughout the year. An initial idea for approaching this goal focused on encouraging new students to ask for help from library staff whenever possible, emphasizing the theme of the library as a place to ask and answer questions with information.

Designing the Delivery

It should be stated here that it was not the goal of the librarians to create and deliver a fully-realized ARG, but rather to use the guidelines of ARG design to create a collaborative and immersive library experience across media, one that bridged new students' pre- and post-arrival experiences of the University. Our final product—by its second iteration in 2007—was a hybrid of an ARG, a self-guided mystery tour, an online multimedia game, and a treasure/scavenger hunt.

Figure 1. "Blood on the Stacks" logo

The librarians agreed upon the theme of Egyptology, chose the name 'Blood on the Stacks' (BOTS), and authored a mystery involving a missing canopic jar stolen from a library exhibit, with the thief at large. With help from a graphic designer, an iconic image of the god Anubis was created to serve as the game's (and, temporarily, the library's) logo and would serve to brand people, materials, and resources that were involved in the game. Using a list of library resources and locations, a list of media we planned to use in delivering clues, and a roster of available participants—including Resident Mentors, librarians, library professional and student staff, and administrators—the core committee of one reference/instruction librarian and the manager of access services drafted a game plan. New students would be introduced to the game by receiving an e-mail directing them to the online "rabbit-hole," or portal site, for the game. This site included an introduction to the mystery, the rules of the game, and the prizes. Centrally located on the homepage was a two-minute movie created with help from a student library employee which dramatized the mystery and established the game's context within the

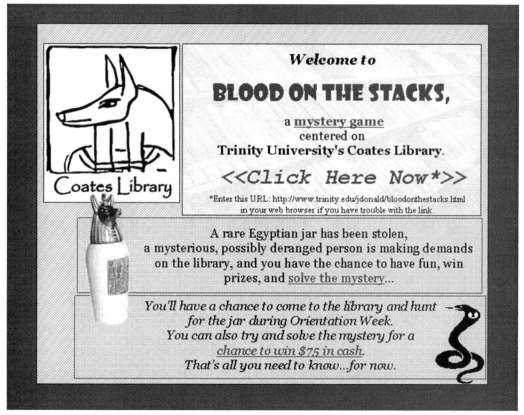

Figure 2. "Blood on the Stacks" E-mail

world of the library and its resources. The site also contained a video clue which players could solve—by following directions to use the online catalog—to earn points for their Resident Mentor (RM) group. A scoring system would allow members of each RM group to gather points collectively and establish a clear winner once all groups had competed. Three days were allotted for the in-house orientation and subsequent work on bonus clues and questions. The prize was to be an all-expenses paid study break (valued at $150) for each of the two top-scoring RM groups.

Coates Library

Suspect Clue:
We have reason to believe that the culprit worships the falcon-headed god Horus. He has a great love of birds.

Find these books with call number
DS62 .F79 2006
DS62 .P385 1983
DS61.7.B37 L85 2006
for your next clue.
Hint: 2ⁿᵈ Floor, Behind the Staircase

3.

Figure 3. "Blood on the Stacks" Suspect Clue

SUSPECT RAP SHEET

Name: Jerry Hernandez

Alias: JH; Officer Friendly;

D.O.B: Same as the birth of Rock 'n Roll

Distinguishing Traits and features:
Bilingual; Works with BC; Name means 'Son of fernando';
works for archaeologist Clint Chamberlain in the Serials
dept; Part Time Wildlife officer; Bird watching addiction

Prior Convictions: Once called the International Space
Station from extension 8307; outstanding warrant for
barbequing w/out requisite safety padding; Repeat offence:
wearing white pants during NIOSA.

Figure 4. "Blood on the Stacks" Suspect Rap Sheet

The in-house orientation would allow several RM groups to compete against each other, with up to one hour to follow a series of clues to various library locations and resources. Each orientation clue also contained a clue about the identity of the culprit. After a brief welcome and introduction by a library staff person, each RM group would split into small teams to follow clues throughout the building. Once reunited, the RM groups would pool their clues and compare them to the traits listed in a series of "suspect rap sheets." Suspects included RMs, librarians, library staff and students, all of whom played slightly embellished versions of themselves, and were encouraged to act as a real suspect might when confronted with ambiguous evidence of their guilt.

Once the RM group had identified a prime suspect, they were guided by a library staff person to the computers in the Information Commons, where they discovered an online tutorial built into the library's homepage. Six different versions of the ten-minute tutorial each posed a game-related question which could be answered by using online databases and the library catalog to find information. The tutorial concluded with the requirement that players print out their result, in keeping with responses from focus group participants that the printing system in the library was a source of significant confusion and intimidation.

RM groups were then invited to finish the game by answering a set of bonus questions which required them to use their new awareness of library resources, including helpful staff, and which emphasized library services—such as laptops and study room keys for checkout—as much as specific information sources. Once finished, RM groups headed to the front of the building to have points awarded based on their success with the mystery clues and the bonus questions, and collect door prizes. Each group's points were tallied on a giant scorecard, and groups were asked to write comments on the blank spaces. Since final scores were too close to establish a clear winner—nearly every group answered all of the bonus questions—a second bonus question was posted on the Web site, and scores were re-tallied the day after the in-house orientation concluded. Two winning groups received top prizes of catered study breaks during mid-term exams and had their pictures taken and published in an announcement in the campus newspaper.

Outcomes

A satisfaction survey, combined with a survey of opinions about the library, was chosen to assess BOTS.[17] Surveys were sent by e-mail to first-year students and to Resident Mentors in the second half of the first semester, approximately two months after the event. Estimates of participation based on door counts indicated that roughly 500 out of 660 new students had participated in BOTS, and all but two of the forty RM groups reported as present. In both cases, the sample sizes from the surveys (forty first-years; fourteen Resident Mentors) were small, though open-ended responses yielded helpful feedback.

Because of the lack of a control group of suitable size, responses to the survey questions are unable to indicate to what extent BOTS improved students' comfort level with the library and its staff in comparison either with a different kind of orientation or with no orientation at all. Responses from new students indicated a favorable appraisal of BOTS as an orientation

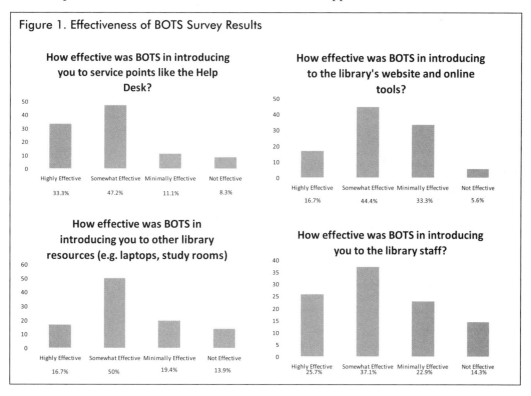

Figure 1. Effectiveness of BOTS Survey Results

How effective was BOTS in introducing you to service points like the Help Desk?

| Highly Effective | Somewhat Effective | Minimally Effective | Not Effective |
| 33.3% | 47.2% | 11.1% | 8.3% |

How effective was BOTS in introducing to the library's website and online tools?

| Highly Effective | Somewhat Effective | Minimally Effective | Not Effective |
| 16.7% | 44.4% | 33.3% | 5.6% |

How effective was BOTS in introducing you to other library resources (e.g. laptops, study rooms)

| Highly Effective | Somewhat Effective | Minimally Effective | Not Effective |
| 16.7% | 50% | 19.4% | 13.9% |

How effective was BOTS in introducing you to the library staff?

| Highly Effective | Somewhat Effective | Minimally Effective | Not Effective |
| 25.7% | 37.1% | 22.9% | 14.3% |

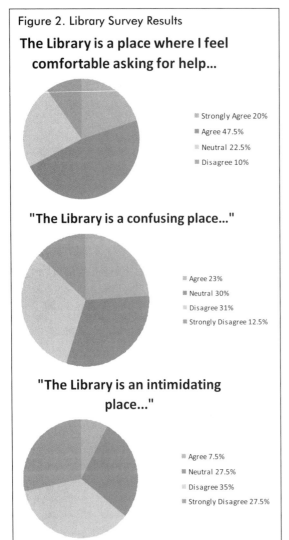

Figure 2. Library Survey Results

The Library is a place where I feel comfortable asking for help...

- Strongly Agree 20%
- Agree 47.5%
- Neutral 22.5%
- Disagree 10%

"The Library is a confusing place..."

- Agree 23%
- Neutral 30%
- Disagree 31%
- Strongly Disagree 12.5%

"The Library is an intimidating place..."

- Agree 7.5%
- Neutral 27.5%
- Disagree 35%
- Strongly Disagree 27.5%

model, and participants indicated positive opinions toward the library's resources and staff. Most (67.5%) agreed that they felt comfortable asking for help in the library, and most (62.5%) disagreed that the library was an intimidating place. Nearly as many respondents found the library confusing as not.

First-Year Students

The majority of students found BOTS to be effective in familiarizing them with library service points, the library Web site, the library staff, and other library resources. The highest number of strongly negative responses was in response to a question on the effectiveness of BOTS in orienting students to other library resources such as laptops and study rooms. A large percentage of students also found the orientation to library staff lacking. (See Figure 1.)

When asked their opinion of the library, nearly seventy percent said that they felt comfortable asking for help there. A sizeable percentage still saw the library as a confusing place, though only a small number (7.5%) thought the library was intimidating. (See Figure 2.)

Open-ended responses to a question about how to improve the event in the future included: requests for clearer instructions, complaints about the state of the building (vendors were still in the process of completing a shifting of the collection at the time of the in-house event), and two requests to more meaningfully connect game locations in the library with collection content. One student asked that maps of the building be included, and another thought serving food would be a good idea, echoing the recommendations of many of the respondents cited above.

Organizers used the bonus questions to gauge the extent to which each RM group engaged with the various activities within the orientation, especially the online tutorials which focused on the library webpage and scholarly databases. Thirty-one out of thirty-nine RM groups stayed to complete the ten printed bonus questions, and forty-nine students submitted e-mail responses to the online bonus question. Regarding the low number of positive satisfaction responses to the survey question about the effectiveness of the orientation to the library Web site and online tools, library staff and RMs both reported that RM groups preferred to delegate two or three members to sit before the computer and interact with the online tutorials, resulting in decreased participation for other group members.

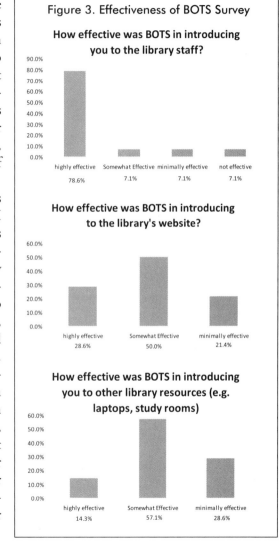

Figure 3. Effectiveness of BOTS Survey

Figure 4. Library Promotion

Do you promote the library to your RM group throughout the year?

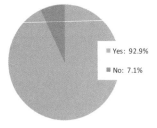

Yes: 92.9%
No: 7.1%

Did BOTS help you promote the library to your new students?

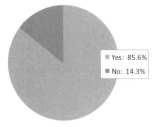

Yes: 85.6%
No: 14.3%

Did BOTS fulfill its goal of making new students more comfortable with the library, its staff, and its resources?

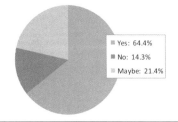

Yes: 64.4%
No: 14.3%
Maybe: 21.4%

Resident Life Staff

Survey responses from RMs indicated some differences in appraisal from the first-years. RMs found the orientation to library staff highly effective, and gave their lowest satisfaction ratings to the orientations to the library Web site and to library resources such as laptops and study rooms. (See Figure 3.)

When asked about their own efforts to promote the library to new students, nearly all said they promoted the library to the students in their group throughout the year. Eighty-six percent said BOTS helped them promote the library to their students. When asked how the event changed their opinion of the library, most said BOTS made them more enthusiastic about introducing their RM group to the library, while roughly one quarter said BOTS did not change their opinion of the library and its staff. A majority agreed that BOTS fulfilled its goal of making new students more comfortable with the library, its staff and its resources. (See Figure 4.)

Some of the most positive feedback came from residential life staff and student Residential Mentors, who appreciated both the energy and the improved focus of the orientation on student-chosen services and resources. One RM wrote to say that BOTS "was a great success, and it really engaged all of my residents."[18] Negative responses dwelt on the time of day (too early) for several of the RMs' scheduled slots to attend BOTS. Others echoed the students' survey responses regarding the amount of contact with library staff, and about the clarity of the instructions given for the time spent in the library.

Conclusions and Implications for Practice

BOTS was a singular success in recruiting residential life staff as library champions and in creating goodwill among the planners of the campus-wide New Student Orientation program of which BOTS is a part. The ARG model as applied to a library orientation for new students presents numerous opportunities for encouraging collaboration between campus residential life staff and librarians, and for capitalizing on the influence Resident Mentors have as role models of student attitudes toward and opinions of the library. The element of immersion—when the game makes use of real world devices and people—central to ARGs is well-suited as a means of including campus role models as active participants in the library's orientation. The ARG model also provides planners of library orientations with a template for combining the most effective elements of the range of library orientation and promotion techniques discussed in the literature, especially mystery tours, scavenger hunts, themed orientations with prizes, and online multimedia games.

A library orientation based on an ARG is what organizers make of it: care must be taken to balance the marketing and outreach potential of the 'virtual' aspects of the ARG model with the execution of the in-house activities, whether self-guided or mediated by library staff. The motivational and social advantages of groups in competition with each other had a negative effect on the rate at which individual students directly engaged with online tutorials, and this undermined the emphasis organizers had hoped to place on the library's Web site and databases. However, survey responses from Resident Mentors indicated that they play an active role in promoting the library to their new student groups throughout the year, and it is the organizers' belief that this influence can continue to be exploited in future—and improved—versions of the ARG-based library orientation.

Positive changes could be made to several aspects of BOTS to address the problems identified by student surveys and librarian observations. Asking students to complete the online tutorials in small groups before rejoining with their RM group to collaborate on the more challenging bonus questions would give each student more familiarity and comfort with the library's online resources. Finding a practical way to tie the content of library materials to the clues—and thereby to the game's solution—would add to the element of immersion and intensity ARGs are known for. Lastly, library staff training and scheduling during the in-house portion of the game should be thorough to the point of redundancy in order to avoid the confusion arising from insufficient support of new students' efforts to complete game tasks and navigate the building.

Notes

1. John Borland. "Blurring the Line between Games and Life." CNET Networks, Inc. http://www.news.com/Blurring-the-line-between-games-and-life/2100-1024_3-5590956.html (accessed July 11, 2007).

2. IGDA Alternate Reality Games SIG, "2006 Alternate Reality Games White Paper," (International Game Developers Association 2006): 56 http://www.igda.org/arg/resources/IGDA-AlternateRealityGames-Whitepaper-2006.pdf

3. Sandra Marcus and Sheila Beck, "A Library Adventure: Comparing a Treasure Hunt with a Traditional Freshman Orientation Tour," *College and Research Libraries* 64 (January 2003): 25.

4. Ibid, 26.

5. Ibid, 25.

6. Ellysa Cahoy and Rebecca Bichel, "A Luau in the Library? A New Model of Library Orientation," College & Undergraduate Libraries, 11 (2004): 50

7. Kristine Kasbohm, David Shoen, and Michelle Dubaj, "Launching the Library Mystery Tour: A Library Component for the First-Year Experience," *College & Undergraduate Libraries*, 13 (2006): 38

8. Eric Resnis, Betsy Butler, and Jennifer Barth, "Follow the Silk Road to Orientation Success: Promoting Miami University's Brill Science Library," *Issues in Science and Technology Librarianship*, 51 (Summer 2007) :11-12.

9. Nancy O'Hanlon, Karen Diaz, and Fred Roecker, "A Game-Based Multimedia Approach to Library Orientation," LOEX Conference, May 2007.

10. John Farquhar, e-mail message to ILI-L listserv, May 13, 2007. http://lists.ala.org/wws/arc/ili-l/2007-05/msg00103.html

11. Office of Residential Life. "Residential Life—First Year Area." Trinity University. http://www.trinity.edu/departments/res_life/fy_area.htm (accessed July 11, 2007).

12. Mimi Benjamin, "Satisfaction of Learning Community Participants with Residentially-Based and

Residentially-and-Course-Based Learning Community Peer Mentors," http://www.lc.iastate.edu/SatisfactionWithPeerMentors.pdf (accessed July 11, 2007)

13. Candyce Reynolds, "Undergraduate Students as Collaborators in Building Student Learning Communities," in *To Improve the Academy V. 22,* eds. Catharine Wehlburg and Sandra Chadwick-Blossey (Bolton, MA: Anker Publishing Company 2004), 233

14. Newhouse, Ben. "What is Orientation?" Trinity University. http://www.trinity.edu/departments/student_activities/firstyear/What%20is%20Orientation.htm (accessed July 2, 2007).

15. George Kuh and Robert Gonyea, "The Role of the Academic Library in Promoting Student Engagement in Learning," *College & Research Libraries*, 64 (July 2003) : 268

16. Wendy Holliday and Cynthia Nordgren, "Extending the reach of librarians: Library peer mentor program at Utah State University," *C&RL News* (April 2005): 284

17. The author used parts of survey instrument created by Marcus & Beck, with permission.

18. Kevin Eaton, e-mail message to author, August 27, 2007.

Appendix A
Focus Group Questions

Moderator agenda for Blood on the Stacks focus groups:

Greet & serve food and drinks.

When everyone has arrived:

> Have everyone introduce themselves.

> Briefly discuss the purpose of the group and the aspirations for the event.

> > "We'd like to accomplish the following with the library orientation:
> > Show them a good time.
> > Brand the library as a positive place.
> > Familiarize FYs with the library staff.
> > Let FYs know we're here to provide personalized help and service.
> > Dial down the intimidation factor for the library.
> > Get people used to the homepage and basic functions, like article searching.
> > Teach them how to print."

Talk about confidentiality, tape recorder, etc.

Turn on tape recorder/start note-taking.

Questions:

A) For you returning RMs, what are some of your impressions of last summer's Library NSO, Blood on the Stacks?

What was successful?

What needed improving?

B) Specifics regarding the game activities:

Winning
Incentives
Accomplishments

Exporting library message
Importing Campus & Community Involvement NSO message

Appendix B
Additional Marketing Materials

In our attempt to reach new students in as many ways as possible, we deployed social networking sites, interactive tutorials, library signage, and an ARG 'rabbit hole' as points of communication for the game with various amounts of game-relevant content.

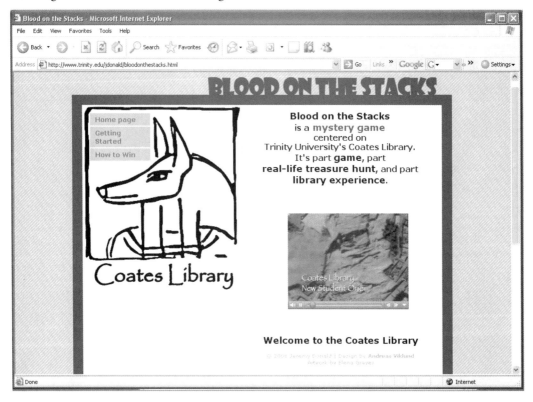

Figure 1. "Blood on the Stacks" Web Site

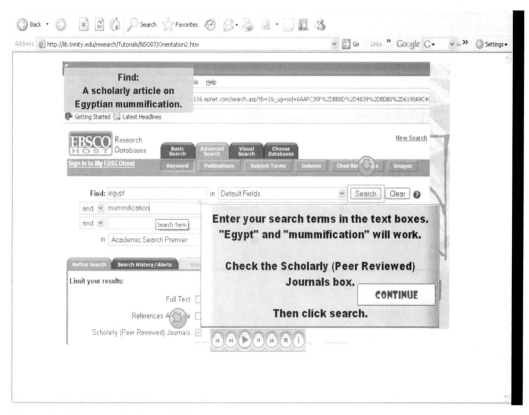

Figure 2. "Blood on the Stacks" Tutorial

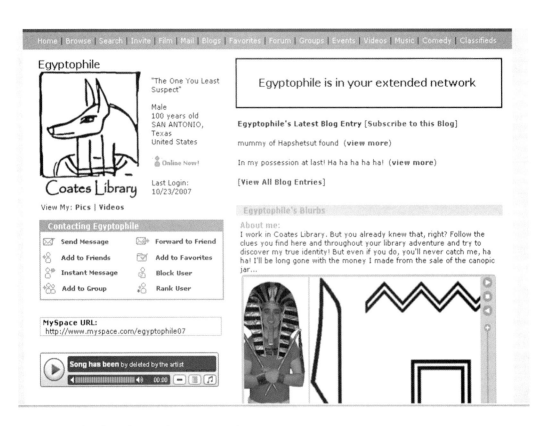

Figure 3. "Blood on the Stacks" Myspace Page

Figure 4. "Blood on the Stacks" Welcome Banner

CHAPTER 16

Leveling Up: Increasing Information Literacy through Videogame Strategies

Paul Waelchli

Videogames provide libraries an innovative way to lead students to learning. They are not merely a way to get students in the doors of a library. Students playing videogames at library events are doing more than building social connections; they are building information literacy skills, just as they do when they gather in a dorm room to play *Halo 3*. Student gamers are not thinking about their games in terms of finding, evaluating, and using information, yet students playing videogames of all kinds and in all places are actually developing their academic skills by exercising critical thinking and information literacy. Uniquely placed, librarians have the opportunity to build on students' gameplay experiences to create that vital link between game and academic success. This link is created in classroom instruction by using the very same strategies designed into games to engage and motivate players. Librarians can incorporate videogame strategies during instruction to create a relevant and meaningful experience for students. Iowa's University of Dubuque library has incorporated such videogame strategies into its information literacy program and witnessed instructional success.

The attention to videogames in education is not without basis. Videogames are a popular form of entertainment and a shared experience that both current and future college students share. Data shows that 47% of players are between the ages of eighteen and forty-nine, and 28% of players are under the age of eighteen.[1] The association between videogames and college students is further supported by Nielsen; statistics found that 66% of males between the ages of eighteen and thirty-four owned videogame systems.[2] While videogames are traditionally seen as a male entertainment, the 2007 Nielsen study also found that 58% of women within the same age group owned a system. The gender gap in system ownership will be nonexistent for future college students. Already 80% of both males and females ages twelve to seventeen owned a videogame system.[3] People are choosing videogames as a form of entertainment and socialization, and whether they are aware of it or not, these same players are learning through videogames. Videogames are not only a popular form of entertainment, but also an arena where scores of learners begin their journey in information literacy. The popularity of videogames alone gives librarians a reason to examine how games are engaging and teaching players. Players learn through videogames in a variety of ways, and this learning creates opportunities for academic libraries to find value in what and how videogames are teaching.

Videogames and Information Literacy

There is educational value within videogames. Regardless of whether the games are social and Flash-based or graphics-intensive console videogames, information literacy skills are applied. Players may not see their games as an exercise in information literacy, but once they begin to describe what is required during their game and how they play the game, information literacy skills begin to appear behind the gameplay. Videogames require players to determine what information they need to solve a puzzle, advance a level, or win a game. Videogames require players to locate that information, determine what information is most valuable, and apply it in order to be successful. This process of determining what information is needed and then locating, evaluating, and applying it to any given game situation parallels the information literacy skills academic librarians teach. Librarians can use these game skills and situations to make information literacy more relevant and meaningful in students' lives as well as contributing to their academic success.

Videogames are a valuable tool in helping patrons and students understand what information literacy is and how they already have the initial skills to be successful. Videogames require players to process both visual and written information in order to determine future actions and decisions. Some information demands immediate action. For example the layout of a map and the opponent's position and weapon in *Call of Duty 4* for Microsoft's Xbox 360 requires the player to process and evaluate the information quickly and move offensively or defensively in order to stay alive. Also, other information has an impact on future decisions. *The Legend of Zelda: Phantom Hourglass*, for the Nintendo DS, provides the player with multiple characters throughout the map that provide pieces of a puzzle. The player needs to decide which information is accurate (since some characters provide false information) and apply the correct information to solve the puzzle and move forward in the quest.

The research process is about moving forward in a quest for information. Some of the sources students find provide false information or distract them from their focused topic. Some information is designed for immediate use and application, while other resources provide information that requires additional background in order to be completely understood. Videogames model many of the stages students go through during the research process: search, evaluation, application, failure, frustration, revision, success. Through this process, videogames help develop basic information literacy skills, but rarely are games considered a tool to promote information literacy.

When librarians understand the inherent skills players require to be successful in video games, a connection to formal information literacy skills and academic success can be constructed. Table 1 shows many of the information literacy skills practiced and applied in three of the most popular and bestselling videogame franchises: EA Sport's *Madden* football series, Bungie's first person shooter action series *Halo*, and Square Enix's role-playing series *Final Fantasy*. The table provides specific examples of how information literacy skills are being applied in each game.

Table 1. Examples of Information Literacy Skills Applied			
ACRL Information Literacy Performance Indicator	Final Fantasy	Halo	Madden
1.1. The information literate student defines and articulates the need for information	⚔	🔫	🏈
1.2. The information literate student identifies a variety of types and formats of potential sources for information.	⚔	🔫	🏈
1.3. The information literate student considers the costs and benefits of acquiring the needed information.		🔫	🏈
1.4. The information literate student reevaluates the nature and extent of the information need	⚔	🔫	🏈
2.1. The information literate student selects the most appropriate investigative methods or information retrieval systems for accessing the needed information.	⚔	🔫	
2.2. The information literate student constructs and implements effectively-designed search strategies	⚔	🔫	
2.3 The information literate student retrieves information online or in person using a variety of methods.		🔫	🏈

Table 1. Examples of Information Literacy Skills Applied			
ACRL Information Literacy Performance Indicator	Final Fantasy	Halo	Madden
2.4. The information literate student refines the search strategy if necessary	⚔	🔫	🏈
2.5. The information literate student extracts, records, and manages the information and its sources	⚔		🏈
3.1. The information literate student summarizes the main ideas to be extracted from the information gathered.	⚔	🔫	
3.2. The information literate student articulates and applies initial criteria for evaluating both the information and its sources.		🔫	🏈
3.3. The information literate student synthesizes main ideas to construct new concepts	⚔	🔫	
3.4. The information literate student compares new knowledge with prior knowledge to determine the value added, contradictions, or other unique characteristics of the information.	⚔	🔫	🏈
3.7 The information literate student determines whether the initial query should be revised	⚔	🔫	
4.1. The information literate student applies new and prior information to the planning and creation of a particular product or performance.	⚔	🔫	🏈
4.2 Reflects on past success, failures, and alternative strategies	⚔	🔫	🏈
4.3. The information literate student communicates the product or performance effectively to others	⚔	🔫	🏈
5.2. The information literate student follows laws, institutional polices, and etiquette related to the access and use of information resources.		🔫	🏈

Librarians can use these videogame skills that students already practice as examples and as a foundation to build further traditional information literacy skills upon.

Videogames and Learning

While the information literacy skills that videogames develop provide excellent examples of the research process, they are more than just tangible metaphors. Videogames and the strategies they use are educational tools that libraries can apply to information literacy programs. There is a large and growing body of research on game-based learning and videogames in education.[4] The process of playing a game creates a learning experience beyond the content communicated on screen. Videogames create opportunities for players to understand and empathize with real-world situations. Games help players learn through doing. This learning experience is described as procedural literacy.[5] Videogame players learn by actively taking part in a process. Players make decisions based on information, experience the results of those decisions, and adjust future strategies based on those results. Videogames are an active learning experience.

This active learning experience has changed the way in which students think and learn. Videogames and other technologies provide information that comes fast, is nonlinear, and contains random access points that provide choices and personalization. Prensky points out that this does not mean that educators dumb down what is taught to make it more appealing; in fact the opposite is true, because reducing the challenge makes the content less appealing.[6] The strategies advocated by Prensky do not change the core content of what librarians teach, but rather how they teach. Prensky encourages educators to get rid of teaching step-by-step and one thing at a time, forcing the students down a teacher-approved path.[7] Prensky discussed teaching strategies that can be successful with current students: engagement before content, an emphasis on decision making, input from students about the teaching process, and the ability to be adaptive in the classroom.[8] Librarians, indeed all educators, need to design lessons to mirror the same type of goal-orientated motivation, choice, and immediate feedback that videogames provide.

In addition to looking at the way students learn, researchers have focused on how videogames teach. Videogames incorporate educational theory and strategies to create games that are successful at engaging players. Leading videogame and literacy scholar, James Paul Gee, identified thirty-six learning principles incorporated in videogames. These principles include well-ordered problems, "just-in-time" information, cycles of challenges, challenges just beyond the comfort level, situated meaning, and lower consequences for failure.[9] The principle of just-in-time information is the way in which videogames provide information close to the time when a player requires it. A videogame shows a player how a skill is executed, provides opportunities for practice, and then allows a player to apply it. This connection provides meaning and lasting understanding. This same concept is applied to education and information literacy. Librarians do not want to teach research skills and evaluation strategies in a vacuum to students.

Gee's principles of cycles of challenge and challenges just beyond the comfort level also mirrors traditional educational theory. Vygotsky's zone of proximal development (ZPD) emphasizes the difference between what students are capable of on their own, given their previous experience compared to what they can grow to achieve with the assistance from others.[10] Vygotsky's ZPD is applied on a regular basis through tutorials and other introductory stages in videogames.[11] Videogames fill the role of peer or teacher when they guide players through the initial stages of a game and help the player learn the gameplay mechanics and strategy. Videogames often take two distinct approaches applying Vygotsky's ZPD: either setting aside the first level or two that step a player through the skills they will need throughout the game; or by staggering the scaffolding throughout the game, introducing new and advanced skills throughout the game that apply to the coming levels and depend upon the understanding of previous skills.

Videogames are designed as active learning experiences. It is this attention to design and active learning that helps create experiences in which players invest time. Information literacy focuses on active learning and engaging students.[12] This active practice, testing, and application of the material is important for understanding and retention. A measure of the success of the application of active learning also includes when it is used. Videogames include active learning throughout the process; players are constantly doing. Videogames do not give players 30 to 40 minutes of instruction before letting them play.

Videogames incorporate good design principles in the structure of gameplay and the active learning involved.[13] Pedagogically, this is important for librarians as well. Students may not be able to define what makes the lesson work, but they can sure tell you when it doesn't. Gameplay and game design are similar experiences for most players who may not be able to identify what "works" about a game, but they can tell when it doesn't. Library instruction needs to incorporate good design to prevent students from struggling in the learning process.

In addition to incorporating traditional educational theory, videogames apply other strategies that further engage and motivate players. Videogames help create a sense of ownership in the player. The sense of ownership and responsibility developed through "agency" also drives a player forward.[14] The sense of agency develops through a series of choices the player is required to make. It is this series of choices that creates ownership. The player and the student will not develop this immediately. The choices need to be continually offered, and they need to be significant to the direction of the game or class. Ownership can begin to grow with a question as simple as, "Where should we start?" The choices should continue throughout a lesson. "What search terms?" "Which source will you use?" Asking questions is important, but it is essential for agency that we follow through on the questions we ask. Nothing will kill a sense of student ownership faster than judging something as the "wrong" answer. Reducing the risk of failure for students is an important videogame strategy. Gee described this as the psychosocial moratorium principle where learners can take risks in a space where real-world consequences are lowered.[15] Not passing the level or finding just the right material on the first try is part of how a videogame is designed. Students need to know they can take risks and fail during the research process. Research is a messy process: taking risks, recovering from failure, learning, and succeeding are part of information literacy. Allowing students to take risks and fail while modeling patience and learning through failure helps create successful, information literate students.

In addition to Gee's work on videogames and learning, the Federation of American Scientists listed specific educational strategies that videogames include that make games well suited for education.[16] The learning strategies identified can be applied to information literacy to create more meaningful and engaging instruction sessions for students. Applied individually, videogame strategies are not unique; most educators are aware of these strategies and attempt to incorporate them in lesson plans. Videogames engage and teach players because they incorporate all these strategies within a single experience (see Table 2).

Videogames incorporate information literacy skills through gameplay experiences, and the design of gameplay parallels traditional teaching strategies. There are a number of excellent videogame projects that libraries are creating, and new ones around the corner. But not all libraries are in a place to invest the money and the time to create their own instructional videogame. The educational strategies applied within videogames provide a structure that any library can apply to their information literacy program in order to gain the engagement and active learning benefits of videogames

Table 2. **Educational Strategies Present in Videogames Identified by the Federation of American Scientists Summit on Educational Games, 2006**

1. Clear learning goals
2. Practice opportunities
3. Monitor progress, provide continual feedback
4. Move player to higher challenges
5. Encourage inquiry and questions
6. Contextual bridging
7. Time on task
8. Motivation
9. Scaffolding
10. Personalization
11. Infinitely patient medium

http://www.fas.org/gamesummit/Resources/Summit%20on%20Educational%20Games.pdf

Videogame Strategies in the Classroom

The University of Dubuque started applying video game strategies with its information literacy program in the fall of 2006. The information literacy program at the University of Dubuque library applied a number of the educational strategies identified by Gee and the Federation of American Scientists to undergraduate classes in Music, English, and Communication. Applying videogame strategies into the existing information literacy program allowed the library to start small but create educational benefits for students. Success in the initial application of video game strategies created additional opportunities to begin applying videogame strategies to additional courses throughout the information literacy program. The reason that videogame strategies worked for instruction was because the lessons did not simply target one or two of the strategies but incorporated many of these strategies at once, allowing students to apply them together. The objectives in each instruction session were mapped to ACRL Information

Literacy Outcomes and were mapped to specific videogames strategies (Appendix A). Adapting videogames strategies to information literacy does not forsake traditional standards.

One instruction session contained an open-ended Web site evaluation for an Introduction to Music course. The lesson (Appendix B) contained the videogame strategies of personalization, contextual bridging, "just-in-time" information, cycles of challenges, and clear learning goals. While the lesson incorporated videogame strategies, the objectives of the lesson still were focused on ACRL information literacy standards, including selecting efficient and effective approaches for accessing the information. This included examining and comparing information from various sources to evaluate; questioning the source of the data, and maintaining a log of research activities. The students worked in groups to find and evaluate Web sites based on their given time period. The activity was to identify two Internet sources on a given musical time period, verify the quality of the sources, and identify one subject from that time period with both a print and online source. The choice of resources and subjects was left for each group to determine. The steps necessary to complete the activity were stated beforehand. Knowing the goals, each group had freedom to personalize the process by what they searched for and where they searched. The groups were required to keep a brief log of their search and be prepared to share the results with the class. The search log and worksheet assessed the students' learning.

The first time this videogame strategy lesson was attempted, the student response ranged from "You want what?" to "What are we doing?" Lacking a specific path for their assignment, the students floundered without a clear direction. Fortunately, videogame strategies emphasize taking risk and being willing to fail. The second time the lesson was taught, the librarian added more explanation and guidance to the structure while still allowing students the personalization the lesson was designed for. The adjustment was successful, and students responded positively with comments like, "I get it, and I like not being told what to do."

A second type of lesson incorporating videogame strategies was a resource review for a research and writing course. The lesson applied the gaming strategies of encouraging inquiry, open-ended exploration, context bridging, scaffolding, and personalization. The students in the course were grouped and given a research question that asked them to find a source within a given format (book, article, Web site; print or online). The goals worked to motivate the groups and kept them working toward the objective. The students quickly ran through the search process to reach the goal, a logical action within the context of games. Given the specific goal, the students worked to reach that goal in order to complete the challenge as quickly as possible. The challenge the librarians faced was to ask questions of the students and expose their search process more. The videogame strategies were effective for engaging the students in discussions about why they took the search path they did. The librarians used a rubric to assess the students' discussion of how they reached their research source. When asked, the students explained the search choices they made and provided examples that met the rubric (Appendix C).

The lesson incorporated gaming strategies to provide an open-ended exercise and allowed students to explore and find their own way. The students were initially challenged by how to get started with this open-ended lesson. The initial session did not clearly define the learning goals, and because of the large degree of personal exploration the lesson encouraged, the students struggled to get started in the activity. The successive attempts at the lesson provided the students with a framework for the activity. By foreshadowing the lesson a little more, each group was much more willing to dive into the activity, explore the search, and complete the goal. The initial setup of some framework not only allowed the students the confidence to jump in and get started but also created more buy-in and motivation for the overall activity.

The librarians taught eight sessions during the fall of 2006 and eleven during the spring of 2007. The vast majority of students felt the content was valuable and enjoyed the way the class was designed. Student comments included, "It was good to get everybody on the same page," and "I thought the activity was useful; however, it seemed to be a big review. I felt like I had been through the process that each group discussed many times before in my other papers. But reviews are always helpful—it made me feel like I knew what I was doing and I feel really confident in my research skills." Another student wrote, "I thought the reviews were helpful and a good way to start with the paper. It aided me in narrowing a topic for my paper." Both the verbal and written comments over the two semesters were overwhelmingly positive and a strong indication that video game strategies work. One student commented on the style of the lesson, "I found the activity to be helpful in showing the various ways to access articles, but more importantly, it got everyone involved, which is FAR AND AWAY (student emphasis) more interesting than being lectured to."

After successful open-ended information literacy sessions applying videogame strategies, the librarians at the University of Dubuque used a student- response system and PowerPoint to create a multiple path, point and click review for an upper division Communication course. The initial design comprised over seventy slides and resulted in a multiple-path review where the students voted to determine the direction of the research process (Figure

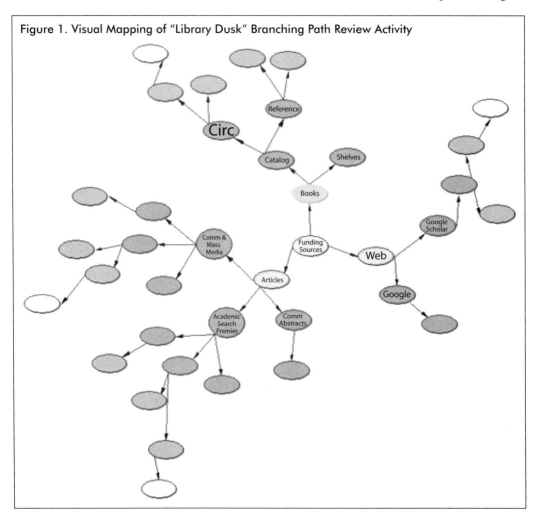

Figure 1. Visual Mapping of "Library Dusk" Branching Path Review Activity

1). The assignment objective was to find two sources from books, articles, or the internet. Every path and choice was hyperlinked within the PowerPoint slides so that any decision the students made was linked to the corresponding choices. Students stayed engaged in voting, reacting to the results, and discussing the choices. Much of the class discussion was peer-led, and the students engaged each other and debated about what path to choose. A short evaluation with open-ended questions was sent to students one week after the information literacy session. Students' responses were overwhelmingly positive and included, "I did like how you gave us an option for going our own paths" and "I thought the voting was great." One student commented that, "It was a lot more fun being able to first handily [*sic*] interact with the research."

Continued Application of Videogames and Information Literacy

Each lesson ultimately was successful, but not without challenges and struggles along the way. The challenges, and even failures, were acceptable and part of the application of videogame strategies. Rarely does a videogame player successfully complete a new challenge on the first attempt. Both Gee and the Federation of American Scientists identify risk taking and failure as strategies that videogames include. Failure and learning from that failure is an important component for librarians applying video game strategies. Librarians need to be willing to take risks, fail, adapt, and succeed in the application of videogame strategies. Videogame strategies improve information literacy instruction, not by simply labeling a skill set we previously taught as a "game." Videogame strategies improve information literacy instruction when they are applied in unison and the strategies are viewed as an entire package.

Starting the process of "leveling up" an information literacy program does not need to be intimidating or daunting. When applying any new strategies or technology, it is best to start small by setting limited goals and focusing on smaller content.[17] King's advice is sound, and while not revolutionary, it is practical. Existing information literacy classes provide jumping off points for those looking to get started with using games and game strategies in the classroom. The University of Dubuque used this message of starting small to place emphasis on success and build upon it. Start small, target a few gaming strategies, include traditional outcomes and do not be afraid of initial failure. These strategies will enhance the learning experiences of students across campus.

Success in videogaming requires information literacy. The skills involved within games create a unique foundation to build future academic success. Librarians are in an excellent position to build that bridge between students, videogame literacy, and traditional information literacy. Creating successful information literate students with videogames goes beyond treating games as a metaphor. Applying videogame strategies created exciting learning opportunities for students at the University of Dubuque, and furthermore, can provide engaging opportunities for any academic library. Videogames can teach a player the research process, and videogame strategies can help librarians teach students.

Notes

1. Entertainment Software Association, "Game Player Data," *ESA Facts and Research,* http://www.theesa.com/facts/gamer_data.php (accessed December 20, 2007).
2. Nielsen Company, "The State of the Console: Video Game Console Usage Fourth Quarter 2006," *Nielsen Wireless and Interactive Services,* http://www.nielsenmedia.com/nc/nmr_static/docs/Nielsen_Report_State_Console_03507.pdf (accessed April 14, 2007).
3. Ibid.
4. David Williamson Shaffer and others, "Video Games and The Future of Learning," *Phi Delta Kappan* 87, no. 2 (2005): 105.; Kurt Squire and others, "Design Principles of Next-Generation Digital Gaming for Education," *Educational Technology* 43, no. 5 (2003): 17; Kurt Squire and others, "From Users to Designers: Building a Self-Organizing Game-Based Learning Environment," *TechTrends: Linking Research & Practice to Improve Learning* 49, no. 5 (2005): 34.; Richard Van Eck, "Digital Game-Based Learning: It's Not Just the Digital Natives Who Are Restless," *EDUCAUSE Review 41,* no. 2 (2006): 17-18.
5. Ian Bogost. *Persuasive Games: The Expressive Power of Videogames* (Cambridge: MIT Press, 2007), 244-45.
6. Mark Prensky. "Digital Natives, Digital Immigrants," *On the Horizon 9,* no. 5 (2001): 3-4.
7. Ibid. 4.
8. Prensky 2005: 10-11
9. James Paul Gee, *What Video Games Have to Teach Us About Learning and Literacy* (New York: Palgrave Macmillan, 2003), 207-12.
10. Lev Semenovich Vygotsky, *Mind in Society: The Development of Higher Psychological Processes* (Cambridge, MA: Harvard University Press, 1978), 86-88.

Appendix A

Library Instruction Session	ACRL Information Literacy Outcomes	Videogame Strategies	Assessment
Music period research—Introduction to Music	• Selects efficient and effective approaches for accessing information • Examines and compares information from various sources in order to evaluate reliability, validity, accuracy, authority, timeliness • Determines probable accuracy by questioning the source of the data • Maintains a log of activities • Participates in peer workgroups	• Scaffolding / Telescoping • Personalization • Monitored progress • Goal orientation	Website evaluation worksheet
Resource Review—Introduction to Research Writing	• Identifies purpose and audience of resource • Investigates scope & content of systems • Assesses the quantity, quality & relevance of results • Identifies gaps in information • Determines if information satisfies needs • Communicates search process	• Decision making • Adaptation • Clear goals • Practice of skills • Personalization	Presentation Rubric

Appendix A

Library Instruction Session	ACRL Information Literacy Outcomes	Videogame Strategies	Assessment
Multiple-path scholarly source search—Speech and Language Barriers	• Identifies key concepts & terms • Identifies the value and differences of potential resources • Identifies keywords, synonyms, and related terms • Selects controlled vocabulary specific to the discipline • Repeats search using revised strategy	• Clear goals • Monitored practiced • Adaptation • Continuous feedback • Individual adjustment • Personalization	E-mail evaluation and assessment

Appendix B
Lesson Plan

Introduction to Music   Time Period Research

Goal: Students will identify a variety of quality resources from each musical period.

Objectives:
—Selects efficient and effective approaches for accessing the information needed
—Examines and compares information from various sources in order to evaluate reliability, validity, accuracy, authority, timeliness
—Determines probable accuracy by questioning the source of the data
—Maintains a log of activities related to the seeking and evaluating process.
—Participates in peer workgroups

Activity: Identify one internet source on a given time period; verify the quality of the source; identify one subject from the period (artist, style, composition) with both a print and online source.

Class Period:
—Introduce the session, goals, and Internet Evaluation *(10 min)*
   o Handout web evaluation worksheet
   o Clarify content and terms of worksheet, using example
—Students organize into groups of two & receive objective worksheet
   o Worksheet describes goal (as listed in the "Activity" above) and the criteria needed to achieve each goal
   o Each group is given a musical period to research
—Students work together to complete each goal *(25 min)*
   o Goal 1: Locate 1 internet source on your time period
      • Use the Web Evaluation worksheet to determine the quality of the source

- Record the search strategy used (terms, search engine, different sites viewed, etc…)
  o Goal 2: Identify 1 focused subject from that period based on the information discovered through Goal 1
  o Goal 3: Locate 1 internet source on your focused subject from Goal 2
    - Use the Web Evaluation worksheet to determine the quality of the source
    - Record the search strategy used (terms, search engine, different sites viewed, etc…)
  o Goal 4: Locate one print resource on the focused subject of Goals 2 & 3
    - List any differences you observe
—Review results of Goals 1, 3 & 4 from selected groups *(15 min)*
  o Each group will describe their results for one of the Goals
    - Using the lab software, a group will be selected to describe the results
    - The software will push the groups screen onto the rest of the class
    - The selected group will described why they choose the Web site/material they did

THE AUTHORS

Tammy Allgood is Web Services Librarian, Fletcher Library, Arizona State University West (Phoenix, AZ).

Tracey Amey is Electronic Resources Librarian, Roger and Peggy Madigan Library, Pennsylvania College of Technology (Williamsport, PA).

David Baker is Classroom Technology Specialist, University of Oregon (Eugene, OR).

Duncan Barth is Assistant Director, Library Systems, University of Oregon (Eugene, OR).

Donna Beck is Engineering Librarian, Carnegie Mellon University (Pittsburgh, PA).

Rachel L. Callison is Research/Reference Librarian, Carnegie Mellon University (Pittsburgh, PA).

Mary Chimato is Head of Access and Delivery Services, North Carolina State University (Raleigh, NC).

Valrie Davis is Outreach Librarian for Agricultural Sciences, George A. Smathers Library, University of Florida (Gainesville, FL).

Chelsea Dinsmore is International Documents Librarian, George A. Smathers Library, University of Florida (Gainesville, FL).

Jeremy Donald is Faculty Technology Liaison, Coates Library, Trinity University (San Antonio, TX).

Vanessa Earp is Liaison Librarian for Education, Kent State University Libraries (Kent, OH).

Paul Earp is Computer Support Assistant, The University of Akron (Akron, OH).

Cynthia Frey is Library Assistant in Government Documents, George A. Smathers Library, University of Florida (Gainesville, FL).

Sheree Fu is Data Services Librarian, Libraries of the Claremont Colleges (Claremont, CA).

John Fudrow is Administrative and Reference Coordinator, Carnegie Mellon University (Pittsburgh, PA).

Bee Gallegos is Education Librarian, Fletcher Library, Arizona State University West (Phoenix, AZ).

Natalie Gick is Campus Librarian, Simon Fraser University Surrey

Amy Harris is First-Year Instruction Librarian, University of North Carolina at Greensboro (Greensboro, NC).

Amy Hughes is Academic Programs Librarian, Cline Library, Northern Arizona University (Flagstaff, AZ).

Dan Hood is Information Literacy Fellow, Carnegie Mellon University (Pittsburgh, PA).

Mary Laskowski is Coordinator of Media Services, Cataloging and Reserves, University of Illinois at Urbana-Champaign.

Sharon Mazure is Reference Librarian, Fairmont State University Libraries (Fairmont, WV).

Linda Musser is Librarian and Head of the Fletcher L. Byrom Earth and Mineral Sciences Library, Pennsylvania State University (State College, PA).

Lara Nesselroad is Science Library Manager, University of Oregon (Eugene, OR).

Carrie Newson is Assistant University Librarian, George A. Smathers Library, University of Florida (Gainesville, FL).

Rosemary Nigro is Acquisitions Librarian, University of Oregon (Eugene, OR).

Scott Rice is E-Learning Librarian, Appalachian State University (Boone, NC).

Lori Robare is Assistant Head, Metadata and Digital Library Services, University of Oregon (Eugene, OR).

Sara Russell Gonzales is Assistant University Librarian, George A. Smathers Library, University of Florida (Gainesville, FL).

Christian Sandvig is Associate Professor, University of Illinois at Urbana-Champaign.

Lynn Sutton is Director of the Z. Smith Reynolds Library, Wake Forest University (Winston-Salem, NC).

Laurie Taylor is Digital Projects Librarian, George A. Smathers Library, University of Florida (Gainesville, FL).

Joe Williams is Director of the Learning Commons, North Carolina State University (Raleigh, NC).

Paul Waelchli is Information Literacy Librarian, Todd Wehr Library, St. Norbert College (DePere, WI).

David Ward is Undergraduate Library Head of Information Services, University of Illinois at Urbana-Champaign.

Giz Womack is Librarian for Instruction and Outreach, Z. Smith Reynolds Library, Wake Forest University (Winston-Salem, NC).

Annie Zeidman-Karpinski is Science and Technical Services Librarian, University of Oregon (Eugene, OR).